A COMPLETE GUIDE
TO COOKING FOR THE DIABETIC

including
**Over 200 Tempting, Taste-tested Recipes**
plus

- Daily menu guides
- Caloric content and exchange-group breakdowns for each measured individual serving
- Nutritive guides to brand-name products
- A simple system for telling the approximate caloric content of any recipe—at a glance
- Information on using diet ingredients, on dining out, on preparing school-or-work box lunches ... and more!

**RECIPES FOR DIABETICS**

THE ART OF JEWISH COOKING by Jennie Grossinger
BEST RECIPES FROM THE BACKS OF BOXES, BOTTLES,
CANS AND JARS by Cell Dyer
BETTER HOMES AND GARDENS ALL-TIME FAVORITE
CASSEROLE RECIPES
BETTER HOMES AND GARDENS CALORIE COUNTER'S COOKBOOK
BETTER HOMES AND GARDENS NEW COOKBOOK
BETTER HOMES AND GARDENS SOUPS & STEWS COOKBOOK
BLEND IT SPLENDID: THE NATURAL FOODS BLENDER BOOK
by Stan and Floss Dworkin
THE CHICKEN AND THE EGG COOKBOOK
by Marla Luisa Scott and Jack Denton Scott
THE COMPLETE CONVECTION OVEN COOKBOOK
by Marla Luisa Scott and Jack Denton Scott
THE COMPLETE INTERNATIONAL SALAD BOOK
by Kay Shaw Nelson
COOKING WITH HERBS AND SPICES by Craig Claiborne
COOKING WITHOUT A GRAIN OF SALT by Elma W. Bagg
COOK'S TOOLS by Susan Campbell
CREPE COOKERY by Mable Hoffman
CROCKERY COOKERY by Mable Hoffman
THE FRENCH CHEF COOKBOOK by Julia Child
THE GREAT POTATO COOKBOOK
by Marla Luisa Scott and Jack Denton Scott
JUEL ANDERSEN'S TOFU KITCHEN by Juel Andersen
KATHY COOKS NATURALLY by Kathy Hoshijo
LAUREL'S KITCHEN by Laurel Robertson,
Carol Flinders and Bronwen Godfrey
MADAME WU'S ART OF CHINESE COOKING by Sylvia Wu
MAKE-A-MIX COOKERY by Nevada Harward,
Madeline Westover and Karine Eliason
MASTERING MICROWAVE COOKING
by Marla Luisa Scott and Jack Denton Scott
MORE-WITH-LESS COOKBOOK by Doris Longacre
MOTHER WONDERFUL'S CHEESECAKES AND OTHER GOODIES
by Myra Chanin
THE OLD-FASHIONED RECIPE BOOK by Carla Emery
PUTTING FOOD BY by Ruth Hertzberg,
Beatrice Vaughan and Janet Greene
RICHARD DEACON'S MICROWAVE COOKERY
THE ROMAGNOLIS' TABLE by Margaret and G. Franco Romagnoli
SOURDOUGH COOKERY by Rita Davenport

# Recipes For DIABETICS

by Billie Little with Penny L. Thorup

BANTAM BOOKS
TORONTO · NEW YORK · LONDON · SYDNEY

*This low-priced Bantam Book
has been completely reset in a type face
designed for easy reading, and printed
from new plates. It contains the complete
text of the original hard-cover edition.*
NOT ONE WORD HAS BEEN OMITTED.

RECIPES FOR DIABETICS

*A Bantam Book / published by arrangement with
Grosset & Dunlap, Inc.*

PRINTING HISTORY

*Grosset & Dunlap edition published March 1972*
*2nd printing ............ October 1973*
*3rd printing ........ December 1974*

*Bantam edition / July 1975*

| | |
|---|---|
| *2nd printing ...... October 1975* | *6th printing :.. December 1977* |
| *3rd printing .......... March 1976* | *7th printing .. September 1978* |
| *4th printing .. November 1976* | *8th printing .... February 1980* |
| *5th printing ........... May 1977* | *9th printing ........... June 1980* |
| *10th printing ........................ July 1981* | |

ISBN 0-553-20447-5

*Published simultaneously in the United States and Canada*

Bantam Books are published by Bantam Books, Inc. Its trademark, consisting of the words "Bantam Books" and the por-
trayal of a bantam, is Registered in U.S. Patent and Trademark
Office and in other countries. Marca Registrada. Bantam
Books, Inc., 666 Fifth Avenue, New York, New York 10103.

PRINTED IN THE UNITED STATES OF AMERICA

19 18 17 16 15 14 13 12

# CONTENTS

# ACKNOWLEDGMENTS

So very many friends, relatives and diabetic patients have contributed their ideas and treasured recipes that we wish to give a special note of thanks to them and to the food companies, firms, newspapers, and magazines whose information appears in this book. We gratefully acknowledge the following permissions:

Alberto Culver Company, Melrose Park, Illinois 60160 (Sugartwin)

Campbell Soup Company, 375 Memorial Ave., Camden, New Jersey 08101

Cumberland Packing Co., 2 Cumberland St., Brooklyn, N. Y. 11205 (Sweet 'n Low Division)

Eli Lilly and Company, Indianapolis, Ind. 46206

Hollywood Foods, 340 Azusa Street, Los Angeles, California 90012 (Safflower Division)

Knox Gelatin Incorporated, Johnstown, N. Y. 12095

Lever Brothers, New York City, N. Y. 10022

Pillsbury Company, Minneapolis, Minn. 55402 (Sprinkle Sweet)

Plough, Incorporated, Memphis, Tennessee 38101 (Ril Sweet)

Spice Island Division, Leslie Foods, Inc., San Francisco, California 94133

Tillie Lewis Foods, Inc., Drawer J, Stockton, California 95201 (Low Calorie Foods)

U. S. Department of Agriculture, Washington, D. C.

U. S. Department of Health, Education, and Welfare, Public Health Service, Washington, D. C.

SPECIAL THANKS TO: Mrs. Editha Carlson, Public Relations Division, Eli Lilly and Company, Indianapolis, Indiana, for her assistance and permission to use information contained in the many excellent booklets distributed by this fine company; to Mr. Frank Schubert of Tillie Lewis; to Dr. Gerson A. Jacobson; the Public Health Service and other sources which have been used; to Marie

Slavens, our typist, for patiently wading through our notes; and last, but not least—Jonathan Bartlett, our faithful and untiring editor.

Additional information on medication, reactions, travel and vacation, food care, etc., will be found in Publication No. 567, "Diabetes and You" (revised 1968; 25 cents), from the Superintendent of Documents, U. S. Government Printing Office, Washington, D. C. 20402.

# FOREWORD

These recipes are intended to help and guide you in preparing and serving attractive, colorful, unusual, and satisfying meals while conforming to your diabetic diet.

It is important that you follow your doctor's diet orders *explicitly* and use only those recipes suited to your particular suggested caloric intake.

The variety of recipes offered is intended to stimulate your interest in following your diet strictly, as your diet need not be monotonous and unappetizing. Many of these recipes can also be enjoyed by the entire family.

# DOCTOR'S PREFACE

Most patients who first learn of having diabetes react with fear, not only to the idea of having a medical disorder, but also to the supposed grim dietary restrictions which they imagine must certainly ensue. To be sure, the more obese patient will require more caloric restriction initially because excess weight is often associated with the need for more stringent maneuvers to obtain precise medical control. Once "ideal weight" is achieved, the cornerstone of good diabetic management is a precise dietary regimen calculated to supply the necessary calories for maintaining this weight.

All too often, new-found diabetics or overweight persons are given a "diet list" of foods allowed, with an admonition to "stay away from sweets." The lack of variety in some of these programs, along with the failure to acquaint the patient with the purpose of diet, brings on a sense of discouragement. Another problem arises with the individual who must eat in restaurants or take a sandwich lunch to work.

This book supplies many helpful bits of dietary information necessary for weight control and diabetic management. The menus are fascinatingly varied, and the general presentation of material should satisfy not only the patient who is able to have his meals prepared at home, but also the individual who is compelled to eat elsewhere. Doctors, too, should find this book a valuable asset in patient education.

*Gerson A. Jacobson*, M.D.
Torrance, California

# AUTHORS' NOTES

We have written this book because many diabetics have expressed their desire for a cookbook with recipes and helpful suggestions specifically related to their dietary needs.

This collection of recipes offers a large variety of unusual and basic recipes which have been kitchen tested and used for hospital patients on diabetic diets. Any of these recipes may be adapted for general use by substituting for the artificial non-caloric sugar substitutes the equivalent amount of regular sugar. Where ingredients which you are unable to tolerate are called for, omit them; the finished product may perhaps be a bit less tasty, but most likely can be eaten with enjoyment just the same.

Each recipe has been carefully calculated to include the caloric content of each measured individual serving, as well as the exchange-group breakdown for each measured individual serving. To help you select recipes suitable for your caloric restrictions, all the recipes have been categorized by calorie count, using asterisks: * 0-100, ** 101-200, *** 201-300 and **** more than 300. The general information chapter includes helpful hints for using diet ingredients, for restaurant dining, and for preparation of box lunches. We have also included reference materials. These include tables of weights and measures, weight tables, diabetic exchange lists, nutritive value of edible parts of food, aids to varying meals, and daily menu guides.

Cookbooks have been published to assist diabetics, but to our knowledge the subject has not been approached from so comprehensive a point of view.

We had you all in mind while writing this, and we hope it will become the most useful book on your cookbook shelf.

*Billie Little*
*Penny Thorup*

# REMEMBER

that while many people (in addition to your doctor)—a dietitian or nurse for example—can assist you in learning to control diabetes, it is up to YOU to:

1. Continue under medical supervision.
2. Use the exact amount and type of medication prescribed for you! Follow this plan, paying special attention to precise amounts and kinds of foods and the time schedule prescribed for you by your doctor.
3. Use the exact diet plan worked out for you.
4. Do some exercise, in the same amounts, each day.
5. Practice good habits of personal hygiene to minimize the possibility of infection.

# RECIPES

# FOR

# DIABETICS

# EQUIVALENTS BY WEIGHT AND VOLUME

The homemaker who is planning meals for a diabetic needs to know something about food values. The following tables will help determine measurements for carbohydrates, fats, and proteins. Also included are equivalents for most of the measures used in these tables. Be sure to use standard measuring utensils such as an 8-ounce measuring cup, tablespoon, teaspoon, and the like. (The "dime" stores also carry a set of spoons as small as 1/8 of a teaspoon.) It is also a good idea to remeasure *after* cooking. There are a few foods that need not be measured; these will be found in the Exchange Lists.

| | |
|---|---|
| 1 pound (16 ounces) | 453.6 grams |
| 1 pound butter or margarine | 16 ounces |
| | 4 sticks |
| | 2 cups |
| | 64 pats or squares |
| 1 stick butter or magarine | ½ cup (approximately) |
| | 16 pats or squares |
| 1000 grams | 1 kilogram |
| 1 kilogram | 2.2 pounds |
| 1 ounce (fluid or solid) | 2 tablespoons |
| | 28.35 grams |
| 1 cup | 16 tablespoons |
| 2 cups | 1 pint |
| 4 cups | 1 quart |
| 4 quarts | 1 gallon |
| 16 tablespoons | 1 cup |
| 12 tablespoons | ¾ cup |
| 10 tablespoons + 2 teaspoons | ⅔ cup |
| 8 tablespoons | ½ cup |
| 5 tablespoons + 1 teaspoon | ⅓ cup |

| | |
|---|---|
| 4 tablespoons | ¼ cup |
| 2 tablespoons | ⅛ cup |
| | 1 fluid ounce |
| | 28.35 grams |
| 1 tablespoon | 3 teaspoons |
| | 14.28 grams |
| 3 teaspoons | 1 tablespoon |
| Dash, or "few grains" | Up to ⅛ teaspoon |

## CALORIES

| | |
|---|---|
| 1 gram carbohydrate | 4 calories |
| 1 gram fat | 9 calories |
| 1 gram protein | 4 calories |
| 1 cup non-dairy whips | 160 Calories (approximately) |

## GENERAL RULES

**MEASURING FOOD:**

All food should be measured. You will need a standard 8-ounce measuring cup and a measuring teaspoon and tablespoon. All measurements are level. Most foods are measured after cooking.

**FOOD PREPARATION:**

Meats may be baked, boiled, broiled or roasted. Do not fry foods except in fat exchange allowed for that meal. Vegetables may be prepared with the family meals, but the portion for the diabetic should be removed before extra fat exchanges or bread exchanges are added.

**SPECIAL FOODS:**

It is not necessary to buy special foods. Select the diet from the same foods purchased for the rest of the family —milk, vegetables, bread, meats, fats, and fruit (fresh, dried, or canned without sugar). "Special dietetic foods" should be used with discretion; be sure to read labels carefully to determine ingredients. Additional calories in special diet foods must also be figured in the diet.

2

# EXCHANGE LISTS

**Special Note:**
**In figuring the exchanges for the recipes**
**in this book, exchanges less than 1/8**
**have been disregarded.**

Your doctor will select items from these food groups according to their carbohydrate, fat, and protein content, calorie count, etc. To insure good nutrition, your diet should include the same essential food, sometimes referred to as the "basic four," recommended for everyone.

Breads and Cereals: Whole-grain, enriched, or restored
Fruits and Vegetables
Meat
Milk

The foods on each list have about the same nutritional value. The groupings are called "exchange lists" because one food may be exchanged for another on the same list, BUT food on one list may NOT be exchanged for foods on another list. Each diet plan includes foods from all exchange lists to give variety.

**LIST 1** (allowed as desired)
(need not be measured)

**Seasonings:** Cinnamon, celery salt, garlic, garlic salt, lemon, mustard, mint, nutmeg, parsley, pepper, saccharin and other sugarless sweeteners, spices, vanilla, and vinegar.

**Other Foods:** Coffee or tea (without sugar or cream), fat-free broth, bouillon, unflavored gelatin, rennet tablets, sour or dill pickles, cranberries (without sugar), rhubarb (without sugar).

**Vegetables:** Group A—insignificant carbohydrate or calories. Eat as much as desired of raw vegetable; if cooked, limit amount to 1 cup.

| | |
|---|---|
| Asparagus | Lettuce |
| Broccoli | Mushrooms |
| Brussels sprouts | Okra |
| Cabbage | Peppers, green or red |
| Cauliflower | Radishes |
| Celery | Sauerkraut |
| Chicory | Squash, summer |
| Cucumbers | String beans |
| Eggplant | Tomatoes |
| Escarole | Watercress |

Greens: beet, chard, collard, dandelion, kale, mustard, spinach, turnip

## LIST 2 Vegetable Exchanges

Each portion supplies approximately 7 gm of carbohydrate and 2 gm of protein, or 36 calories.

**Vegetables:** Group B—One serving equals 1/2 cup or 100 gm

| | |
|---|---|
| Beets | Pumpkin |
| Carrots | Rutabagas |
| Onions | Squash, winter |
| Peas, green | Turnips |

## LIST 3 Fruit Exchanges

(fresh, dried, or canned without sugar)
Each portion supplies approximately 10 gm of carbohydrate, or 40 calories.

| | Household Measurement | Weight of Portion |
|---|---|---|
| Apple | 1 small (2″ dia.) | 80 gm |
| Applesauce | 1/2 cup | 100 gm |
| Apricots, fresh | 2 med. | 100 gm |
| Apricots, dried | 4 halves | 20 gm |
| Banana | 1/2 small | 50 gm |
| Berries | 1 cup | 150 gm |
| Blueberries | 2/3 cup | 100 gm |

| | | |
|---|---|---|
| Cantaloupe | 1/4 (6″ dia.) | 200 gm |
| Cherries | 10 large | 75 gm |
| Dates | 2 | 15 gm |
| Figs, fresh | 2 large | 50 gm |
| Figs, dried | 1 small | 15 gm |
| Grapefruit | 1/2 small | 125 gm |
| Grapefruit juice | 1/2 cup | 100 gm |
| Grapes | 12 | 75 gm |
| Grape juice | 1/4 cup | 60 gm |
| Honeydew melon | 1/8 (7″) | 150 gm |
| Mango | 1/2 small | 70 gm |
| Orange | 1 small | 100 gm |
| Orange juice | 1/2 cup | 100 gm |
| Papaya | 1/3 med. | 100 gm |
| Peach | 1 med. | 100 gm |
| Pear | 1 small | 100 gm |
| Pineapple | 1/2 cup | 80 gm |
| Pineapple juice | 1/3 cup | 80 gm |
| Plums | 2 med. | 100 gm |
| Prunes, dried | 2 | 25 gm |
| Raisins | 2 tablespoons | 15 gm |
| Tangerine | 1 large | 100 gm |
| Watermelon | 1 cup | 175 gm |

## LIST 4 Bread Exchanges

Each portion supplies approximately 15 gm of carbohydrate and 2 gm of protein, or 68 calories.

| | Household Measurement | Weight of Portion |
|---|---|---|
| Bread | 1 slice | 25 gm |
| Biscuit, roll | 1 (2″ diameter) | 35 gm |
| Muffin | 1 (2″ diameter) | 35 gm |
| Cornbread | 1 1/2″ cube | 35 gm |
| Flour | 2 1/2 tablespoons | 20 gm |
| Cereal, cooked | 1/2 cup | 100 gm |
| Cereal, dry (flakes or puffed) | 3/4 cup | 20 gm |
| Rice or grits, cooked | 1/2 cup | 100 gm |
| Spaghetti, noodles, etc. | 1/2 cup | 100 gm |

| | | |
|---|---|---|
| Crackers, graham | 2 | 20 gm |
| Crackers, oyster | 20 (1/2 cup) | 20 gm |
| Crackers, saltine | 5 | 20 gm |
| Crackers, soda | 3 | 20 gm |
| Crackers, round | 6-8 | 20 gm |
| Vegetables | | |
| Beans, (lima, navy, etc.), dry, cooked | 1/2 cup | 90 gm |
| Peas (split peas, etc.), dry, cooked | 1/2 cup | 90 gm |
| Baked beans, no pork | 1/4 cup | 50 gm |
| Corn | 1/3 cup | 80 gm |
| Parsnips | 2/3 cup | 125 gm |
| Potato, white, baked or boiled | 1 (2" diam.) | 100 gm |
| Potatoes, white, mashed | 1/2 cup | 100 gm |
| Potatoes, sweet, or yams | 1/4 cup | 50 gm |
| Sponge cake, plain | 1 1/2" cube | 25 gm |
| Ice cream (Unless specially prepared for diabetics, omit 2 fat exchanges) | 1/2 cup | 70 gm |

## LIST 5 Meat Exchanges

Each portion supplies approximately 7 gm of protein and 5 gm of fat, or 73 calories. (30 gm equal 1 ounce)

| | Household Measurement | Weight of Portion |
|---|---|---|
| Meat and poultry (beef, lamb, pork, liver, chicken, etc.) (med. fat) | 1 slice (3" x 2" x 1/8") | 30 gm |
| Cold cuts | 1 slice (4 1/2" sq., 1/8" thick) | 45 gm |
| Frankfurter | 1 (8-9 per lb.) | 50 gm |
| Codfish, mackerel, etc. | 1 slice (2" x 2" x 1") | 30 gm |

6

| | | |
|---|---|---|
| Salmon, tuna, crab | 1/4 cup | 30 gm |
| Oysters, shrimp, clams | 5 small | 45 gm |
| Sardines | 3 medium | 30 gm |
| Cheese, cheddar, American | 1 slice (3 1/2" x 1 1/2" x 1/4") | 30 gm |
| Cheese, cottage | 1/4 cup | 45 gm |
| Egg | 1 | 50 gm |
| Peanut butter | 2 tablespoons | 30 gm |

Limit peanut butter to one exchange per day unless diet plan allows for carbohydrate.

## LIST 6 Fat Exchanges

Each portion supplies approximately 5 gm of fat, or 45 calories.

| | Household Measurement | Weight of Portion |
|---|---|---|
| Butter or margarine | 1 tsp. | 5 gm |
| Bacon, crisp | 1 slice | 10 gm |
| Cream, light | 2 tbsp. | 30 gm |
| Cream, heavy | 1 tbsp. | 15 gm |
| Cream cheese | 1 tbsp. | 15 gm |
| French dressing | 1 tbsp. | 15 gm |
| Mayonnaise | 1 tsp. | 5 gm |
| Oil or cooking fat | 1 tsp. | 5 gm |
| Nuts | 6 small | 10 gm |
| Olives | 5 small | 50 gm |
| Avocado | 1/8 (4" diam.) | 25 gm |

## LIST 7 Milk Exchanges

Each portion supplies approximately 12 gm of carbohydrate, 8 gm of protein, and 10 gm of fat, or 170 calories.

| | Household Measurement | Weight of Portion |
|---|---|---|
| Milk, whole | 1 cup | 240 gm |
| Milk, evaporated | 1/2 cup | 120 gm |
| *Milk, powdered | 1/4 cup | 35 gm |
| *Buttermilk | 1 cup | 240 gm |
| *Milk, skim | 1 cup | 240 gm |

*Add 2 fat exchanges if milk is fat-free.

## FOODS TO AVOID:

Sugar
Candy
Honey
Jam
Jelly
Marmalade
Syrups
Fried, scalloped, or
    creamed foods

Beer, wine, or other alcoholic
    beverages
Pie
Cake
Cookies
Pastries
Condensed Milk
Soft Drinks
Candy-Coated Gum

EAT ONLY
those foods which are on the diet list.
the amounts of foods on diet.
DO NOT
skip meals.
eat between meals.

The use of the exchange list is based upon the recommendation of the American Dietetic Association and The American Diabetic Association in cooperation with the Diabetes Branch of the U. S. Public Health Service, Department of Health, Education, and Welfare.

# NOTES ON SPECIAL INGREDIENTS
# USED IN RECIPES

1. In order to reduce the caloric content of numerous recipes without affecting quality, we have included various diet ingredients available in local supermarkets. We have calculated the calories and exchange groupings in our recipes using the following diet products:

   diet margarine
   diet mayonnaise
   diet salad dressings
   imitation dairy and non-dairy products
   diet puddings
   diet sauces and toppings

   If you prefer to use an ingredient other than the diet supplement, you will have to adjust the calories and exchanges.

2. **Sweeteners:** No-calorie sweeteners may be substituted for sugar in many recipes, and also used on foods that need a certain amount of sweetening. They are sold in granulated, liquid, and tablet form. Granulated sweetener may be sprinkled on cereals and fresh fruits; it dissolves immediately. For cold beverages the liquid is most convenient, and either the tablet or the granulated may be used in cooking or in hot beverages. For best results, add the sweetening agent toward the end of the cooking process, since the sweetening power is lessened when exposed to high or low temperatures for any long period of time.

   Some sweeteners are available with either a calcium base or a sodium base. Calcium base sweeteners are slightly less sweet than sodium form. They are suggested for the diabetic who is on a low-sodium diet.

   If you find too much substitute has been used, and

that it leaves a bitter taste in the mouth, counteract it with a little salt (providing you are permitted salt).

The many sugar substitutes on the market include Sweeta, Sucaryl, Saccharin, Sweetness and Light, Sweet 'N, Sprinkle Sweet, Sugartwin, Sweet 'n Low, and Ril Sweet. There are others also, which you may prefer.

For SUBSTITUTE SUGAR SYRUP, combine equal quantities of water and the sugar substitute. Bring to a boil; boil 5 minutes or so. Store in a covered jar in your refrigerator and use for sweetening cold drinks. (This may be used in place of the commercial liquid sweetener.)

**Syrups:** (May be used to sweeten fruits for canning.)
**Light:** 7 teaspoons of sugar substitute and 4 cups of water. Boil together 5 minutes. Skim. Makes 4 1/2 cups.
**Medium:** 13 teaspoons substitute, 3 cups water. Boil 5 minutes. Skim. Makes 3 3/4 cups.
**Heavy:** 20 teaspoons substitute, 2 cups water. Boil 5 minutes. Skim. Makes 2 2/3 cups.
**Glazes:** Non-nutritive sweetener equivalent to 1 cup brown sugar; juice and rind (grated) of 1 orange.
Non-nutritive sweetener equivalent to 1 cup sugar; 1/2 cup cider, dietetic maraschino cherry juice or sweet pickle juice.
1 glass dietetic currant jelly, melted.
1/2 cup dietetic orange marmalade, softened.

There are several brown sugar substitutes available, but if you cannot locate any and brown sugar is called for in a recipe, put granulated white sugar substitute in a frying pan over VERY LOW HEAT, and stir constantly until caramelized.

Use bulk non-nutritives for cakes, cookies, bread, etc. For drinks use liquid non-nutritive sweeteners.

*Using a liquid rather than a granulated sweetener will reduce the number of cups of sugar in a recipe. For example: 1 1/2 cups of granulated regular sugar, or granulated sugar substitute, is the equivalent of one tablespoon of liquid sweetener.*

3. All diet margarines contain less than half the calories of regular margarine—17 per teaspoon (5 gms), 50

per tablespoon (14 gms). Although it is not recommended for frying, it is, with proper care, usable (first melt *SLOWLY* in a frying pan, add food, cover and cook over *LOW* heat). When baking, remember that it has only half the fat content of regular margarines, so in recipes calling for more than two tablespoons of margarine, we suggest the regular soft-form or stick-form margarines.

4. **Wine and Liquor Notes.** The recipes containing alcohol are not for diabetics without the explicit consent of their own doctor. Each recipe containing beer, liqueurs, liquor, or wine is specially marked.

## AIDS TO VARYING MEALS

☐ Bake, broil, or roast meats.
  Bake, broil, or poach fish.
☐ Add herbs to meats and vegetables. (Use 1/4 teaspoon dry herbs for each 6 servings of fish, meat, or vegetables.)
☐ Try basil, rosemary, garlic salt, dry mustard, or curry powder with beef or lamb; rosemary or savory with chicken, fish, or veal.
☐ Season tomatoes with curry powder, basil, or oregano; turnips with rosemary; cabbage with savory; zucchini or carrots with thyme or nutmeg; cauliflower with dill; spinach with marjoram or nutmeg.
☐ The addition of seasoning salt and lemon pepper to recipes gives an entirely new taste.
☐ To enhance dishes use a variety of condiments: Chervil for soups and eggs (1/2 teaspoon for 4 servings); Beau Monde for eggs, fish, meats, sauces, and stuffing (1/2 teaspoon for 4 servings).
  Mei Yen in shrimp soufflé (1 1/2 teaspoons) or 1 tablespoon to either 4 eggs or 3 cups milk.
  Bay leaf, celery salt, or marjoram (1 teaspoon to 1 teaspoon salt) for stews.
  Green onion seasoning (1 teaspoon to 4-6 pound chicken).
  Tarragon (2 teaspoons to 4-6 pound chicken), for stuffing.

11

☐ Add herbs and spices to liquids and be sure you thoroughly crush any whole spices such as anise seed, basil, bay leaf, oregano, rosemary, thyme, etc., or in the case of leaves, such as bay leaf, remove before serving.

☐ Interesting meals may be prepared if you are careful in selecting from your exchange lists. For instance, you may prepare a stew if you select one small potato from the Bread Exchange (List 4) . . . vegetables and meat may be added according to your own meal plan; or you might wish to have a spaghetti dinner by using spaghetti from Bread Exchange (List 1) or (List 2), cheese from Meat Exchange (List 5) and meat sauce.

☐ Soy margarine or Soyamaise are good substitutes for margarine or butter as there is less fat content (if you are able to tolerate soy derivatives).

☐ Use nondairy whips. Each cup averages about 160 calories.

☐ Good sauces may be made from Sweet 'n Sour Barbecue Sauce or Teriyaki Barbecue Marinade, but be sure to check the sugar content.

☐ Low-calorie diet spreads are available and may be used for sandwiches, hors d'oeuvres, etc.

☐ Unusual low-calorie or water-packed fruits such as bing cherries, fruits for salads, Kadota figs, mandarin oranges, pineapple spears, purple plums, etc., are also available.

# ADDITIONAL SUGGESTIONS

☐ Measure dry ingredients before liquid; this will save washing utensils!
☐ Sift flour **before** you measure when the recipe calls for sifted flour. Sift the flour into a bowl, then spoon into measuring utensil. Level with a spatula or knife.
☐ Molasses or syrup flow more easily if measuring utensil is rinsed in cold water and then lightly greased.
☐ 1 medium egg = 1/4 cup eggs.
☐ Have eggs at room temperature.
☐ Arrowroot: 1 tablespoon = 1 slice of bread. (May be used for fruit juices.)
☐ Arrowroot powder may be used in place of flour. In recipes where we use arrowroot, flour may also be used, but be sure to double the amount.
☐ Cornstarch: 2 tablespoons = 1 slice bread. (May be used for fruit juices.)
☐ Egg Yolk: Use this in place of 1 tablespoon flour. Yields 3 gms protein and 5 gms fat, no carbohydrate.)
☐ Flour: 1 tablespoon = 1/3 slice of bread. (Use all-purpose flour, sifted.) 2 1/2 tablespoons = 1 slice bread. (Use all-purpose flour, sifted.)
☐ Tapioca: 1 teaspoon, no exchange necessary. (This is used mostly for sweet sauces. In thickening power this is equivalent to 1 tablespoon flour.)

# EATING OUT

**Suggestions for restaurant dining and for preparing lunches to be eaten away from home**

The questions frequently asked by people on diabetic diets is, "How do I make this diet fit my normal, daily routine?" This is extremely important both to children and adults. Size of portions will depend upon individual calorie requirements and allowed food exchanges.

## LUNCH-BOX MEALS

1. Bread exchange: use either bread or crackers.
2. Fat exchange: butter or mayonnaise; cream for beverages.
3. Fruit exchange: use fresh fruit, unsweetened canned fruits, or fruit juices.
4. Meat exchange: hard-boiled eggs, cold cuts, roast beef, turkey, chicken, ham, cheese, cottage cheese, peanut butter.
5. Milk exchange: as beverage.
6. Vegetables List 1 or 2: raw vegetables such as carrots, celery, cherry tomatoes, cucumber sticks, green pepper rings, radishes, whole tomatoes.

## LUNCH-BOX SUGGESTIONS

**Sandwich:** composed of bread exchange (1 or 2 slices of bread), meat exchange (turkey or beef), fat exchange (butter or mayonnaise), and lettuce, sliced tomato, or other vegetable.

**Sandwich fillings:** for people on high-calorie diets, use chicken, egg, or tuna salad, for example.

14

**Snacks:** graham crackers and butter
    cheese and crackers
    peanut butter and crackers
    crackers and cold cuts, fish, or poultry.

## EXAMPLES

Milk (thermos or purchased at school)

Sandwich of turkey, peanut butter, etc.

Fresh fruit, apple or tangerine

Carrot and celery sticks

Sandwich or cheese and crackers or cottage cheese

Fresh fruit, pear

Fresh tomato

Coffee with cream, or milk

## HOT LUNCH PROGRAMS

Straight meat entrees with vegetables
    or
Plain hamburger sandwich
    or
Plain hot dog on a bun
Fresh fruit
Salad without salad dressing

Beverages, fruit juice or milk, coffee or tea

Assorted List 1: raw vegetable relishes

Cold baked chicken

Bread and butter

Fresh fruit

Milk or hot beverage, as desired

## DINING OUT HINTS

It can be easy to dine out on your calorie-restricted diet comfortably if you keep your exchange groupings in mind. Avoid dishes you are unsure of, such as casseroles, creamed foods, and other dishes that might have "hidden" ingredients.

1. Order plain soups such as consommés, French onion, vegetable.
2. When ordering a salad, ask for your dressing to be brought in a side dish so you can measure the amount according to the fat exchanges you are allowed for that meal. If your fat exchanges are limited, lemon

15

wedges or vinegar (wine or cider) are usually available upon request.

Sliced tomatoes are usually available upon request. Order them without dressing or with the dressing in a side dish.

3. In selecting entrees, take meat items that are either baked, broiled, poached, or roasted. Ask the restaurant to eliminate butter from their preparation. The following are recommended:

   a. Baked or broiled chicken.
   b. Broiled shish kabob or brochette without marinade.
   c. Broiled or baked seafood or fish.
   d. Broiled steak.
   e. Hamburger steak.
   f. Prime rib, roast beef.
   g. Roast turkey (omit dressing and gravy).

   Request that sauces and gravies be eliminated from your entree or brought separately.

4. Order hot and cold cereals plain. Use milk or cream on cereals according to your exchange pattern.

5. Order bread or rolls without fat, according to exchange pattern. Order toast dry.

6. Plain potatoes are readily available either baked or boiled. For oven browned or mashed potato, figure one bread exchange plus one fat exchange.

7. Order cooked vegetables plain; if not available figure one extra fat exchange per serving of vegetables.

8. Recommended vegetables commonly served in restaurants include green beans, tomatoes, carrots, peas, corn on the cob, mixed vegetables, asparagus.

9. Broiled steak is often suitable for breakfast.

10. Order eggs poached or soft cooked; for fried or scrambled eggs, if prepared in a skillet, add one fat exchange.

11. Order bacon or sausage crisp.

12. Fresh fruit is usually available (in season); choose banana, half grapefruit (plain), melon wedge, or fresh strawberries. Stewed prunes are often available without sugar syrup.

13. Order unsweetened fruit juice, or fresh fruit juice.

# EXAMPLES

## Breakfast

1/2 fresh grapefruit
3/4 cup cold cereal with
   cream or milk
1 poached egg

1 slice dry toast
1 strip crisp bacon
1 pat butter
Coffee or tea

### OR

1/2 glass fresh orange juice
1/2 cup oatmeal with
   cream or milk
1 fried egg prepared in pan
   with 1 pat butter

1 strip bacon
Dry toast
Butter
Coffee or tea

## Lunch

Tossed green salad with
   French dressing or
   wine vinegar
Broiled hamburger steak

Toasted dry bun
Sliced tomatoes
Cantaloupe wedge
Milk, coffee, tea

### OR

Cup of bouillon or French
   onion soup

Chef's salad with dressing
   in side dish

### OR

Crab Louis with dressing
   in side dish
Dinner roll or soda cracker

Butter
Fruit juice or serving of
   fresh fruit

## Dinner

Green or spinach salad, or
   salad of your choice
   without dressing
Dressing of your choice
   in side dish

Tomato or "V-8" juice
   cocktail

OR Fresh fruit cup or melon
   wedge

Broiled New York Steak or Prime Rib au jus
Baked potato
Green beans
Dinner roll or bread
Milk or hot beverage
Fruit as desired, or later at home.

Broiled lobster tail, butter in side dish
Mashed potatoes or potato
Broiled tomato
Dinner roll or crackers
Milk or beverage

### OR

Tossed salad with dressing separate
Charcoal broiled hamburger sandwich, plain (have condiments brought separately)
Milk or beverage
Fruit as desired, or later at home

# DAILY MENU GUIDE

The sample diets listed below show some of the ways that the exchange lists may be used to add variety to your meals. Use the exchange lists to plan different menus.

## CALORIE DIETS

The following suggested diets include a breakdown of exchange lists for breakfast, lunch, and dinner. Liquid diets are suggested to replace any meal for those who are sick or dieting.

**1000 Calories** (approximately)

| | |
|---|---|
| carbohydrate | 90 gm |
| protein | 60 gm |
| fat | 45 gm |

## Liquid Diet

**Full Liquid:**
Eggnog (milk ......................1/2 cup ..................120 gm
         (egg ......................1 ............................. 50 gm
Orange juice ......................3/4 cup ..................150 gm
Milk ......................3/4 cup ..................180 gm

**Clear Liquid:**
Clear bouillon ......................1 cup
Orange juice ......................1 cup ......................200 gm
Gelatin dessert ......................1/2 cup ..................100 gm

**Bedtime Feeding** (when directed by doctor):
1/2 milk exchange (1/2 cup milk)

1/2 bread exchange (2 crackers)

will add approximately 120 calories to the daily diet.

### Breakfast
1 fruit exchange (List 3)
1 bread exchange (List 4)
1 meat exchange (List 5)
1 milk exchange (List 7)
Coffee or tea (any amount)

*Example:*
Orange juice ......1/2 cup
Toast ..................1 slice
Egg .....................1
Milk, whole ........1 cup

### Lunch
2 meat exchanges (List 5)
1 1/2 bread exchanges
  (List 4)
Vegetable(s) as desired
  (List 1)
1 fruit exchange (List 3)
1 milk (skim) exchange
  (List 7)
2 fat exchanges (List 6)
Coffee or tea (any amount)

*Example:*
Meat ..................2 slices
  (3" x 2" x 1/8" ea.)
Potatoes .............1/2 cup
Lettuce and
  tomato salad....as desired
Bread ..................1/2 slice
Pineapple ............1/2 cup
Milk, skim ..........1 cup
French dressing....1 tbsp.

### Dinner
2 meat exchanges (List 5)
1 1/2 bread exchanges
  (List 4)
Vegetable(s) as desired
  (List 1)
1 vegetable exchange
  (List 2)
1 fruit exchange (List 3)
1 fat exchange (List 6)
Coffee or tea (any amount)

*Example:*
Tomato juice ......3 oz.
Chicken ..............2 slices
  (3" x 2" x 1/8" ea.)
Noodles ..............1/2 cup
Asparagus ..........as desired
Peas .....................1/2 cup
Bread ..................1/2 slice
Butter ................1/2 tsp.
Banana ..............1/2 small

**1200 Calories** (approximately)   carbohydrate  125 gm
  protein         60 gm
  fat             50 gm

### Liquid Diet

**Full Liquid:**
  Eggnog (milk ...................1/2 cup ...................120 gm
         (egg ......................1 ............................. 50 gm

| Orange juice | 1 cup | 200 gm |
|---|---|---|
| Milk | 3/4 cup | 180 gm |

**Clear Liquid:**

| Clear bouillon | 1 cup | |
|---|---|---|
| Orange juice | 1 cup | 200 gm |
| Grapefruit juice | 1/2 cup | 100 gm |
| Gelatin dessert | 1/2 cup | 100 gm |

**Bedtime Feeding** (when directed by physician):

1/2 milk exchange (1/2 cup milk)

1/2 bread exchange (2 crackers)

will add approximately 120 calories to the daily diet.

### Breakfast

*Example:*

| 1 fruit exchange( List 3) | Orange juice | 1/2 cup |
|---|---|---|
| 1 bread exchange (List 4) | Toast | 1 slice |
| 2 meat exchanges (List 5) | Eggs | 2 |
| 1/2 milk exchange (List 7) | Milk, whole | 1/2 cup |

### Lunch

*Example:*

2 meat exchanges (List 5) — Meat ......2 slices (3″ x 2″ x 1/8″ ea.)

1 bread exchange (List 4)

Vegetable(s) as desired (List 1) — Broccoli ......as desired

1 fruit exchange (List 3) — Lettuce and tomato salad....as desired

1/2 milk (skim) exchange (List 7) — Bread ......1 slice

1 fat exchange (List 6) — Butter ......1 tsp.

Coffee or tea (any amount) — Pineapple ......1/2 cup

Milk, skim ......1/2 cup

### Dinner

*Example:*

2 meat exchanges (List 5) — Tomato juice ......3 oz.

1 bread exchange (List 4) — Chicken ......2 slices (3″ x 2″ x 1/8″ ea.)

Vegetable(s) as desired (List 1) — Noodles ......1/2 cup

1 vegetable exchange (List 2) — Asparagus ......as desired

Peas ......1/2 cup

1 fruit exchange (List 3)  Butter ................1 tsp.
1 fat exchange (List 6)   Banana ..............1/2 small
Coffee or tea (any amount)

**1500 Calories** (approximately) carbohydrate 150 gm
             protein   70 gm
             fat     70 gm

## Liquid Diet

**Full Liquid:**

Eggnog (milk ....................1/2 cup ..................120 gm
    (egg ....................1 ..................... 50 gm
Orange juice ........................1 cup .....................200 gm
Gelatin dessert .....................1/2 cup .................100 gm
Milk .....................................1/2 cup ..................120 gm

**Clear Liquid:**

Bouillon (if desired) ...........1 cup
Orange juice ........................1 cup .....................200 gm
Grapefruit juice ...................1/2 cup .................100 gm
 with sugar .......................2 tsp. ...................... 10 gm
Gelatin dessert .....................1/2 cup .................100 gm

**Bedtime Feeding** (when directed by physician):

1/2 milk exchange (1/2 cup milk)
1/2 bread exchange (2 crackers)
 will add approximately 120 calories to the daily diet.

## Breakfast

*Example:*

2 fruit exchanges (List 3) Orange juice ......1 cup
2 bread exchanges (List 4) Toast ..................2 slices
2 meat exchanges (List 5) Eggs .....................2
1 milk exchange (List 7)  Bacon, crisp ........2 slices
2 fat exchanges (List 6)  Milk ....................1 cup
Coffee or tea (any amount) Butter ................1 tsp.

## Lunch

*Example:*

2 meat exchanges (List 5) Cold cuts ............1 slice
2 bread exchanges (List 4) (4 1/2" sq. x 1/8" thick)

Vegetable(s) as desired (List 1)

1 vegetable exchange (List 2)

1 fruit exchange (List 3)

1 milk exchange (List 7)

1 fat exchange (List 6)

Coffee or tea (any amount)

| | |
|---|---|
| Bread | 2 slices |
| Butter | 1 tsp. |
| Lettuce salad with cottage cheese | 1/4 cup |
| Beets | 1/2 cup |
| Pear | 1 small |
| Milk | 1 cup |

## Dinner

2 meat exchanges (List 5)

2 bread exchanges (List 4)

Vegetable(s) as desired (List 1)

1 vegetable exchange (List 2)

1 fruit exchange (List 3)

1 milk exchange (List 7)

1 fat exchange (List 6)

Coffee or tea (any amount)

*Example:*

| | |
|---|---|
| Roast Beef (3″ x 2″ x 1/8″ ea.) | 2 slices |
| Potatoes | 1/2 cup |
| Squash | 1/2 cup |
| Relish—celery, radishes | as desired |
| Bread | 1 slice |
| Butter | 1 tsp. |
| Cherries | 10 large |
| Milk | 1 cup |

**1800 Calories** (approximately)

| | | |
|---|---|---|
| carbohydrate | 180 gm |
| protein | 80 gm |
| fat | 80 gm |

## Liquid Diet

**Full Liquid:**

| | | |
|---|---|---|
| Eggnog (milk | 2/3 cup | 160 gm |
| (egg | 1 | 50 gm |
| Orange juice | 1 cup | 200 gm |
| Custard (milk | 1/2 cup | 120 gm |
| (egg | 1 | 50 gm |
| Grape juice | 3/4 cup | 180 gm |

**Clear Liquid:**

| | | |
|---|---|---|
| Orange juice | 1 cup | 200 gm |
| with sugar | 2 tsp. | 10 gm |
| Grapefruit juice | 1/2 cup | 100 gm |
| with sugar | 2 tsp. | 10 gm |
| Gelatin dessert | 1/2 cup | 100 gm |

**Bedtime Feeding** (when directed by physician):

1/2 milk exchange (1/2 cup milk)

1/2 bread exchange (2 crackers)

⎱ will add approximately 120 calories to the daily diet.

**Breakfast**

2 fruit exchanges (List 3)
2 bread exchanges (List 4)
2 meat exchanges (List 5)
1 milk exchange (List 7)
2 fat exchanges (List 6)
Coffee or tea (any amount)

*Example:*

Orange juice ...... 1 cup
Toast ..................2 slices
Eggs ..................2
Bacon, crisp ......1 slice
Milk ....................1 cup
Butter ................1 tsp.

**Lunch**

2 meat exchanges (List 5)
2 bread exchanges (List 4)
Vegetable(s) as desired (List 1)
1 vegetable exchange (List 2)
1 fruit exchange (List 3)
1 milk exchange (List 7)
1 fat exchange (List 6)
Coffee or tea (any amount)

*Example:*

Cold cuts ............1 slice
  (4 1/2" sq. x 1/8" thick)
Bread ..................2 slices
Butter ................1 tsp.
Lettuce salad with
  cottage cheese..1/4 cup
Beets ..................1/2 cup
Pear ....................1 small
Milk ....................1 cup

**Dinner**

2 meat exchanges (List 5)
2 bread exchanges (List 4)
Vegetable(s) as desired (List 1)
1 vegetable exchange (List 2)
1 fruit exchange (List 3)
1 milk exchange (List 7)
1 fat exchange (List 6)
Coffee or tea (any amount)

*Example:*

Roast Beef ..........2 slices
  (3" x 2" x 1/8" ea.)
Potatoes ..............1/2 cup
Squash ................1/2 cup
Relish—celery,
  radishes ..........as desired
Bread ..................1 slice
Butter ................1 tsp.
Cherries ..............10 large
Milk ....................1 cup

24

**2000 Calories** (approximately)     carbohydrate 210 gm
                                      protein         90 gm
                                      fat             90 gm

## Liquid Diet

### Full Liquid:
Milk (milk ..........................1/2 cup ....................120 gm
Toast (bread ........................1 slice .................... 25 gm
Eggnog (milk ...................... 1/2 cup ....................120 gm
     (egg ............................1 ............................ 50 gm
Milk ....................................1 cup .......................240 gm
Orange juice ........................1 cup .......................200 gm

### Clear Liquid:
Orange juice ........................1 cup .......................200 gm
   with sugar ........................2 tsp. ...................... 10 gm
Grapefruit juice ...................1 cup .......................200 gm
   with sugar ........................2 tsp. ...................... 10 gm
Gelatin dessert .....................1/2 cup .....................100 gm

**Bedtime Feeding** (when directed by physician):
1/2 milk exchange (1/2
   cup milk)                     will add approximately 120
                                 calories to the daily diet.
1/2 bread exchange (2
   crackers)

| **Breakfast** | **Example:** |
|---|---|
| 1 fruit exchange (List 3) | Orange ...............1 |
| 3 bread exchanges (List 4) | Cereal, cooked ....1 cup |
| 2 meat exchanges (List 5) | Toast ...................1 slice |
| 1 milk exchange (List 7) | Eggs .....................2 |
| 2 fat exchanges (List 6) | Butter ...............1 tsp. |
| Coffee or tea (any amount) | Bacon, crisp ........1 slice |
|  | Milk ....................1 cup |

| **Lunch** | **Example:** |
|---|---|
| 2 meat exchanges (List 5) | Cold cuts ............2 slices |
| 2 bread exchanges (List 4) | (4 1/2″ sq. x 1/8″ thick) |

25

Vegetable(s) as desired (List 1)      Baked potato ......1 (2")

| | |
|---|---|
| Vegetable(s) as desired (List 1) | Baked potato ......1 (2") |
| | Asparagus ..........as desired |
| 1 vegetable exchange (List 2) | Carrots .............1/2 cup |
| | Bread ..................1 slice |
| 2 fruit exchanges (List 3) | Butter ................2 tsp. |
| 1 milk exchange (List 7) | Apricots ..............1 cup |
| 2 fat exchanges (List 6) | Milk .....................1 cup |
| Coffee or tea (any amount) | |

## Dinner      **Example:**

| | |
|---|---|
| 3 meat exchanges (List 5) | Liver, broiled ......3 slices |
| | (3" x 2" x 1/8" ea.) |
| 2 bread exchanges (List 4) | Potatoes .............1/2 cup |
| Vegetable(s) as desired (List 1) | Onions ...............1/2 cup |
| 1 vegetable exchange (List 2) | Broccoli ..............as desired |
| | Bread ..................1 slice |
| 2 fruit exchanges (List 3) | Butter ................1 tsp. |
| 1 milk exchange (List 7) | Banana .............1 small |
| 2 fat exchanges (List 6) | with cream ......1 oz. |
| Coffee or tea (any amount) | Milk .....................1 cup |

**2200 Calories** (approximately)

| | | |
|---|---|---|
| | carbohydrate | 250 gm |
| | protein | 90 gm |
| | fat | 90 gm |

## Liquid Diet

### Full Liquid:

| | | |
|---|---|---|
| Milk (milk | 1/2 cup | 120 gm |
| Toast (bread | 1 1/2 slices | 38 gm |
| Eggnog or (milk | 1/2 cup | 120 gm |
| Custard (egg | 1 | 50 gm |
| Milk | 1 cup | 240 gm |
| Orange juice | 1 cup | 200 gm |
| with sugar | 2 tsp. | 10 gm |

### Clear Liquid:

| | | |
|---|---|---|
| Orange juice | 1 cup | 200 gm |
| with sugar | 2 tsp. | 10 gm |
| Grapefruit juice | 1 cup | 200 gm |
| with sugar | 2 tsp. | 10 gm |

Orange juice ........................1/2 cup ..................100 gm
Gelatin dessert .....................1/3 cup .................. 65 gm

**Bedtime Feeding** (when directed by physician):

1/2 milk exchange (1/2 cup milk)

1/2 bread exchange (2 crackers)

will add approximately 120 calories to the daily diet.

## Breakfast
2 fruit exchanges (List 3)
3 1/2 bread exchanges (List 4)
2 meat exchanges (List 5)
1 milk exchange (List 7)
2 fat exchanges (List 6)
Coffee or tea (any amount)

**Example:**
Orange juice ...1 cup
Cornflakes .......3/4 cup
Toast ...............2 1/2 slices
Eggs ..................2
Butter .............1 tsp.
Cream .............1 oz.
Milk .................1 cup

## Lunch
2 meat exchanges (List 5)
4 bread exchanges (List 4)
Vegetable(s) as desired (List 1)
1 fruit exchange (List 3)
1 milk exchange (List 7)
2 fat exchanges (List 6)
Coffee or tea (any amount)

**Example:**
Cheese ...........1 oz.
Bread ......2 slices, sandwich
Butter ...........1 tsp.
Roast Beef .....1 slice
      (3" x 2" x 1/8")
Bread ......2 slices, sandwich
Mayonnaise ...1 tsp.
Celery and
   radishes .....as desired
Apple.. ...........1 small
Milk ...............1 cup

## Dinner
2 meat exchanges (List 5)
3 bread exchanges (List 4)
Vegetable(s) as desired (List 1)
1 vegetable exchange (List 2)
2 fruit exchanges (List 3)
1 milk exchange (List 7)

**Example:**
Hamburger ........2 patties
   (3" diam., 1/4" thick ea.)
Whole-kernel
   corn .................1/3 cup
Tomatoes ............as desired
Carrots ...............1/2 cup
Bread ...................2 slices
Butter ................2 tsp.

2 fat exchanges (List 6)          Plums ................ 4 med.
Coffee or tea (any amount)        Milk ..................... 1 cup


**2500 Calories** (approximately)   carbohydrate  250 gm
                                    protein       100 gm
                                    fat           120 gm

**Bedtime Feeding** (when directed by physician):
  1/2 milk exchange (1/2
      cup milk)                 ⎫
                                 ⎬ will add approximately 120
  1/2 bread exchange (2           calories to the daily diet.
      crackers)                 ⎭


## Breakfast

2 fruit exchanges (List 3)
3 1/2 bread exchanges
  (List 4)
3 meat exchanges (List 5)
1 milk exchange (List 7)
3 fat exchanges (List 6)
Coffee or tea (any amount)

**Example:**
Orange juice ...... 1 cup
Cereal, cooked .... 3/4 cup
Toast .................. 2 slices
Eggs ..................... 2
Ham ............... 1 slice
    (3" x 2" x 1/8")
Butter ............... 2 tsp.
Cream ............... 1 oz.
Milk ..................... 1 cup


## Dinner

2 meat exchanges (List 5)
3 bread exchanges (List 4)
Vegetable(s) as desired
  (List 1)
1 vegetable exchange
  (List 2)
2 fruit exchanges (List 3)
1 milk exchange (List 7)
4 fat exchanges (List 6)
Coffee or tea (any amount)

**Example:**
Grapefruit juice .. 1 cup
Tuna fish ............. 1/2 cup
  with
  mayonnaise .... 2 tsp.
Potato, baked .... 1 (2")
  with butter ...... 1 tsp.
Peas ................... 1/2 cup
Lettuce salad ...... as desired
Bread ................. 2 slices
Butter ............... 1 tsp.
Pear ................... 1 small
Milk ..................... 1 cup

**3000 Calories** (approximately)     carbohydrate   300 gm
                                      protein        130 gm
                                      fat            140 gm

## Breakfast
2 fruit exchanges (List 3)
2 bread exchanges (List 4)
2 meat exchanges (List 5)
1 milk exchange (List 7)
3 fat exchanges (List 6)
Coffee or tea (any amount)

**Example:**
Orange juice ......1 cup
Cereal, cooked .... 1/2 cup
Toast ..................1 slice
Egg ......................1
Ham ..................1 slice
     (3″ x 2″ x 1/8″)
Butter .................2 tsp.
Milk .....................1 cup
Cream, light ........2 tbsp.

## Lunch
3 meat exchanges (List 5)
4 bread exchanges (List 4)
Vegetable(s) as desired
   (List 1)
2 fruit exchanges (List 3)
1 milk exchange (List 7)
2 fat exchanges (List 6)
Coffee or tea (any amount)

**Example:**
Egg, hard-cooked
   and chopped....1
   mixed with
   mayonnaise ....1 tsp.
Bread ..................2 slices
Luncheon meat....2 slices
(4 1/2″ sq. x 1/8″ thick ea.)
Mayonnaise ........1 tsp.
Bread ..................2 slices
Dill pickle, sliced;
   radishes ..........as desired
Orange ................1
Milk .....................1 cup
Apple ..................1 small

## Midafternoon Feeding
1 meat exchange (List 5)
1 bread exchange (List 4)
1/2 milk exchange (List 7)
1 fat exchange (List 6)

**Example:**
American cheese..1 slice
   (3 1/2″ x 1 1/2″ x 1/4″)
Soda crackers ....3
Butter .................1 tsp.
Milk .....................1/2 cup
Coffee or tea ...... (any
                       amount)

## Dinner

3 meat exchanges (List 5)
4 bread exchanges (List 4)
Vegetable(s) as desired
  (List 1)
1 vegetable exchange
  (List 2)
2 fruit exchanges (List 3)
1 milk exchange (List 7)
3 fat exchanges ( List 6)
Coffee or tea (any amount)

**Example:**

Grapefruit juice....1/2 cup
Tuna fish ............3/4 cup
Potato, baked ....1 (4")
  with butter ......1 tsp.
Peas ....................1/2 cup
Lettuce salad ......as desired
Bread ..................2 slices
Butter ................2 tsp.
Pear ....................1 small
Milk ....................1 cup

## Bedtime Feeding

2 bread exchanges (List 4)
2 meat exchanges (List 5)
1 fat exchange (List 6)

**Example:**

Rye bread ..........2 slices
Ham ..................2 slices
  (3" x 2" x 1/8" ea.)
Mayonnaise ........1 tsp.

# APPETIZERS AND BEVERAGES

100 grams are equivalent to 3 1/2 ounces. This makes one serving when prepared according to the directions on the label.

When using basic ingredients such as arrowroot, eggs, flour, margarine, and tapioca, refer to General Information and to Table of Weights and Measures.

## *APPLE FOAM

Exchanges per serving: 1 cup = 1/2 fruit.
Calories per serving: 20                    Yield: 2 servings

2 cups apple juice
1 teaspoon lemon juice
1/4 cup (1-2 medium)
   egg whites

Non-nutritive sweetener
   equivalent to 1 1/2 cups
   sugar
1/16 teaspoon cinnamon

Chill juices. Beat egg whites until stiff; add sweetener while beating. Add apple and lemon juices; pour into fruit cups. Mix sugar substitute and cinnamon, enough to sprinkle on fruit juice mixture.

## *HONOLULU DIP

Exchanges per serving: 1/4 cup = 1/2 fat, 1/4 fruit.
Calories per serving: 43 (for dip only)   Yield: 1 1/3 cups

1/2 cup chopped fresh (or
   crushed, artificially
   sweetened) pineapple

3 ounces cream cheese
2 tablespoons safflower
   mayonnaise

31

2 tablespoons chopped
   mint

Blend ingredients together and serve with crisp carrot and celery sticks and crackers.

## *CHEESE NIBBLERS

Exchanges per serving: 1 ball = 1/4 bread, 2/3 fat,
                       1/4 meat.
Calories per serving: 60                Yield: 36 nibblers

1/2 cup sharp cheddar        1/2 cup diet margarine
   cheese, grated            1 cup flour

Mix the ingredients together and roll into balls. These can be made ahead of time and frozen—just freeze on a cookie sheet and then store in bags. To bake, place them, frozen, in an oven that has been preheated to 375° for 20-25 minutes.

## *GOLDEN SHOYU DIP

Exchanges per serving: 2 tablespoons = 2 fat.
Calories per serving: 90                Yield: 1 1/4 cups

1 cup safflower             1/2 teaspoon instant onion
   mayonnaise               1/4 teaspoon arrowroot
1/4 cup soy sauce              powder

Blend all ingredients until smooth. Chill and restir before serving as dip for all fish "pupus" or with grilled or fried fish.

## **RUMAKI

Exchanges per serving: 4 Rumaki = 2 fat, 1/2 meat.
Calories per serving: 120               Yield: 48 Rumakis

12 chicken livers (see note)   1 cup water chestnuts,
1 teaspoon seasoned salt          drained
1/8 teaspoon ginger            16 slices bacon

Cut livers into small bite-size pieces and season with salt and ginger; cut water chestnuts into halves and bacon into thirds; wrap a piece of liver and a half chestnut in bacon and secure with a pick. Broil or bake in 425° oven until golden brown (25-30 minutes). Serve hot with fruit chutney, chili sauce, Chinese Mustard, or Hot Shoyu Sauce.

**Note:** Chicken livers can be eliminated and just the water chestnuts fixed as above, in which case omit meat exchange.

### ***CHEESE AND PINEAPPLE PUPUS

Exchanges per serving: 1/3 cup dip = 3 fat, 1/2 meat,
                              1/2 cup pineapple = 1 fruit.
Calories per serving: 225        Yield: Fruit, 2 cups
                                           Sauce, 3 cups

| | |
|---|---|
| 1 fresh pineapple, cubed | 1 cup cheddar cheese, |
| 1 1/2 cups Luau | grated |
| mayonnaise | 1/2 cup shredded coconut |

Serve pineapple chunks on picks with bowls of other ingredients. Dip pineapple first in mayonnaise, then in cheese and coconut.

### *CRANBERRY SIP

Exchanges per serving: 1/2 cup = 3/4 fruit.
Calories per serving: 30        Yield: 2 1/2 cups

| | |
|---|---|
| 1 cup cranberries, washed | Non-nutritive sweetener |
| 1 1/2 cloves, whole | equivalent to 1 1/2 cups |
| 1 teaspoon cinnamon | sugar |
| 1 cup water | 1/4 cup orange juice |
| | 1/4 cup lemon juice |
| | 1/16 teaspoon salt |

Combine cranberries, spices, water, and sweetener; cook until cranberry skins burst. Strain and add rest of ingredients. Chill.

### *LOU'S LEMONADE

Exchanges per serving: 1/2 cup = 1/2 fruit.
Calories per serving: 20        Yield: 8 cups

1 cup unsweetened lemon
  juice
Non-nutritive sweetener
  equivalent to 3/4 cup
  sugar

6 cups water
1 cup low-calorie cran-
  berry juice cocktail

Combine ingredients and mix well. Add ice cubes just prior to serving.

## *QUICK DRINK

Exchanges per serving: 1 cup = 1/2 fruit, 1 skim milk.
Calories per serving: 100                Yield: 1 1/4 cups

2/3 cup dry instant
  powdered milk
1/2 cup frozen fruit,
  unsweetened

Non-nutritive sweetener
  equivalent to 2 table-
  spoons sugar
2 ice cubes
1/8 cup water

Blend in blender until ice cubes are dissolved.

## *HOT CHOCOLATE

Exchanges per serving: 1/2 cup = 1/2 fat,
                       1/2 skim milk.
Calories per serving: 58                 Yield: 2 1/2 cups

1 1/2 ounces unsweetened
  chocolate
3/4 cup water
1/16 teaspoon salt

Non-nutritive sweetener
  equivalent to 1/2 cup
  sugar
2 1/4 cups skim milk

Combine chocolate, water and cook, stirring constantly until chocolate is melted. Add salt and sweetener; bring to boiling point and boil 4 minutes, stirring constantly. Place over boiling water, and gradually add milk, still stirring constantly. Heat. Just before serving beat with rotary beater until frothy.

## *APRICOT ORANGE PUNCH

Exchanges per serving: 1/2 cup = 1 fruit.
Calories per serving: 40                 Yield: 7 cups

34

1 1/2 cups unsweetened
   apricot nectar
3 cups fresh orange juice
1/2 cup fresh lemon juice

Non-nutritive sweetener
   equivalent to 1/2 cup
   sugar
2 cups low-calorie ginger
   ale

Combine first four ingredients. Chill well and just before placing in punch bowl, add well-chilled ginger ale.

## *"DELISHUS" PUNCH

Exchanges per serving: 1/2 cup = 1 fruit.
Calories per serving: 40                   Yield: 8 cups

1 dozen cloves, whole
1 orange, thinly sliced
1 lemon, thinly sliced
4 cups low-calorie cran-
   berry juice cocktail

1 cinnamon stick
1 teaspoon allspice
2 tablespoons lemon juice
Non-nutritive sweetener to
   taste

Put a clove in each slice of lemon and orange. Place in a pitcher. Combine cocktail, cinnamon, and allspice and heat to boiling over low heat. Add lemon juice. Add sweetener to taste and strain hot into pitcher over the fruit. Serve in punch cups garnished with fruit slices.

## *NONNIE'S CRANBERRY COCKTAIL

Exchanges per serving: 1 cup = 1 fruit.
Calories per serving: 40                   Yield: 5 cups

4 cups low-calorie cran-
   berry juice
3 cloves
1 stick cinnamon

Non-nutritive sweetener
   equivalent to 1 cup sugar
1/4 cup fresh lemon juice
2/3 cup fresh orange juice
1/16 teaspoon salt

Combine first four ingredients and bring to a boil. Reduce heat; simmer a few minutes, then remove from heat. Add juices and salt. Chill. Serve very cold.

## *OLGA'S MINTY DRINK

Exchanges per serving: 1 cup = 1 fruit.
Calories per serving: 40                   Yield: 8 cups

1/4 cup mint leaves, chopped fine
Non-nutritive sweetener equivalent to 1/2 cup sugar

1 cup water
1/2 cup fresh lemon juice
2 cups fresh orange juice
4 cups low-calorie ginger ale

Combine first three ingredients and bring to a boil. Cool and strain. When ready to serve, add remaining ingredients and pour over crushed ice in chilled glasses.

## *YUMMY COFFEE DRINK

Exchanges per serving: 1 cup = 2 fat.
Calories per serving: 90                Yield: 4 1/2 cups

2 cups strong iced coffee
Non-nutritive sweetener equivalent to 1/3 cup sugar

1/2 cup nondairy whipping cream
2 cups low-calorie ginger ale

Mix coffee and sweetener. Fill 4 large glasses about 1/4 full with crushed ice. Whip cream. Add 1/4 cup cream and 1/4 cup coffee mixture, then 1/2 cup ginger ale. Stir slightly.

## *NONALCOHOLIC EGGNOG

Exchanges per serving: 1 cup = 1/3 skim milk, 1/2 meat.
Calories per serving: 62                Yield: 4 cups

1/2 cup (2 medium) eggs
1/2 cup dry nonfat instant powdered milk
2 2/3 cups water, ice cold

Non-nutritive sweetener equivalent to 2 table- spoons sugar
3 teaspoons vanilla
1 teaspoon rum flavoring

Mix all ingredients well, pour into cups and serve.

## *LEMONADE

Exchanges per serving: 1/2 cup = 1/2 fruit.
Calories per serving: 20                Yield: 2 cups

2/3 cup unsweetened lemon juice
1 1/2 cups cold water

Sugar syrup substitute
Lemon slices

Combine lemon juice and water. Sweeten with sugar syrup substitute, and add ice. Pour into large glasses on top of ice. Garnish with lemon slice.

## *COLA DRINK

Exchanges per serving: 1 cup = 1 skim milk.
Calories per serving: 75                    Yield: 2 cups

2 sugarfree, non-caloric        Non-nutritive sweetener
  cola tablets                      equivalent to 1 teaspoon
2 cups skim milk                sugar

Mix all ingredients well until tablets dissolve.

## *CRANBERRY PUNCH

Exchanges per serving: 1/2 cup = 1/2 fruit.
Calories per serving: 20                    Yield: 15 cups

8 cups low-calorie cran-        Non-nutritive sweetener
  berry juice cocktail            equivalent to 1/3 cup
3 cups unsweetened pine-        sugar
  apple juice                     4 cups low-calorie ginger
                                            ale

Combine juices and sweetener. Chill and stir in ginger ale, which has been well chilled, just before serving; add ice cubes.

## *IMITATION WINE

Exchanges per serving: 1/2 cup = 1/2 fruit.
Calories per serving: 20                    Yield: 8 cups

2 cups unsweetened grape        2 cups low-calorie fruit
  juice                           carbonated beverage,
Non-nutritive sweetener         chilled
  equivalent to 1/3 cup           4 cups low-calorie ginger
  sugar                           ale, chilled

Combine juice and sweetener and chill. Stir in carbonated beverage and ginger ale just before serving. Add ice cubes.

# *JOAN'S FRUIT SHAKE

Exchanges per serving: 1 cup = 1 fruit, 1/2 skim milk.
Calories per serving: 80                     Yield: 4 cups

| | |
|---|---|
| 2 bananas | Non-nutritive sweetener |
| 3 tablespoons fresh orange | equivalent to 1/2 cup |
| juice | sugar |
| 1/16 teaspoon salt | 1/8 teaspoon vanilla |
| | 2 cups skim milk |

Blend all ingredients until smooth and foamy. Place in refrigerator until chilled, then serve.

# *COFFEE PUNCH

Exchanges per serving: 1 cup = 1/4 milk.
Calories per serving: 45                 Yield: 24 6-ounce cups

| | |
|---|---|
| 2 cups skim milk | 4 cups ice milk (vanilla, |
| 8 cups strong coffee, cold | chocolate, or coffee) |
| 2 teaspoons vanilla | 1 cup nondairy cream, |
| Non-nutritive sweetener | whipped |
| equivalent to 1/2 cup | 1/16 teaspoon cinnamon |
| sugar | or nutmeg |

Combine milk, coffee, vanilla, and sweetener in large pitcher; stir until sweetener dissolves, then chill. Place chunks of ice milk in punch bowl just before serving. Add coffee mix, put nondairy whipped cream on top, stir lightly; add cinnamon or nutmeg.

# *COCOA

Exchanges per serving: 1 cup = 1 skim milk.
Calories per serving: 75                     Yield: 8 cups

| | |
|---|---|
| 6 tablespoons unsweetened | 6 cups skim milk |
| cocoa | Non-nutritive sweetener |
| 1/2 teaspoon salt | equivalent to 1/2 cup |
| 2 cups water | sugar |

Mix cocoa, salt, and water. Stir constantly over very low heat for 2 minutes. Add milk and sweetener; continue stirring until cocoa again boils; serve.

## **WINE LEMONADE

(Not for diabetics without consent of doctor.)
Exchanges per serving: 1 cup = 1/2 fruit.
Calories per serving: 20 + alcohol (approx. 148)

Yield: 6 cups

3 cups water
1/2 cup fresh lemon juice

Non-nutritive sweetener
   equivalent to 1/2 cup
   sugar
2 cups white wine

Combine all ingredients and pour over crushed ice in chilled glasses.


## **EGGNOG DEVINE

(Not for diabetics without consent of doctor.)
Exchanges per serving: 1/2 cup = 1/2 meat, 1 skim milk.
Calories per serving: 116 + alcohol    Yield: 4 cups

3/4 cup (3 medium) eggs,
   separated
4 cups skim milk

Non-nutritive sweetener
   equivalent to 1/2 cup
   sugar
1/2 cup rum

Beat egg yolks until thick and lemony and combine all ingredients except whites of eggs. Beat whites until stiff and fold in carefully just before serving.


## ****CHAMPAGNE PUNCH

(Not for diabetics without consent of doctor.)
Exchanges per serving: 1 cup = 1/4 fruit.
Calories per serving: 10 + alcohol (approx. 1246)

Yield: 50 cups

1 "fifth" bottle white rum
Non-nutritive sweetener
   equivalent to 1/2 cup
   sugar
2 cups fresh peaches,
   sliced thin

1/2 cup orange-flavored
   liqueur
6 "fifth" bottles champagne
   chilled

39

The day before serving, place rum in bowl; stir in sugar substitute; add peaches as you slice, to prevent their turning brown. Just before serving stir in the orange liqueur; pour over ice in a large punch bowl, add champagne, and serve at once.

# SOUPS

Many soup companies can help you plan meals using as a base one of their products. On these you can generally obtain 3 servings per can, with 1 serving equaling 7 ounces (except where noted). If you make the soup with milk, you must, of course, subtract that amount of milk from what is allotted you for that meal. The following, through the courtesy of the Campbell Soup Company, are examples. There are, of course, other varieties manufactured.

## PROXIMATE COMPOSITION OF
## CAMPBELL SOUP COMPANY PRODUCTS
(Contents of 100 grams, undiluted)*

| VARIETY | Calories | Protein | Fat | Carbohydrate | Sodium | Vitamin A |
|---|---|---|---|---|---|---|
| Heat Processed Soups | | gm | gm | gm | mg | I. U. |
| Asparagus, Cream of | 70 | 1.9 | 2.8 | 9.4 | 890 | 321 |
| Bean with Bacon | 133 | 6.8 | 4.2 | 17.1 | 750 | 550 |
| Beef | 87 | 8.0 | 2.0 | 9.2 | 773 | 1067 |
| Beef Broth | 22 | 3.6 | 0.0 | 2.1 | 708 | trace |
| Beef Noodle | 58 | 3.2 | 1.9 | 7.2 | 795 | 52 |
| Black Bean | 80 | 4.7 | 1.4 | 12.2 | 860 | 258 |
| Celery, Cream of | 66 | 1.4 | 3.9 | 6.4 | 860 | 173 |

(*) 100 grams are equivalent to 3 1/2 ounces or 1/3 can of soup. This makes one serving when prepared according to the directions on the label. If soup is prepared with milk, add the nutrients listed opposite the type of milk used. No nutrients are added if soup is prepared with water.

| | | | | | | |
|---|---|---|---|---|---|---|
| Cheddar Cheese | 142 | 4.8 | 9.9 | 8.3 | 780 | 300 |
| Chicken Broth | 36 | 5.5 | 1.0 | 1.2 | 785 | |
| Chicken, Cream of | 76 | 2.8 | 4.4 | 6.3 | 800 | 48 |
| Chicken Gumbo | 49 | 2.2 | 1.1 | 7.5 | 900 | 17 |
| Chicken 'n Dumplings | 83 | 5.8 | 4.8 | 4.2 | 860 | 17 |
| Chicken Noodle | 55 | 3.3 | 1.6 | 6.9 | 870 | 4 |
| Chicken with Rice | 43 | 2.8 | 1.3 | 4.9 | 756 | 13 |
| Chicken and Stars | 50 | 3.4 | 1.3 | 6.1 | 930 | 13 |
| Chicken Vegetable | 60 | 3.4 | 1.8 | 7.6 | 820 | 207 |
| Chili Beef | 131 | 6.2 | 3.7 | 18.3 | 860 | 61 |
| Clam Chowder (Manhattan Style) | 63 | 1.9 | 2.1 | 9.2 | 720 | 71 |
| Consommé | 28 | 4.7 | 0.0 | 2.5 | 550 | trace |
| Golden Mushroom | 70 | 2.9 | 3.5 | 6.8 | 840 | 1170 |
| Green Pea | 116 | 6.9 | 1.6 | 18.5 | 760 | 206 |
| Hot Dog Bean | 153 | 8.4 | 5.3 | 18.0 | 805 | 510 |
| Minestrone | 72 | 3.5 | 2.4 | 9.2 | 788 | 2167 |
| Mushroom, Cream of | 115 | 1.7 | 8.7 | 7.5 | 842 | 79 |
| Noodles and Ground Beef | 80 | 3.6 | 3.7 | 8.1 | 760 | 470 |
| Onion | 37 | 3.5 | 1.4 | 2.7 | 810 | trace |
| Oyster Stew | 57 | 1.8 | 3.2 | 5.3 | 780 | trace |
| Pepper Pot | 83 | 6.1 | 3.2 | 7.6 | 1000 | 478 |
| Potato, Cream of | 59 | 1.4 | 1.9 | 9.0 | 914 | trace |
| Scotch Broth | 74 | 4.6 | 2.4 | 8.6 | 1000 | 1867 |
| Split Pea with Ham | 141 | 10.2 | 2.6 | 19.1 | 803 | 480 |
| Tomato | 69 | 1.4 | 1.6 | 12.3 | 810 | 946 |
| Tomato, Bisque of | 101 | 2.2 | 2.1 | 18.4 | 870 | 695 |
| Tomato Rice, Old-Fashioned | 87 | 1.6 | 2.5 | 14.7 | 662 | 917 |
| Turkey Noodle | 63 | 3.3 | 2.6 | 6.6 | 760 | 120 |
| Turkey Vegetable | 64 | 2.7 | 2.8 | 7.0 | 710 | 2572 |
| Vegetable | 68 | 2.7 | 1.4 | 11.1 | 730 | 2579 |
| Vegetable Beef | 66 | 5.0 | 2.3 | 6.4 | 755 | 2795 |
| Vegetable and Beef Stockpot | 79 | 4.5 | 3.4 | 7.5 | 785 | 3235 |
| Vegetable, Old-Fashioned | 53 | 2.2 | 1.7 | 7.2 | 713 | 2242 |
| Vegetarian Vegetable | 62 | 1.8 | 1.5 | 10.4 | 594 | 2494 |

## Frozen Soups

| | | | | | | |
|---|---|---|---|---|---|---|
| Clam Chowder (New England Style) | 108 | 3.7 | 6.4 | 8.9 | 870 | 50 |
| Green Pea with Ham | 109 | 7.6 | 2.3 | 14.5 | 750 | 185 |
| Oyster Stew | 102 | 4.6 | 6.3 | 6.9 | 680 | 191 |
| Potato, Cream of | 90 | 2.7 | 4.3 | 10.1 | 944 | 345 |

| | | | | | | |
|---|---|---|---|---|---|---|
| Shrimp, Cream of | 132 | 4.0 | 9.9 | 6.9 | 860 | 93 |
| Vegetable with Beef, Old-Fashioned | 68 | 5.4 | 2.3 | 6.6 | 856 | 2272 |

## CONDENSED SOUPS IN EXCHANGE LISTS FOR DIABETICS AND OTHER PATIENTS

The following recommendations have been developed by Campbell Soup Company, based on the Standard Exchange Units set forth by American Dietetic Association, American Diabetic Association, and Public Health Service, Department of Health, Education, and Welfare.

## RECOMMENDATIONS FOR PLACING CAMPBELL'S SOUPS INTO EXCHANGE LISTS

These recommendations are based on a 100-gram portion, which is equivalent of 3 1/2 ounces or 1/3 can of soup. This makes a 7-ounce serving when prepared according to directions on the label. If milk is used in the preparation, use part of your daily allotment. NOTE: When serving a portion, be sure the soup is well blended.

Exchange Substitution for 1 Bread and 1/2 Fat

Frozen Green Pea with Ham
Green Pea
Tomato, Bisque of

Exchange Substitution for 1 Bread

Black Bean
Tomato
Tomato Rice, Old-Fashioned
Vegetable

Exchange Substitution for 1/2 Meat and 1/2 Bread

Beef Soup
Chicken Vegetable
Clam Chowder, Manhattan Style
Noodles and Ground Beef
Pepper Pot
Scotch Broth
Vegetable Beef
Frozen Vegetable with Beef, Old-Fashioned

Exchange Substitution for 1/2 Bread and 1/2 Fat

43

Exchange Substitution for
  1/2 Bread and 1 Fat

Celery, Cream of
Chicken, Cream of
Minestrone
Frozen Potato, Cream of

Exchange Substitution for 1
  Meat and 1 Bread

Split Pea with Ham

Asparagus, Cream of
Beef Noodle
Chicken Gumbo
Chicken Noodle
Chicken and Stars
Potato, Cream of
Turkey Noodle
Turkey Vegetable
Vegetarian Vegetable
Vegetable, Old-Fashioned

## *JOAN'S JELLIED TOMATO CONSOMME

Exchanges per serving: 2/3 cup = 1 fat, 1/2 fruit,
                1 "A" vegetable.

Calories per serving: 65                  Yield: 3 cups

1 envelope unflavored
  gelatin
2 1/4 cups tomato juice
1 bouillon cube, any flavor
1/2 teaspoon salt
Non-nutritive sweetener
  equivalent to 1/4 cup
  sugar

1/2 teaspoon Worcester-
  shire sauce
1/8 teaspoon Tabasco
  sauce
2 tablespoons lemon juice
1/4 cup cucumbers,
  unpeeled and diced
1/2 cup imitation sour
  cream (optional)

Sprinkle gelatin over half the tomato juice in a saucepan.
Add bouillon cube and place over low heat, stirring constantly until gelatin and cube are dissolved (about 3 minutes). Remove from heat. Add rest of tomato juice, salt,
sweetener, Worcestershire and Tabasco sauces, cucumbers,
and lemon juice. Pour into 2" x 8" x 8" pan and chill
until firm. Spoon into serving dishes. Serve with imitation
sour cream topping, if desired.

## *ASPARAGUS SOUP

Exchanges per serving: 1/2 cup = No exchange necessary.
Calories per serving: 0                   Yield: 5 cups

44

| 2 cups asparagus | 1/16 teaspoon thyme |
| 3 cups water | 1/8 teaspoon salt |
| 4 bouillon cubes, any flavor | 1/16 teaspoon pepper |

Puree asparagus. Boil water and combine with bouillon cubes, thyme, salt, and pepper. Add asparagus and simmer 5 minutes.

## *CUCUMBER SOUP

Exchanges per serving: 1 cup = 1 1/2 fat,
1 "A" vegetable.

Calories per serving: 68                Yield: 3 cups

| 2 beef or chicken bouillon cubes | 1/4 teaspoon lemon peel, dried |
| 2 cups water | 1/16 teaspoon seasoned salt |
| 1 cucumber, sliced | 1/16 teaspoon pepper |
| 1/2 cup imitation sour cream | 1/16 teaspoon thyme |

Bring bouillon, water, and cucumber slices to boil. Cover and simmer until tender (about 10 minutes). Cool and place in refrigerator. When cold, blend and add sour cream, lemon peel, and condiments. Blend until smooth. Serve cold.

## *VEGETABLE SOUP, COLD
### (Gazpacho)

Exchanges per serving: No exchange necessary.
Calories per serving: 0                Yield: 6 servings

| 1 cup tomatoes, peeled and finely chopped | 1 small clove garlic (minced or run through garlic press) |
| 1/2 cup green pepper, finely chopped | 3 tablespoons tarragon wine vinegar |
| 1/2 cup celery, finely chopped | 1 teaspoon garlic salt |
| 1/2 cup cucumber, peeled and finely chopped | 1/4 teaspoon pepper |
| 1/4 cup green onion, finely chopped | 1 teaspoon Worcestershire sauce |
| | 2 cups tomato juice |

45

| 2 teaspoons parsley, snipped | Hot sauce to taste (approximately 2 teaspoons) |
| 1 teaspoon chives, snipped | |

Combine ingredients in either a glass or stainless steel bowl. Take half the mixture and put through blender. When thoroughly blended return to bowl; mix well. Cover bowl and place in refrigerator to chill at least 4 hours, and serve in chilled cups. This may also be used in place of a salad.

## *GREAT CARROT or BEAN SOUP

Exchanges per serving: 1 cup carrot = 1 "B" vegetable.
                        1 cup bean = 1 "A" vegetable.
Calories per serving: Carrots, 20; Beans, 0   Yield: 4 cups

| 1 cup water | 1/4 teaspoon thyme |
| 2 bouillon cubes, any flavor | 1/16 teaspoon salt |
| 2 scant cups carrots (or green beans, if preferred) | 1/16 teaspoon pepper |

Heat water with bouillon cubes in saucepan and stir occasionally. Add carrots and puree until smooth. Add thyme, salt, and pepper.

## *TARRAGON-THYME SOUP

Exchanges per serving: 2/3 cup = 1 fat, 1 "A" vegetable.
Calories per serving: 45                 Yield: 2 1/3 cups

| 2 tablespoons onion, chopped | 1/2 teaspoon dried tarragon |
| 2 tablespoons celery, chopped very fine | 1/2 teaspoon salt |
| 1 tablespoon diet margarine | 1/8 teaspoon pepper |
| 2 cups tomato juice | 1/16 teaspoon Tabasco sauce, if desired |

Sauté onion and celery in margarine until onion is golden, then add rest of ingredients. Bring to a boil. Lower heat and simmer 5 minutes.

## *EASY PEANUT SOUP

Exchanges per serving: 2/3 cup = 1 bread, 1/2 meat.
Calories per serving: 100          Yield: 4 3/4 cups

1 1/2 cups condensed
   cream of chicken soup
1 1/2 cups condensed
   cream of celery soup

1/4 cup chunky peanut
   butter
1 1/2 cups water

Blend all ingredients well; let simmer 5 minutes.

## **POTATO AND WATERCRESS SOUP

Exchanges per serving: 1 cup = 1/2 bread, 1/2 milk.
Calories per serving: 120          Yield: 3 1/3 cups

1 1/3 cups cream of
   potato soup
1 1/3 cups skim milk
1/2 cup watercress,
   chopped fine (packed
   tightly)

1/2 teaspoon thyme
1/16 teaspoon salt
1/16 teaspoon pepper

Heat cream of potato soup with skim milk in saucepan.
Puree watercress and thyme. Mix with soup until well
blended. Add salt and pepper. Cover. Cook and serve hot
or cold.

## *CELERY BEAN SOUP

Exchanges per serving: 1 cup = 1/2 fat, 1/2 skim milk,
                  1/2 "A" vegetable.
Calories per serving: 98          Yield: 4 cups

1 cup string beans, cut fine
2 tablespoons onion,
   chopped fine
1 1/4 cups condensed
   cream of celery soup

1/16 teaspoon salt
2/3 teaspoon arrowroot
   powder
1 1/2 cups skim milk

Combine beans and onion with 1/8 cup water, the soup,
and half the salt. Cook in tightly covered saucepan about
6-7 minutes, until onions soften. In another saucepan combine remaining salt and arrowroot powder; stir in skim

milk gradually to make a smooth mixture. Add to first mixture and cook over low heat, stirring occasionally until thickened.

## **FESTIVE TOMATO SOUP

Exchanges per serving: 1 scant cup = 1 bread, 1 fruit.
Calories per serving: 110                    Yield: 5 2/3 cups

**2 2/3 cups tomato soup**
**(do not add water)**

**2/3 cup unsweetened**
**orange juice concentrate**
**2 1/2 cups water**

Put tomato soup in pan, add mixture of orange juice and water. Boil gently. Serve hot or cold.

## ***SHRIMP CHOWDER

Exchanges per serving: 1/2 cup = 1 bread, 2 meat,
                    1/2 skim milk, 1 "B" vegetable.
Calories per serving: 288                    Yield: 8 1/4 cups

**1/2 cup onion, finely**
**chopped**
**1 tablespoon diet margarine**
**2 cups water**
**2 teaspoons salt**
**1 1/4 cups potatoes, pared**
**and cubed (about 1/2"**
**thick)**

**2 cups skim milk, scalded**
**1 2/3 cups shrimp, drained**
**and shelled**
**1/2 tablespoon arrowroot**
**powder**
**1 tablespoon water**
**1/6 teaspoon salt**
**1/16 teaspoon pepper**

Sauté onion in margarine until golden. Add water, salt, and potatoes. Boil gently, covered, until potatoes are tender (about 20 minutes). Add scalded skim milk and shrimp, stirring occasionally. Bring to boil, reduce heat and simmer until shrimp are pink and cooked (about 5 minutes). Make smooth thin paste of arrowroot and water; add to first mixture and stir until slightly thickened. Add pepper and remaining salt, to taste.

## **SPLIT PEA SOUP

Exchanges per serving: 1 cup = 1 1/2 bread,
                    1/2 "B" vegetable.
Calories per serving: 123                    Yield: 6 cups

| 1 cup green split peas, | 3 beef or chicken bouillon |
|---|---|
| drained | cubes |
| 1 carrot, sliced thin | 1 teaspoon salt |
| 1 onion, sliced thin | 1/16 teaspoon pepper |
| 5 cups water | 1 teaspoon curry powder |
| | (optional) |

Mix everything except the curry powder together in saucepan. Cover and boil gently until peas are very soft (about 3/4 hour). Stir in curry powder; press mixture through sieve and return puree to saucepan. Reheat and serve.

### ***TURKEY-WATERCRESS SOUP

Exchanges per serving: 1 cup = 3 meat, 1 "A" and
1 "B" vegetable.
Calories per serving: 260        Yield: 3 cups

| 1 cup water | 1 1/2 cups cooked turkey, |
|---|---|
| 1 1/3 cups turkey broth, | cut in small pieces |
| condensed | 1 cup watercress, packed |
| 2 tablespoons onion, | firm (chopped fine) |
| chopped fine | 1 1/2 teaspoons arrowroot |
| 1/4 cup celery, chopped | powder |
| fine | 2 tablespoons water |
| 1/2 teaspoon salt | |

Simmer first six ingredients about 15 minutes. Add watercress and simmer again until watercress is wilted. Mix arrowroot powder and two tablespoons water into a smooth paste and stir into soup. Cook until clear and smooth (a few minutes).

### ***QUICK AND TASTY CHICKEN SOUP

Exchanges per serving: 1 cup = 3 meat.
Calories per serving: 277        Yield: 4 cups

| 1 1/2 cups chicken or | 1/4 cup celery, diced fine |
|---|---|
| turkey, cooked and diced | 1/2 teaspoon salt |
| 1 1/3 cups chicken or | 1/2 teaspoon thyme |
| turkey broth | 1/2 tablespoon arrowroot |
| 1 cup water | powder |

| 2 tablespoons onion, chopped fine | 1 tablespoon water |

Simmer first seven ingredients for about 10 minutes. Make paste with arrowroot and water; add to soup. Cook until clear and smooth (takes just a few seconds).

# SALADS

## *CUCUMBER SALAD, SWEET AND SOUR

Exchanges per serving: 1/2 cup = 1 "A" vegetable.
Calories per serving: 0                     Yield: 2 cups

| | |
|---|---|
| 1/2 cup water | 1/8 cup dill pickle, |
| 1 cup cider vinegar | chopped fine |
| Non-nutritive sweetener | 1 1/2 teaspoons salt |
| equivalent to 1/8 cup | 2 cucumbers, sliced thin |
| sugar | 1 stalk celery, sliced thin |

Boil the water, vinegar, sweetener, pickle, and salt. Place cucumbers and celery slices in glass jar; pour boiling liquid over them, cover and refrigerate overnight. Drain before serving.

## *MARINATED VEGETABLE TOSS

Exchanges per serving: 1/2 cup = 1 "A" vegetable.
Calories per serving: 0 (exclusive of dressing)
                                        Yield: 8 servings

| | |
|---|---|
| 2 cups fresh tomato | 1/2 medium red onion, |
| wedges, peeled | thinly sliced |
| 1/2 cup radishes, sliced | 1/2 cup celery crescents |
| | 1/2 cup cucumber chunks |

Combine all vegetables in salad bowl, pour Italian dressing over. Refrigerate overnight.

## *SWEET AND SOUR BEETS

Exchanges per serving: 1 serving = 1/2 meat, 1 "A" and
                        1 "B" vegetable.
Calories per serving: 70                 Yield: 6 servings

4 cups sliced beets (reserve
    juice)
Non-nutritive sweetener
    equivalent to 3 table-
    spoons sugar
1 teaspoon salt

1/4 teaspoon black pepper
1 tablespoon allspice
1/2 cup vinegar
3 eggs, hard-boiled and
    shelled
Lettuce

Mix 1/2 cup beet juice with sweetener, salt, pepper, and
allspice. Boil gently about 5 minutes. Strain, stir in vinegar.
Place eggs and beet slices in baking dish. Pour beet-juice
mixture over them and refrigerate overnight, turning both
beets and eggs occasionally. Slice eggs with egg slicer; drain
beets and divide into 6 servings; place on lettuce leaves.
Top each with liquid, then sliced half egg.


## *RADISH CELERY SALAD

Exchanges per serving: 1/2 cup = 1 "A" vegetable.
Calories per serving: 0 (exclusive of dressing)

Yield: 2 cups

1 bunch radishes, sliced
    thin
1 cup celery, sliced thin

1/4 cup French dressing
    (low calorie)
Lettuce leaves

Toss radishes, celery, and dressing together. Refrigerate
an hour or so before placing on lettuce leaves.


## *TOMATO AND HERB SALAD

Exchanges per serving: 1 serving = 1 "A" vegetable.
Calories per serving: 0                           Yield: 6 servings

6 tomatoes, peeled
1 1/2 teaspoons oregano
Non-nutritive sweetener
    equivalent to 1 table-
    spoon sugar

4 tablespoons malt vinegar
1/2 teaspoon seasoned salt
1/4 teaspoon pepper
Lettuce leaves

Chop 1 1/2 tomatoes fine; combine with oregano, sweetener, vinegar, and salt. Slice remaining tomatoes, place on
top of lettuce leaves; top with vinegar mix; refrigerate
until ready to serve.

## *PEPPER SLAW

Exchanges per serving: 1/2 cup = 1 "A" vegetable.
Calories per serving: 0 (exclusive of dressing)

Yield: 3 cups

1/2 head cabbage
1 carrot, chopped fine

1/4 green pepper,
  chopped fine
2 cups water

Cut cabbage into small wedges. Place half in blender along with carrot and pepper. Blend quickly; turn off and drain at once, using liquid for blending with balance of cabbage. Mix with salad dressing.

## *MOLDED VEGETABLE SALAD

Exchanges per serving: 1/2 cup = 1 "A" vegetable.
Calories per serving: 10 (+ 9 calories in gelatin)

Yield: 4 servings

1 envelope dietetic orange
  gelatin
2 cups boiling water
1/2 cup white cabbage,
  chopped

1/2 cup carrots, shredded
1/4 cup celery, finely
  chopped
1/4 teaspoon celery seeds

Dissolve gelatin in boiling water. Chill until consistency of egg whites. Fold in vegetables and celery seeds. Pour in pan or molds and refrigerate until firm.

## *RASPBERRY RHUBARB SALAD

Exchanges per serving: 1/2 cup = 1/8 fruit.
Calories per serving: 5 (exclusive of dressing)

Yield: 2 cups

1 cup boiling water
1 envelope dietetic rasp-
  berry gelatin
1/2 cup artificially
  sweetened rhubarb sauce
1/2 teaspoon anise seed,
  crushed fine

1/2 cup apples, chopped
  fine
1/2 cup celery, chopped
  fine
1 or 2 drops red vegetable
  coloring
Lettuce

Dissolve gelatin in water. Add rhubarb and anise seed, mix well, and cool until congealed slightly. Add apples and celery; mix well. Pour into slightly oiled salad mold and chill until firm. Divide equally on lettuce and serve with fruit salad dressing, if desired.


## *CUCUMBER-PINEAPPLE-GELATIN SALAD

Exchanges per serving: 1/2 cup = 1/2 fruit.
Calories per serving: 20                        Yield: 3 1/2 cups

1 envelope dietetic lemon or       1/8 teaspoon salt
  orange-flavored gelatin          1 cup artificially sweetened
1/2 cup hot water                    dietetic pineapple tidbits
1/4 cup liquid, drained            1 1/2 cups cucumber,
  from pineapple tidbits             shredded and drained
1/4 cup lemon or orange
  juice

Dissolve gelatin in hot water. Add pineapple liquid, orange or lemon juice, and salt. Chill until thickened and consistency of syrup. Then fold in pineapple and cucumber. Pour into mold and chill.


## *LAURA'S JELLIED VEGETABLE SALAD

Exchanges per serving: 1 serving = 1 "A" vegetable.
Calories per serving: 20                        Yield: 8 servings

2 envelopes unflavored             1 tablespoon tarragon
  gelatin                            vinegar
1/2 cup cold water                 1 teaspoon salt
3 cups boiling water               3 drops food coloring
1/2 cup fresh lemon juice          1/2 cucumber, diced fine
Non-nutritive sweetener            8-9 radishes, sliced
  equivalent to 2/3 cup            8-9 scallions, sliced
  sugar

Soften gelatin in cold water; add boiling water and stir to dissolve. Blend in lemon juice, sweetener, vinegar, salt, and coloring; chill until mixture begins to thicken. Fold in vegetables and place in a lightly oiled mold. Chill until set.

# *CARROT SLICES

Exchanges per serving: 2/3 cup = 1/2 bread,
1 "B" vegetable.

Calories per serving: 70                          Yield: 3 cups

2 cups carrots, scraped
and cut into 1" slices
3/4 cup water
1/4 cup cider vinegar
1/2 teaspoon dill pickle,
chopped fine
1 tablespoon green onion
seasoning

1/2 teaspoon poultry
seasoning
1/2 teaspoon thyme
1/4 teaspoon garlic salt
1/2 teaspoon marjoram
1/2 teaspoon seasoned salt
1/16 teaspoon lemon
pepper
1 cup prepared croutons

Simmer first nine ingredients covered, until carrots are
tender. Add salt, pepper, and croutons. Cool. Place in
refrigerator for an hour, drain, and serve.

# *GOLDEN GLOW SALAD

Exchanges per serving: 1/2 cup = 1 fruit, 1 "A" and
1 "B" vegetable.

Calories per serving: 75                          Yield: 4 cups

1 envelope unflavored
gelatin
1/8 cup lemon juice
2 cups artificially sweetened pineapple tidbits
(reserve syrup)

1/4 teaspoon salt
1 tablespoon vinegar
1 cup carrots, grated
1/2 cup boiling water
Lettuce

Mix gelatin, lemon juice, and syrup from pineapple tidbits.
Soften a few minutes; stir in salt, vinegar, carrots, pineapple, and boiling water. Pour into loaf pan and refrigerate
until firm (about 4-5 hours). Serve on lettuce leaves.

# *APPLE-CELERY-CRANBERRY-NUT MOLD

Exchanges per serving: 3/4 cup = 1 fat, 1 fruit.
Calories per serving: 85                          Yield: 4 1/4 cups

2 cups cranberries
1 1/4 cups water

1 cup apples, peeled and
diced

Non-nutritive sweetener
equivalent to 1 cup
sugar
1 package unflavored
gelatin

1/2 cup celery, chopped
fine
1/2 cup pecans, chopped
very fine
Lettuce

Cook cranberries in 1 cup water. When skins are broken rub through sieve. Add sweetener and reheat. Soften gelatin in remaining 1/4 cup water, add to cranberry puree and cool. When mixture starts to thicken add apples, celery, and pecans. Pour into mold. Chill. Serve on lettuce.

## *PEACH-Y SALAD

Exchanges per serving: 2/3 cup = 1 fruit,
1 "A" vegetable.
Calories per serving: 40                  Yield: 4 cups

4 cups artificially sweetened peaches, halved
1 tablespoon vinegar

2 sticks cinnamon
1/2 teaspoon allspice
1 teaspoon cloves, whole
Lettuce

Mix peaches, vinegar, cinnamon, and allspice. Boil gently 5 minutes. Place in refrigerator 5-6 hours. Drain thoroughly; stick a clove in each peach half; serve on lettuce leaves.

## *SUPER SALAD

Exchanges per serving: 1 serving = 1 fruit, 1 "A" and
1 "B" vegetable.
Calories per serving: 75                  Yield: 3 1/2 cups

1 cup carrots, grated
2 cups unsweetened
pineapple tidbits
(reserve syrup)
1/4 teaspoon salt
1/2 teaspoon anise seed,
crushed

1 tablespoon white vinegar
1/2 cup boiling water
1/8 cup lemon juice
1 envelope unflavored
gelatin
Lettuce

Mix carrots, pineapple, salt, anise seed, vinegar, and water. Stir together lemon juice, gelatin, syrup from pineapple;

56

let soften, then add to first mixture and pour into lightly oiled salad mold. Refrigerate until firm. Loosen mold in hot water; run table knife along inside edges, invert on lettuce.

## *JELLIED APPLESAUCE SALAD

Exchanges per serving: 1/2 cup = 1 fruit,
1 "A" vegetable.
Calories per serving: 40 (+ 9 calories in gelatin)
Yield: 4 servings

1 envelope diet raspberry
gelatin
1 3/4 cups boiling water
1 cup water-packed
applesauce

1/2 cup water-packed
crushed pineapple,
drained
1/2 cup celery, chopped

Dissolve gelatin in hot water. Let cool in refrigerator until the consistency of egg whites. Add fruit and celery; stir well. Pour into pan or molds and refrigerate until set (4-5 hours).

## *JELLIED FRUIT SALAD

Exchanges per serving: 2/3 cup = 1/2 fruit.
Calories per serving: 20
Yield: 4 cups

1 envelope low-calorie
strawberry gelatin
dessert
1 3/4 cups boiling water
1/4 cup fresh lemon juice

Non-nutritive sweetener
equivalent to 1/2 cup
sugar
1 cup fresh peaches, sliced
fine
1 cup cantaloupe balls

Dissolve gelatin in boiling water. Add lemon juice and sweetener. Chill until consistency of thick syrup; add fruit. Place in lightly oiled mold and chill until set.

## *ANN'S APPLE SALAD

Exchanges per serving: 1/2 cup = 1 1/2 fat, 1/2 fruit,
1/4 meat, 1 "A" vegetable.
Calories per serving: 100
Yield: 2 cups

| 1/2 cup apples, thinly sliced | 1/2 cup carrots, grated |
| 1/2 cup creamed cottage cheese | 1/2 cup celery, chopped fine |
| 2 tablespoons salad dressing | 1/16 teaspoon salt |
| | Lettuce |

Toss together first six ingredients. Divide mixture and place about 1/2 cup portions on lettuce leaves. Refrigerate before serving.

## *SLAW

Exchanges per serving: 1 cup = 1 "A" vegetable.
Calories per serving: 8 (exclusive of dressing)

Yield: 4 cups

| 1/2 head cabbage | 1/2 cup green pepper, chopped fine |
| 1/2 cup carrots, chopped fine | 2 cups water |

Shred cabbage. Place half in blender along with carrots, pepper, and water. Blend quickly; turn off and drain at once, using liquid for blending with balance of cabbage. Mix with salad dressing of your choosing.

## *MOLDED BEET-ONION SALAD

Exchanges per serving: 1/2 cup = 1 "B" vegetable.
Calories per serving: 35 (+ 9 calories in gelatin)

Yield: 4 servings

| 1 envelope black raspberry diet gelatin | 1 cup shoestring beets, drained |
| 2 cups boiling water | 1 small jar cocktail pickled onions |

Dissolve gelatin in boiling water. Chill until consistency of egg whites. Fold in vegetables. Pour in pan or molds and refrigerate until firm (5-6 hours).

## **MARGARET'S GELATIN WITH FRUIT

(Not for diabetics without consent of doctor.)
Exchanges per serving: 1 cup = 4 fruit.
Calories per serving: 160 (+ alcohol)      Yield: 6 cups

1 cup unsweetened peaches, sliced and drained
1 cup unsweetened pineapple tidbits, drained
1 1/2 tablespoons unflavored gelatin
1 1/4 cups unsweetened grapefruit juice
Non-nutritive sweetener equivalent to 1 cup sugar
1/2 cup wine
3 drops red food coloring
1 cup fresh orange sections
1 cup seedless grapes
2 medium bananas, sliced
2 pears, pared, cored, and diced

Set aside peaches and pineapple. Using liquid from fruit, soften gelatin. Bring grapefruit juice to a boil; add to softened gelatin. Stir to dissolve gelatin, then add sweetener, wine, and food coloring. Refrigerate 3/4 hour. Place peaches, pineapple, and the other fruit in compote and pour chilled gelatin over them. Refrigerate until gelatin thickens, but do not allow to get too firm.

## **FROZEN ORANGE FRUIT SALAD

Exchanges per serving: 1/2 filled orange = 2 fat, 1 fruit.
Calories per serving: 130 (+ whipped topping)
Yield: 8 servings

4 oranges
3/4 cup cream cheese
1/2 cup diet mayonnaise or salad dressing
1 tablespoon lemon juice
1/4 teaspoon prepared mustard
1/4 teaspoon salt
1 cup unsweetened fruit cocktail or mixed unsweetened fruits
1/4 cup slivered almonds
1/2 cup diet topping, whipped and sweetened

Cut oranges in half and scoop out pulp. Combine cream cheese, mayonnaise, lemon juice, mustard, and salt. Add almonds, drained orange pulp and fruit cocktail. Fold in whipped topping. Heap salad in orange halves and freeze until firm. Wrap individually in foil and keep frozen until needed. Remove from freezer 1/2 hour before serving. Garnish with endive or mint.

## **MOTHER'S RAW SPINACH SALAD

Exchanges per serving: 1 cup = 3 1/2 fat,
1 "A" vegetable.

Calories per serving: 158                    Yield: 5 servin|

| | |
|---|---|
| 2 bunches fresh spinach | 1/2 cup diet mayonnaise |
| 1/2 medium red onion, sliced thin and ringed | 1/2 cup wine vinegar |
| 6 slices bacon, chopped and fried crisp | Non-nutritive sweetener equivalent to 1/2 cup granulated sugar |

Wash spinach thoroughly; cut off stems, crisp. Cut in bite
size pieces in salad bowl; add onion rings and bacon bit|
Combine mayonnaise, vinegar, and sweetener; mix well i|
blender or mixer. Pour over greens. Toss and serve a
once.

## **HOT POTATO SALAD

Exchanges per serving: 1 cup = 1 bread, 1 meat,
               1 "A" vegetable.
Calories per serving: 140                    Yield: 4 cup|

| | |
|---|---|
| 2 cups potatoes, pared and cubed | 1 stalk celery, chopped fine |
| Water (to cover potatoes) | 1/4 cup green pepper, chopped fine |
| 2 1/2 teaspoons salt | 1 cup nonfat creamed cottage cheese |
| 1 onion, chopped fine | Lettuce |

Place potatoes in water to cover; cook until tender; drain|
Toss potato cubes and rest of ingredients together and mi|
well. Serve on lettuce leaves.

## ***MEAT or SEAFOOD SALAD

Suitable for Salads or Sandwich fillings

Exchanges per serving: 3 tablespoons = 2 fat, 2 meat.
Calories per serving: 236                    Yield: 3 cup|

| | |
|---|---|
| 2 cups minced meat, shell-fish, or flaked fish | 1 egg, hard-cooked, chopped fine |
| 1 tablespoon green onion, minced | 1 teaspoon capers, minced |
| 1/4 cup celery, minced | 1/2-3/4 cup diet mayon-naise or diet salad dressing |
| 1 teaspoon pimiento, minced | Salt and pepper to taste |

60

| 1 teaspoon fresh parsley, minced, or parsley flakes | Garlic salt to taste |

Combine all ingredients. Mix with mayonnaise or salad dressing: season to taste. Chill.

Suggestions: Serve as sandwich filling with plain bread or toasted bun. Serve as main-plate salad:
1. On bed of chopped lettuce, garnished with "A" vegetables.
2. Stuffed in tomato or avocado.

### ***SEAFOOD SALAD

Exchanges per serving: 1/2 cup = 2 fat, 2 meat.
Calories per serving: 236                     Yield: 2 cups

| | |
|---|---|
| 1/2 pound deveined shrimp, shelled, cooked, chilled, and cut in 2" pieces | 1/2 cup chopped nuts |
| | 1 cup nonfat creamed cottage cheese |
| | Lettuce |
| 1 tablespoon green onion, minced | 1 tomato, cut in wedges |
| 3 tablespoons diet salad dressing | 1 teaspoon parsley sprigs, chopped fine |
| 3 tablespoons diet French dressing | |

Mix first six ingredients. Divide evenly on lettuce leaves, garnish with tomato and parsley.

### **CAESAR SALAD

Exchanges per serving: 1 cup = 2 fat, 1 meat,
                       1 "A" vegetable.
Calories per serving: 185                     Yield: 6 servings

| | |
|---|---|
| 1 clove garlic | 1 2-ounce can anchovy fillets, drained and chopped |
| 2 heads romaine lettuce or | |
| 1 head iceberg lettuce | 1/4 cup Parmesan cheese |
| 1/4 cup olive oil | 1/2 cup prepared croutons |
| Juice of 1 lemon | 1 egg, well beaten |
| 1/4 cup wine vinegar | Salt and pepper to taste |

61

Rub salad bowl with cut clove of garlic. Tear cleaned a
crisped lettuce into bite-size pieces in salad bowl. Po
olive oil, lemon juice, and vinegar over greens; toss light
Sprinkle chopped anchovies, grated cheese, and crouto
on top; add beaten egg. Season. Toss and serve at once.

## ****LOTTIE'S COTTAGE CHEESE MOLD

Exchanges per serving: 1 serving = 1/2 skim milk,
4 meat.

Calories per serving: 332          Yield: 3 servin;

2 cups minced clams
1 envelope unflavored
  gelatin
1 1/4 cups skim milk
1/2 teaspoon Worcester-
  shire sauce
1/2 teaspoon salt
1/16 teaspoon Tabasco
  sauce

1/16 teaspoon allspice
2/3 cup nonfat cottage
  cheese
1 tablespoon green pepper,
  chopped fine
1/2 tablespoon onion,
  chopped fine

Drain clams, reserve 1/2 cup liquid. Sprinkle gelatin o
clam liquid in saucepan to soften; place over low heat an
stir until gelatin dissolves (2-3 minutes). Remove fror
heat. Add milk, Worcestershire sauce, salt, Tabasco an
allspice. Chill until mixture has the consistency of unbeate
egg whites. Add clams, cottage cheese, pepper, and onior
Place in small loaf pan and chill until firm. Unmold t
serve.

## ****NUT AND CHEESE SALAD

Exchanges per serving: 3/4 cup = 2 fat, 2 meat,
1 "A" vegetable.

Calories per serving: 336          Yield: 3 cup

2 cups nonfat creamed
  cottage cheese
1 cup chopped nuts

2 small dill pickles,
  chopped fine
Lettuce

Mix first three ingredients well and serve on lettuce leaves

# ****FISH AND POTATO SALAD

Exchanges per serving: 1 serving = 1 bread, 2 fat, 3 meat,
1 "A" vegetable.

Calories per serving: 377                    Yield: 3 servings

3 potatoes
2 cups fish, flaked
2 tablespoons pimiento,
chopped
2 tablespoons onion,
minced
2 tablespoons parsley,
snipped

1 cup celery, sliced thin
1/4 cup vinegar
2 tablespoons salad oil
1 teaspoon salt
1/8 teaspoon pepper
Lettuce

Wash, pare, and slice potatoes thin. Boil gently about 5-6
minutes in salted boiling water to cover until nearly tender.
When potatoes are almost done, add fish. Bring water back
to boil, cover, and gently boil about 5 minutes. Drain
liquid, cool potatoes slightly, then place in refrigerator
until serving. Toss remaining ingredients (except lettuce)
in large bowl and mix well. Cover and place in refrigerator
until time to serve. Add potatoes and fish to dressing; toss
and mix. Serve on lettuce leaves.

# *EASY SALAD DRESSING

Exchanges per serving: 1 tablespoon = None.
Calories per serving: 0                    Yield: 1 1/4 cups

1/4 cup eggs, well beaten
1/2 teaspoon salt
1/16 teaspoon pepper
1/2 teaspoon dry mustard
1/2 cup vinegar

1/2 cup skim milk
Non-nutritive sweetener
equivalent to 1/2 cup
sugar

Mix all ingredients except sweetener and cook until mixture comes to a racing boil, over low heat. Add sweetener
and cool. Use for salads.

# *VINEGAR DRESSING

Exchanges per serving: None.
Calories per serving: 0                    Yield: 1/3 cup

1/4 cup vinegar
2 tablespoons water
1 clove garlic, crushed
1/8 teaspoon salt
1/8 teaspoon paprika

Non-nutritive sweetener
    equivalent to 3 1/2
    teaspoons sugar
1/2 teaspoon dill or tar-
    ragon or a combination
    of rosemary and thyme

Combine all ingredients. Store in jar in refrigerator. Shake
well before using.

## *FRUIT SALAD DRESSING

Exchanges per serving: 1 tablespoon = None.
Calories per serving: 5                          Yield: 3/4 cup

Non-nutritive sweetener
    equivalent to 3 cups
    sugar
1/2 cup unsweetened
    lemon juice
1/2 cup water

1/2 tablespoon arrowroot
    powder
1/2 teaspoon celery seed
1/2 teaspoon chervil
1 teaspoon celery salt
1/2 teaspoon dry mustard
1/2 teaspoon paprika

Combine sweetener, lemon juice, water, and arrowroot
powder in a small pan and stir to blend. Add rest of ingredients and bring to a boil, cooking until thick and clear
(about 3-4 minutes), stirring constantly. Cool, store in
refrigerator.

## *SKIM MILK DRESSING

Exchanges per serving: 1 tablespoon = None.
Calories per serving: 7                          Yield: 3 cups

1 cup white vinegar
Non-nutritive sweetener
    equivalent to 3/4 cup
    sugar

2 cups skim milk

Beat all ingredients thoroughly with rotary beater. Store in
refrigerator. May be used for lettuce, coleslaw, etc.

## *SALLY'S SALAD DRESSING

Exchanges per serving: 1 tablespoon = None.
Calories per serving: 8     Yield: 3 ounces or 5 tablespoons

2 teaspoons minced onion
4 tablespoons malt or
   cider vinegar

Non-nutritive sweetener
   equivalent to 1/2 cup
   sugar
2 teaspoons seasoned salt
1/8 teaspoon lemon pepper

Mix all ingredients well. Serve on fruit or vegetable salads or for coleslaw mix.

## *LOW-CALORIE DRESSING

Exchanges per serving: 2 tablespoons = None.
Calories per serving: 10          Yield: 1 1/2 cups

1 1/4 cups condensed
   tomato soup, undiluted
1/4 teaspoon onion salt
1/8 teaspoon black pepper

1/4 teaspoon garlic powder
3 tablespoons wine vinegar
1 tablespoon corn relish

Mix all ingredients together in large jar. Cover and refrigerate. Shake before using.

## *MARGE'S SALAD DRESSING

Exchanges per serving: 1 tablespoon = None.
Calories per serving: 10          Yield: 1 1/2 cups

1/4 cup (1 medium) egg,
   well beaten
Non-nutritive sweetener
   equivalent to 2/3 cup
   sugar
2/3 cup skim milk

1/2 cup malt vinegar
1 teaspoon mustard
1/2 teaspoon salt
1/8 teaspoon pepper
1/2 teaspoon diet
   margarine

Combine all ingredients in top of double boiler and cook over hot water. Stir until thick and smooth. Chill. Use for vegetable salads.

## *DRESSING A LA BLANCHE

Exchanges per serving: 1 tablespoon = None.
Calories per serving: 16          Yield: 3 cups

1 cup white vinegar
2 cups skim milk

Non-nutritive sweetener
   equivalent to 3/4 cup
   sugar

Place all ingredients in covered glass jar; shake until well mixed. Store in refrigerator. Use for lettuce, coleslaw, etc.

## *FRUIT DRESSING

Exchanges per serving: 1 tablespoon = 1/2 fat.
Calories per serving: 20                    Yield: 3 cups

| | |
|---|---|
| 1/4 teaspoon dry mustard | 1 1/2 cups water |
| 1/4 teaspoon salt | 1/2 cup oil |
| 1 teaspoon onion juice | Non-nutritive sweetener |
| 1 cup cider vinegar | equivalent to 3 cups |
| 4 teaspoons paprika | sugar |
| 4 tablespoons celery seed | |

Combine first five ingredients. Bring to boil. Simmer over low heat about 5 minutes; remove from heat and add remaining ingredients. Chill. Serve on fruit salads.

## *LOUISE'S SALAD DRESSING

Exchanges per serving: 1 tablespoon = 1/2 fat.
Calories per serving: 20                    Yield: 1 cup

| | |
|---|---|
| 1/4 cup (3 medium) egg yolk, beaten well | 1/2 cup fresh lemon juice |
| 2 tablespoons skim milk | 2 teaspoons diet margarine, melted |
| Non-nutritive sweetener equivalent to 1/2 cup sugar | 1/8 teaspoon salt |

Mix all ingredients in saucepan and cook over medium heat. Stir constantly, until mixture comes to a boil and is slightly thick. Chill.

## *GOURMET SOUR CREAM DRESSING

Exchanges per serving: 1 tablespoon = 1 fat.
Calories per serving: 45                    Yield: 1 1/4 cups

| | |
|---|---|
| 2 tablespoons green onion, minced | 1 teaspoon salt |
| 3 tablespoons wine vinegar | 1 teaspoon prepared mustard |

Non-caloric sweetener
equivalent to 2 table-
spoons sugar

1/8 teaspoon pepper
Dash of pepper sauce
1 cup sour cream

Combine all ingredients. Chill at least 1/2 hour to blend
flavors.

## *GINNY'S SALAD DRESSING

Exchanges per serving: 1 tablespoon = None.
Calories per serving: 0                    Yield: 5 tablespoons

2 teaspoons onion juice
4 tablespoons cider vinegar
Non-nutritive sweetener
equivalent to 1/2 cup
sugar

1/8 teaspoon dry mustard
1/8 teaspoon pepper
1/8 teaspoon salt

Mix all ingredients well. Serve on fruit or vegetable salads
or for coleslaw mix.

## *SALAD DRESSING

Exchanges per serving: 1 tablespoon = None.
Calories per serving: 10                         Yield: 2 cups

1/2 cup (2 medium) eggs,
well beaten
1 teaspoon salt
1/8 teaspoon lemon
pepper

1 teaspoon dry mustard
1 cup malt or cider vinegar
1 cup skim milk
Non-nutritive sweetener
equivalent to 1 cup sugar

Mix first six ingredients. Cook until mixture comes to a
racing boil, over low heat. Add sweetener; cool.

## *CHUTNEY AND CURRY MAYONNAISE

Exchanges per serving: 1 tablespoon = 1 fat.
Calories per serving: 45                          Yield: 1 cup

1 cup safflower mayonnaise
1 teaspoon any minced
fruit

1 teaspoon chutney,
chopped, or curry
powder

Blend all ingredients together for spicy sauce for seafoods
and chicken salad.

# *FRENCH VINEGAR STYLE DRESSING

Exchanges per serving: 1 tablespoon = 1 1/2 fat.
Calories per serving: 65                    Yield: 3/4 cup

2 tablespoons vinegar
1/2 teaspoon salt
1 teaspoon paprika
4 tablespoons lemon juice

1/2 onion, grated fine
6 tablespoons oil
Non-nutritive sweetener
equivalent to 1 cup sugar

Bring vinegar, salt, paprika, lemon juice, and onion to a
boil. Cool. Add oil and sweetener and cook until thick as
desired.

# *BLEU CHEESE TOPPING

Exchanges per serving: 1 tablespoon = None.
Calories per serving: 19                    Yield: 2 1/4 cups

2 cups unflavored low-
calorie yogurt

3 tablespoons low-calorie
bleu cheese dressing
1/2 teaspoon salt

Combine ingredients, then chill. Serve on lettuce leaves.

# *THOUSAND ISLAND DRESSING

Exchanges per serving: 1 tablespoon = None.
Calories per serving: 23                    Yield: 1 1/3 cups

1 cup unflavored low-
calorie yogurt
1/4 cup low-calorie catsup
2 tablespoons celery, diced
fine
1 tablespoon green pepper,
diced fine

1 tablespoon onion,
chopped fine
Non-nutritive sweetener
equivalent to 1/2 cup
sugar
1/4 teaspoon seasoned salt
1/4 teaspoon pepper

Mix all ingredients and blend well. Chill overnight in refrigerator.

# *LUAU MAYONNAISE

Exchanges per serving: 1 ounce = 1 1/2 fat.
Calories per serving: 80                    Yield: 1 1/4 cups

| 1 cup safflower mayonnaise | 1 tablespoon maraschino |
| 2 tablespoons artificially sweetened pineapple juice | cherry syrup |

Thin mayonnaise with juice and syrup and blend to smooth pink color.

## *DOTTIE'S FRENCH DRESSING

Exchanges per serving: 1 tablespoon = 2 fat.
Calories per serving: 90                                    Yield: 3/4 cup

| 1/2 cup olive oil | 1/16 teaspoon paprika |
| 1/4 cup malt vinegar | 1/16 teaspoon lemon |
| 1/4 teaspoon dry mustard | pepper |
| 1 teaspoon salt | |

Place all ingredients in glass jar. Blend or shake until well mixed. Chill.

# CHEESE AND EGG DISHES

Fried eggs and omelets can be cooked beautifully in a Teflon-coated pan without the addition of fat.

When using basic ingredients such as arrowroot, eggs, flour, margarine, and tapioca, refer to General Information and to Table of Weights and Measures.

## *FLUFF OMELET

Exchanges per serving: 1 serving = 1 meat.
Calories per serving: 75                           Yield: 1 serving

    1/4 cup (1 medium) egg      1/16 tablespoon salt
    1 tablespoon water

Using a wire whip, beat all ingredients together. Place in Teflon pan and cook until done.

**VARIATIONS:** Diet Jelly: No additional calories.
Cheese: 1/2 ounce grated cheese, add 35 calories to above.
Ham and Green Pepper: 20 grams ham and green pepper, chopped, add 35 calories to above.

## *SCRAMBLED EGGS

Exchanges per serving: 1 serving = 1 meat.
Calories per serving: 85                           Yield: 1 serving

    1/4 cup (1 medium) egg      salt
    1 tablespoon skim or      pepper
      whole milk

To eliminate the use of fat, scramble eggs in a double boiler (or use Teflon-coated pan). Mix egg and milk with wire whip or fork; add salt and pepper and for variety, a dash of curry powder or chopped chives, green onion, or parsley. For a marvelous variation, add 2 tablespoons Spanish sauce to raw egg mixture, then cook.

## *BLINTZES WITH CHEESE FILLING

Exchanges per serving: 1 blintze = 1/2 bread, 3/4 meat.
Calories per serving: 85                    Yield: 1 dozen

| | |
|---|---|
| 1 cup flour | 2 cups low-calorie cottage |
| 1/2 teaspoon salt | cheese, sieved |
| 1/2 teaspoon baking | Non-nutritive sweetener |
| powder | equivalent to 2 table- |
| 1 cup skim milk | spoons sugar |
| 3/4 cup (3 medium) eggs | 1/2 teaspoon cinnamon |
| 2 tablespoons diet mar- | 1/4 teaspoon allspice or |
| garine, melted | nutmeg |

Sift flour, salt, and baking powder together. Beat milk, 1/2 cup (2 medium) eggs, and margarine. Slowly add to flour mixture; stir to form thin batter. Grease 6" frying pan lightly, then pour 1/8 cup batter into skillet and cover bottom completely. Cook until top of pancake is bubbly, then turn onto paper towel. Make rest of pancakes, greasing skillet as necessary. Mix cottage cheese, sweetener, cinnamon, allspice or nutmeg, and remaining egg. Top each pancake, which has been turned brown side up, with tablespoon of filling. Fold over sides, then the ends to make small drugstore-type package; set to one side. Refrigerate until ready to serve. A few minutes before serving, melt margarine in skillet and lightly brown each blintze, starting with flap side down. Then turn and brown other side. Serve warm.

## **SALLY'S CHEESE FONDUE

(Not for diabetics without consent of doctor.)
Exchanges per serving: 1 slice = 1 bread, 2/3 meat,
                            1/3 milk.
Calories per serving: 175 (+ wine)    Yield: 12 servings

| | |
|---|---|
| 1 clove garlic, peeled | 1/16 teaspoon pepper |
| 2 cups dry white wine | 1/16 teaspoon salt |

| 2 cups cheese, shredded fine | 1/16 teaspoon nutmeg |
| 1/4 teaspoon arrowroot powder | 12 slices bread, cut into cubes leaving one side of crust on each cube |
| 2 tablespoons Kirschwasser (if approved by doctor) | |

Rub an earthenware casserole with garlic, then add wine. Heat slowly over chafing dish burner. Mix cheese lightly with arrowroot powder; when bubbles in wine rise to surface, add cheese mix a handful at a time. Stir until each handful melts and continue until all cheese is melted; add Kirschwasser and seasonings. Stir well. Turn heat low but keep fondue slowly bubbling. Each person takes a cube of bread on the end of his fork and twirls it in the bubbling fondue. If fondue is too thick, add a little *hot* wine.

## **HAM AND CHEESE ON BUNS

Exchanges per serving: 1/2 bun = 1/2 bread, 2 meat.
Calories per serving: 185                    Yield: 3 buns

| 3 buns, cut in half | 1/4 cup dietetic cranberry sauce |
| 6 slices ham, baked | 6 slices Mozarella cheese |

Toast halves of bun slightly, then top with slice of ham. Spread each with cranberry sauce and place thin slice of cheese over this; put under broiler until cheese melts and is lightly browned.

## **EGGS ON TOAST, OVEN STYLE

Exchanges per serving: 1 serving = 1 bread, 1 fat, 1 meat.
Calories per serving: 190                    Yield: 6 servings

| 6 slices bread | 1 tablespoon chervil |
| 6 teaspoons diet margarine | 1/8 teaspoon salt |
| 1 1/2 cups (6 medium) eggs, separated | 1/8 teaspoon pepper |

Preheat oven to 350°. Butter each slice of bread with margarine and place buttered side up on cookie sheet. Beat

72

egg whites until stiff and distribute evenly on each slice of bread. Make a hollow in center of white, then fill with yolk. Sprinkle eggs with chervil, salt, and pepper. Bake until yolk is nearly set and white is lightly browned (about 15 minutes). Serve at once.

### ***EGGS WITH CHEESE SAUCE

Exchanges per serving: 2/3 cup = 1 1/2 bread,
                       1/2 fat, 2 meat.
Calories per serving: 278          Yield: 4 cups

1 1/4 tablespoons arrow-
  root powder
1/2 teaspoon salt
1/16 teaspoon cayenne
1 tablespoon prepared
  mustard
1 tablespoon chervil
1/2 cup milk

1 tablespoon diet
  margarine
1 1/2 cups cheese, grated
  fine
1 1/2 cups (6 medium)
  eggs
6 slices bread

Preheat oven to 350°. Butter individual custard cups. Mix first five ingredients together. Stir in milk slowly; continue stirring until thick and smooth, over medium heat. Remove from heat and stir in margarine and cheese. Stir until cheese has melted and sauce is smooth. Into each cup break one egg; cover with 1/4 cup cheese sauce and bake until firm (15-20 minutes). Toast bread, cut in half, and serve egg with toast.

### ***CHEESE TOAST AND EGGS

Exchanges per serving: 1 serving = 1 bread, 2 meat.
Calories per serving: 220       Yield: 4 servings

4 slices bread
4 ounces Mozarella cheese

1 cup (4 medium) eggs,
  poached

Preheat oven to 350°. Toast bread, top with 1/4 of cheese for each slice. Put on cookie sheet and place in oven until cheese just melts (2-3 minutes). Add poached egg on top. Serve at once.

### ***EGGS CURRY

Exchanges per serving: 1 serving = 1 bread, 1 fat, 1 meat,
　　　　　　　　　　　　1 skim milk, 1 "B" vegetable.
Calories per serving: 260　　　　　　　　　Yield: 4 servings

6 hard-boiled eggs
1/4 cup almonds, slivered
2 tablespoons diet
　margarine
1 onion, chopped fine
1/2 cup celery, chopped
　fine

1 1/2 tablespoons arrow-
　root powder
1 teaspoon salt
1 1/2 teaspoons curry
　powder
2 cups skim milk
4 slices toast

Thinly slice shelled eggs. Brown almonds in margarine until
golden brown. Remove and drain on absorbent paper. In
same pan sauté onion and celery until golden, then stir in
arrowroot, salt, and curry powder. Stir in milk slowly;
cook, stirring constantly until thick and smooth. Stir in
sliced eggs and heat to boil. Place a slice of toast in the
bottom of each of four, individual, heated casseroles.
Divide the eggs evenly over the toast and sprinkle with
almonds.

### ***OMELET WITH COTTAGE CHEESE

Exchanges per serving: 1 serving = 1 fat, 3 meat.
Calories per serving: 270　　　　　　　　　Yield: 2 servings

2 tablespoons diet
　margarine
1 cup (4 medium) eggs,
　separated
1/16 teaspoon salt

1/2 cup low-calorie cot-
　tage cheese, sieved
1/16 teaspoon pepper
1 tablespoon chervil

Preheat oven to 350°. Melt margarine in skillet. Beat egg
whites and salt until stiff, but not dry. Beat yolks separately
until lemon-colored and thick, then add cheese and pepper
and beat until smooth. Fold in egg whites and chervil.
Place mixture in skillet and cook over medium heat until
lightly browned on bottom and fluffy (about 3-4 minutes).
Place in oven 15 minutes; make a crease down center
with knife and fold over. Serve at once.

## ****CHEESE FONDUE

Exchanges per serving: 1 serving = 1 bread,
3 meat, 1/4 milk.
Calories per serving: 329                    Yield: 4 servings

| | |
|---|---|
| 1 cup milk | 1 1/2 cups bread cubes |
| 1 tablespoon diet | 2/3 cup cheddar cheese, |
| margarine | grated |
| 1/8 teaspoon pepper | 3/4 cup (3 medium) eggs, |
| 1/4 teaspoon salt | separated |

Preheat oven to 375°. Place a 2" x 9" x 9" cake pan,
filled about 1/2" deep with hot water, in oven. Scald milk,
add margarine, pepper, and salt. Stir to melt margarine,
then stir in bread cubes and cheese until completely mixed.
Add yolks of eggs and stir until smooth, let cool. Beat
whites of eggs until stiff enough to form peaks. Pour milk-
bread mixture over egg whites and fold in gently. Pour into greased casserole; place casserole in water in the cake
pan and bake until browned (about 3/4 hour). Serve at
once.

# FISH, MEAT, AND POULTRY

## PROXIMATE COMPOSITION OF CAMPBELL SOUP COMPANY PRODUCTS

(Contents of 100 grams, equivalent to one 3 1/2-ounc
can. This makes one serving when prepared according t
the directions.)

**VARIETY**

| Heat Processed Soups | Calories | Protein gm | Fat gm | Carbohydrate gm | Sodium mg | Vitamin A I. U |
|---|---|---|---|---|---|---|
| Barbecue Beans | 126 | 5.7 | 1.5 | 22.5 | 406 | 22: |
| Beans and Franks | 160 | 8.4 | 7.1 | 15.7 | 481 | 128 |
| Beans and Ground Beef | 114 | 7.1 | 2.7 | 15.3 | 500 | 860 |
| Pork and Beans | 115 | 7.1 | 1.3 | 18.8 | 420 | 11: |

### Bounty Main Dish Products:

| | Calories | Protein gm | Fat gm | Carbohydrate gm | Sodium mg | Vitamin A I. U |
|---|---|---|---|---|---|---|
| Beef Stew | 79 | 7.2 | 2.5 | 7.0 | 440 | 1923 |
| Chicken Stew | 82 | 6.1 | 3.4 | 6.8 | 420 | 1942 |
| Chili Con Carne (with beans) | 119 | 7.0 | 5.8 | 9.6 | 470 | 583 |
| Chili Mac | 114 | 5.6 | 4.4 | 13.0 | 550 | 526 |
| Corned Beef Hash | 184 | 11.5 | 10.6 | 10.7 | 650 | trace |

### Franco-American Products:

| | Calories | Protein gm | Fat gm | Carbohydrate gm | Sodium mg | Vitamin A I. U |
|---|---|---|---|---|---|---|
| Beef Gravy | 49 | 3.1 | 1.9 | 4.9 | 562 | trace |
| Chicken Giblet Gravy | 48 | 1.8 | 2.3 | 4.9 | 590 | 490 |
| Chicken Gravy | 88 | 2.3 | 6.3 | 5.5 | 480 | 583 |

| | | | | | | |
|---|---|---|---|---|---|---|
| Italian Style Spaghetti | 77 | 3.5 | 0.9 | 13.6 | 432 | 255 |
| Macaroni with Cheese Sauce | 97 | 3.7 | 4.2 | 11.0 | 440 | 228 |
| Macaroni 'n Beef | 99 | 5.4 | 3.7 | 11.0 | 610 | 353 |
| MacaroniO's | 75 | 3.4 | 2.5 | 9.8 | 485 | 270 |
| Spaghetti with Ground Beef | 119 | 4.9 | 6.1 | 11.2 | 507 | 750 |
| Spaghetti with Meatballs | 116 | 4.9 | 6.0 | 10.7 | 488 | 485 |
| Spaghetti with Tomato Sauce | 81 | 3.2 | 0.7 | 15.6 | 403 | 200 |
| SpaghettiO's | 81 | 2.7 | 1.0 | 15.2 | 475 | 350 |
| SpaghettiO's with Franks | 111 | 3.9 | 5.6 | 11.3 | 577 | 280 |
| SpaghettiO's with Meatballs | 94 | 4.7 | 3.9 | 10.1 | 560 | 425 |
| Spaghetti Sauce with Meat | 96 | 4.6 | 5.2 | 7.9 | 740 | 2614 |
| Spaghetti Sauce with Mushrooms | 77 | 1.5 | 3.0 | 10.9 | 880 | 935 |

## OTHER CAMPBELL PRODUCTS IN EXCHANGE LISTS

(100 gram portion measures between 1/3 and 1/2 cup)

Exchange Substitution for
1 1/2 Meat and 1 Bread

Bounty Corned Beef Hash

Exchange Substitution for
1 Meat and 1/2 Bread

Bounty Chili Con Carne

Exchange Substitution for
1/2 Meat and
1 Vegetable "B"

Bounty Beef Stew
Bounty Chicken Stew

Other products that you may serve but do not need to measure are:

Beef Broth
Consommé

Tomato Juice
"V-8" Cocktail Vegetable Juice

## **CHOP SUEY WITH TUNA

Exchanges per serving: 1 cup = 1 bread, 1 meat.
Calories per serving: 145          Yield: 4 servings

2 stalks celery, cut small
1/2 onion, chopped fine

1/6 teaspoon pepper
2 tablespoons soy sauce

| | |
|---|---|
| 2 cups + 2 tablespoons water | 3/4 cup water-packed tuna, drained |
| 3/4 cup rice | |
| Non-nutritive sweetener equivalent to 1/2 teaspoon sugar | |

Cook celery and onion in 2 tablespoons water over low heat, covered. When tender, remove from heat; add rice, 2 cups water, and seasonings. Bring to boil. Turn heat to low and cook, covered, until rice is tender and liquid absorbed (about 1/2 hour). Add tuna. Mix and remove from heat. Set aside, covered, for a few minutes before serving.

### ***CHEESE AND CRAB ORIENTAL STYLE

Exchanges per serving: 1 serving = 1/4 bread,
2 1/2 meat, 2 "A" and
1/4 "B" vegetables.

Calories per serving: 220                    Yield: 5 servings

| | |
|---|---|
| 1/2 cup mushrooms, sliced | 1 teaspoon salt |
| 1/2 carrot, sliced thin | 1 bay leaf |
| 1/4 cup green pepper, diced | 4 cups tomatoes |
| 1 cup celery, sliced | 3/4 cup rice, precooked |
| 1 cup onion, chopped fine | 1 1/2 cups crab meat, frozen, thawed, and |
| 2 tablespoons oil | drained |
| Non-nutritive sweetener equivalent to 1 tablespoon sugar | 1/2 cup sharp cheeese, grated |

Preheat oven to 350°. Sauté first five ingredients in oil in Dutch oven or other oven-proof container until the onion is golden brown. Add sweetener, salt, bay leaf and tomatoes and boil for 5 minutes, gently. Stir in rice and crab meat. Sprinkle entire mixture with grated cheese. Bake 20-25 minutes.

### ***FISH AND MUSHROOMS

Exchanges per serving: 1 serving = 1 fat, 3 meat,
1 "A" vegetable.

Calories per serving: 260 (plus sherry)   Yield: 4 servings

| | |
|---|---|
| **1 onion, sliced thin** | **1/6 teaspoon salt** |
| **1 tablespoon oil** | **1/16 teaspoon pepper** |
| **1 1/2 cups mushrooms, sliced thin** | **1 stalk celery, sliced thin** |
| | **1 tablespoon soy sauce** |
| **1 pound fish fillets (cod, halibut, sole) cut in 1" slices** | **1 tablespoon dry sherry (if permitted by doctor)** |

Preheat skillet and sauté onion in oil. Add mushrooms and sauté about 2 minutes, stirring all the while, until mushrooms have wilted. Then spread half of fillet slices on mushrooms; sprinkle with salt and pepper, add remaining fillets, sprinkle these with salt and pepper. Add celery, soy sauce and sherry and cook gently, covered, for ten minutes.

### ***HARRIET'S FISH DISH

Exchanges per serving: 1 serving = 1/2 fat, 3 meat,
                    1 "A" and 1 "B" vegetable.
Calories per serving: 270                    Yield: 4 servings

| | |
|---|---|
| **2 onions, sliced thin** | **2 cups canned tomatoes** |
| **1 clove garlic, crushed** | **1 tablespoon tomato paste** |
| **1 tablespoon diet margarine** | **2 chicken bouillon cubes** |
| **1/2 cup parsley, snipped** | **4 4-ounce fish fillets or steaks** |
| **1/2 teaspoon salt** | **3 slices tomato, cut thin** |
| **1/8 teaspoon pepper** | **3 slices lemon, cut thin** |

Preheat oven to 300°. Sauté onions and garlic in margarine until golden; add parsley, salt, pepper, tomatoes with juice, tomato paste, and bouillon cubes. Simmer gently, uncovered, about 20 minutes. Then place fish steaks, cut about 3/4" thick, in medium baking dish. Cover with sauce, top with slices of tomatoes and lemons. Bake until tender.

### ***BAKED FISH STEAKS

Exchanges per serving: 3 ounces = 1 fat, 3 meat,
                    1/4 "B" vegetable.
Calories per serving: 280                    Yield: 4 servings

4 3-ounce fish steaks
  (halibut, swordfish, etc.)
4 tablespoons oil
1 onion, sliced thin
1 potato, sliced thin

1/2 carrot, sliced thin
1/16 teaspoon salt
1/16 teaspoon pepper
1/2 teaspoon parsley,
  snipped

Preheat oven to 450°. Remove skin from fish steaks and cut meat away from bone. Pour oil in center of 4 pieces of heavy-duty foil and place steaks on oil. Top each piece with slice of onion, potato, carrot, and salt and pepper. Using drugstore folds, wrap each piece separately. Put on cookie sheet and bake until fish flakes easily and is tender. Garnish with parsley.

### ***HILO FILLET OF SOLE

Exchanges per serving: 3 ounces = 3 fat, 2 meat.
Calories per serving: 275         Yield: 8 servings

1 1/2 pound fish fillets
  (cod, halibut, sole)
1/4 teaspoon salt
2 teaspoons instant minced
  onion
1 1/2 teaspoons water
3/4 cup safflower
  mayonnaise

1 teaspoon lemon juice
1/4 teaspoon seasoned salt
1 teaspoon parsley, finely
  chopped
1/3 cup macadamia nuts,
  chopped, or slivered
  almonds

Wipe fillets with a damp cloth. Sprinkle with salt. Roll and secure each with toothpick. Place rolls in steamer or on wire rack above boiling water; cover and steam 15 minutes. Mix onion, water, mayonnaise, lemon juice, seasoned salt, and parsley. Remove fillets carefully from steamer and spread quickly with mayonnaise mixture. Top with nuts and serve at once.

### ****TASTY FILLETS

Exchanges per serving: 1 serving = 1 fat, 4 meat.
Calories per serving: 320        Yield: 3 servings

1 pound fish fillets
1/2 cup sour cream

1/8 teaspoon ginger
1/8 teaspoon dry mustard

1/8 teaspoon thyme          1/8 teaspoon parsley,
1/4 teaspoon salt              snipped fine
1/6 teaspoon paprika

Preheat oven to 400°. Grease 2" x 6" x 10" baking dish. Divide fillets into 3 servings. Sprinkle with salt on both sides and place in baking dish in one layer. Mix sour cream, ginger, mustard, thyme, and salt and spread mixture on top of fillets. Bake until fish is tender and easily flaked (about 20-25 minutes). Top with paprika and parsley. Serve at once.

### ***SHRIMP AND RICE

Exchanges per serving: 2/3 cup rice and 3/4 cup sauce =
            1 bread, 3 meat, 1 "A" vegetable.
Calories per serving: 287              Yield: 5 servings

2 cups tomatoes                  1/2 teaspoon oregano
2 tablespoons parsley flakes     1 3-ounce can tomato paste
2 cups celery, sliced thin       1/2 cup long-grain rice
1/4 teaspoon basil               2 7-ounce packages frozen,
1 1/2 teaspoons salt                deveined, shelled shrimp
1/8 teaspoon pepper

Mix everything except rice and shrimp in large skillet. Stir occasionally. Boil gently, uncovered, until celery is nearly tender (about 1/2 hour). Stir in shrimp and boil until shrimp are cooked but still tender (about 5-10 minutes). Cook rice as directed, omitting margarine or butter. Serve shrimp over rice.

### ***CRAB, SHRIMP, RICE SUPREME

Exchanges per serving: 3/4 cup = 1/2 bread, 3 fat,
            1 1/3 meat.
Calories per serving: 270              Yield: 8-10 servings

2 cups cooked rice               1/4 cup toasted almonds,
1 cup diet mayonnaise               slivered
1/2 cup green onion,             8-ounces fresh, frozen, or
   chopped                          canned crab meat
1/4 cup green pepper,            8-ounces fresh, frozen, or
   chopped                          canned shrimp
1 cup tomato juice               1/4 cup prepared bread
                                    crumbs

Preheat oven to 350°. Mix all ingredients (except bread crumbs) together, place in casserole, top with the bread crumbs. Bake 1 hour. Use fresh seafood if available. This is an excellent party casserole as it can be made a day ahead and refrigerated.

### ***TUNA (or SALMON) PIE WITH CRUST

Exchanges per serving: 1 serving = 1 bread, 1/2 fat,
3 meat.

Calories per serving: 300        Yield: 6 servings

| | |
|---|---|
| 1 cup long-grain white rice, uncooked | 1/4 teaspoon salt |
| 2 tablespoons diet margarine | 1/8 teaspoon pepper |
| 3/4 cup (3 medium) eggs | 1/8 teaspoon nutmeg |
| 1 1/4 cups water-packed tuna (or pink salmon), drained and flaked | 3/4 cup American cheese, grated |
| | 3/4 cup skim milk, scalded |
| | 1/2 teaspoon parsley |

Preheat oven to 400°. Cook rice as directed, then mix with margarine and half the egg. Line a 9″ pie pan and mound rice mixture up to about 1″ above rim of plate. Spread tuna (or salmon) in shell, sprinkle with salt, pepper, nutmeg, and cheese. Beat remaining egg in small bowl and stir in scalded milk. Heat until smooth, then pour mixture over cheese. Bake until cheese is dark golden brown (about 1/2 hour). Sprinkle parsley over top, if desired.

### ***SALMON (or TUNA) CASSEROLE

Exchanges per serving: 1/2 cup = 1/2 bread, 1/2 fat,
1/2 milk, 1 1/2 meat.

Calories per serving: 260        Yield: 24 servings

| | |
|---|---|
| 1 cup noodles | 1/2 cup flour |
| 2 cups mushrooms, sliced thin | 2 teaspoons paprika |
| 4 tablespoons onion, chopped fine | 2 cups milk |
| 4 tablespoons diet margarine | 2 cups light cream |
| | 4 cups pink salmon (or tuna, water-packed and well drained) |

82

1 teaspoon salt                 1 cup Parmesan cheese,
1/4 teaspoon pepper             grated

Preheat oven to 375°. Cook noodles according to directions on the package. Sauté mushrooms and onions in
margarine until tender. Stir in salt, pepper, flour, and
paprika. Then stir in milk slowly, cooking and stirring
constantly until thick and smooth. Remove from heat. Stir
in light cream. Remove skin and bones from drained
salmon (or tuna), then flake. Mix fish with noodles, mushroom mixture, and all but a little of the grated cheese.
Pour into casserole, sprinkle remaining grated cheese on
top. Bake 20-25 minutes.

## ****CRAB CASSEROLE

Exchanges per serving: 1 serving = 1 bread, 1 fat,
                       1/2 fruit, 3 meat.
Calories per serving: 325          Yield: 6 servings

2 cups wild rice mix            2 1/4 cups frozen crab
1 onion, chopped fine            meat
1 stalk celery, chopped fine   1/2 teaspoon monosodium
2 tablespoons salad oil          glutamate (optional)
1 apple, pared and chopped     1/4 cup raisins
1 1/2 teaspoons curry
  powder

Preheat oven to 375°. Cook rice as directed but omit
margarine or butter and decrease cooking time to 20 minutes (it will be moist). In a large skillet sauté onion and
celery in oil until onion is golden. Stir in apple, curry
powder, crab meat (which has been thawed and drained
thoroughly), monosodium glutamate, and raisins. Divide
mixture into small casserole dishes. Cover and bake 15
minutes.

## ****FISH OVEN STYLE

Exchanges per serving: 1 serving = 1 fat, 4 meat.
Calories per serving: 337          Yield: 3 servings

1 pound fish steaks (sword-    1 tablespoon diet margarine
  fish, halibut, haddock,      1/16 teaspoon salt
  etc.) cut into 3 serving     1/16 teaspoon pepper
  pieces

Preheat oven to 350°. Remove skin from fish steaks, if necessary, and place wihout touching one another in the bottom of shallow baking dish. Dot with margarine, then sprinkle salt and pepper on top. Bake until fish flakes with a fork (about 15-20 minutes).

## ****CRAB (or LOBSTER) AND TOMATOES

Exchanges per serving: 1 serving = 1 1/2 fat, 3 meat,
                      1/2 milk, 1 "A" vegetable.
Calories per serving: 350              Yield: 4 servings

| | |
|---|---|
| 4 tomatoes, salted to taste | 1 1/2 cups crab (or lobster) meat |
| 3 tablespoons onion, chopped fine | 1 teaspoon Worcestershire sauce |
| 3 tablespoons green pepper, chopped fine | 1/16 teaspoon cayenne pepper |
| 2 tablespoons diet margarine | 1/2 teaspoon salt |
| 3/4 tablespoon arrowroot powder | 1/2 cup milk cheese, well grated |
| 1 1/2 cups milk | |

Preheat oven to 350°. Cut off stem of tomato; cut around inside (be careful not to break shell). Scoop out pulp (this leaves the shell which is about 1/2" thick). Salt to taste, let drain upside down about 10 minutes. Sauté onion and pepper in margarine until onion is golden brown. Mix in arrowroot, stirring constantly. Add milk and heat until this is thick and smooth; then stir in crab (or lobster) meat, Worcestershire sauce, cayenne, and salt. Heat to boil. Fill tomato shells with mixture and garnish with cheese. Place tomatoes in shallow baking pan; add 1/4" water to pan and bake until cheese melts (about 10 minutes). Serve at once.

## *SWEET-SOUR TONGUE

Exchanges per serving: 1 slice = 1 meat, 1/4 fat.
Calories per serving: 88              Yield: 4 servings

| | |
|---|---|
| 2 tablespoons diet margarine | Non-nutritive sweetener equivalent to 2 tablespoons sugar |

| 1 tablespoon arrowroot | 2 tablespoons malt vinegar |
| powder | 1/4 teaspoon pepper |
| 1/2 teaspoon salt | 8 slices cooked smoked |
| 1 cup stock | tongue (3 ounces) |

Blend margarine, arrowroot powder, seasonings with stock and cook until thickened. Add tongue and heat together.

## **STUFFED BUNS

Exchanges per serving: 1 bun = 1 bread, 1 1/2 fat,
1 meat.

Calories per serving: 200          Yield: 8 servings

| 1 6-ounce diet water- | 1 tablespoon ripe olives, |
| packed tuna (or chicken | chopped |
| or turkey) | Minced dill pickle to taste |
| 2 tablespoons green onions, | 1/2 cup diet mayonnaise |
| minced | 1/4 cup cheddar cheese, |
| 2 tablespoons celery, | grated |
| minced | 8 hot dog buns |

Mix all ingredients; fill inside of bun. Wrap in foil. Place in 350° oven about 10-15 minutes until hot and cheese has melted.

## **LIVER A LA BOURGEOISE

Exchanges per serving: 3 ounces = 1 fat, 1 1/2 meat,
1/2 "B" vegetable.

Calories per serving: 187          Yield: 8 servings

| 1 carrot, shredded | 2 1/2 pounds liver |
| 1 onion, minced | 2 cups water |
| 1 turnip, diced | 1/16 teaspoon seasoned |
| 1 bay leaf | salt |
| 2 tablespoons diet | 1/16 teaspoon lemon |
| margarine | pepper |
| 1 tablespoon arrowroot | |
| powder | |

Brown carrot, onion, and turnip with the bay leaf in margarine. Add arrowroot powder and blend; then add liver and water. Season, then simmer 1 1/2 to 1 3/4 hours.

### ***ONION, LIVER, AND CHEESE

Exchanges per serving: 1 serving = 1/2 fat, 3 meat.
Calories per serving: 239                    Yield: 6 servings

1 pound beef liver,
  quartered
1 tablespoon flour
1/16 teaspoon salt
1/16 teaspoon pepper
1/16 teaspoon garlic salt

2 tablespoons diet
  margarine
1/2 cup cheddar cheese,
  grated
1 onion, sliced very thin

Remove the skin and veins from the beef liver and cut
liver into 1/2" serving pieces. Sprinkle lightly with flour.
Shake off excess and sprinkle salt, pepper and garlic salt
on each side. Sauté liver and margarine a few minutes over
medium heat. Turn off heat. Pour off most of margarine
and return pan to burner; sprinkle pieces with cheese, then
thin rounds of onion. Cover. Heat until cheese is melted,
then serve.

### ***FRANKFURTER CASSEROLE

Exchanges per serving: 1 serving = 1 bread, 2 fat,
                        1 meat, 1 "B" vegetable.
Calories per serving: 260                    Yield: 8 servings

1 1/4 cups bean and
  bacon soup, undiluted
1 1/4 cups water
2 cups all-meat frank-
  furters, cut into 1/2"
  slices
1 onion, chopped fine

1 green pepper, chopped
  fine
1/2 cup celery, chopped
  fine
2 tablespoons prepared
  mustard
1 cup ready-mix type
  biscuits

Preheat oven to 375°. Mix all ingredients except biscuits.
Boil gently 5 minutes. Put about 3/4 cup mixture into
each of 8 individual baking dishes and top each with biscuit. Bake until biscuits are dark golden brown (about 20
minutes). Serve at once.

### **CALIFORNIA POT ROAST

Exchanges per serving: 2 ounces = 2 meat.
Calories per serving: 150                    Yield: 20 servings

4 pounds beef rump
2 tablespoons flour
1 teaspoon salt
1/16 teaspoon pepper
1 tablespoon oil
1 onion, chopped fine
2 carrots, sliced

1 tablespoon Worcester-
shire sauce
1 cup water
Non-nutritive sweetener
equivalent to 1/2 cup
sugar

Dredge meat well in flour, salt, and pepper. Brown in oil in skillet; add remaining ingredients. Cover. Simmer about 4 hours over low heat.

## **ROAST BEEF WITH FRUIT SAUCE

Exchanges per serving: 1 ounce = 1 meat exchange.
1/4 cup sauce = 1 fruit exchange.
Calories per serving: 40 (sauce)      Yield: 3 cups (or
75 (meat)       1 dozen 1/4 cups)

Trim fat from beef before roasting. Salt and pepper. After roasting, trim remaining fat.

Sauce

4 cups artificially sweetened plums (reserve
syrup)
1/4 teaspoon salt
1/8 teaspoon pepper
1 tablespoon arrowroot
powder

1/3 cup unsweetened
frozen orange juice
concentrate
2 tablespoons Worcester-
shire sauce
1/8 teaspoon Tabasco
sauce

Drain plums, and pit. Save 3/4 cup of the syrup. Puree plums until smooth; add syrup and balance of ingredients. Blend until smooth. In medium saucepan heat to boiling. Serve over Roast Beef.

## ***HAMBURGER CORNMEAL SHEPHERD'S PIE

Exchanges per serving: 1 serving = 1/2 bread, 2 fat,
1 1/2 meat, 1/2 "B" vegetable.
Calories per serving: 240       Yield: 8 servings

1/2 cup green pepper,
chopped fine

1/2 cup flour, sifted
3/4 cup yellow cornmeal

| | |
|---|---|
| 1/4 cup onion, minced fine | Non-nutritive sweetener |
| 2 cups ground round | equivalent to 1 table- |
| 5 tablespoons oil | spoon sugar |
| 1 cup tomato sauce | 2 teaspoons baking powder |
| 2 tablespoons catsup | 1/2 teaspoon thyme |
| 2 teaspoons salt | 1/4 cup (1 medium) egg |
| Dash lemon pepper | 1/2 cup skim milk |
| 1 teaspoon chili powder | |

Preheat oven to 400°. Sauté pepper, onion, beef in 2 tablespoons of oil in skillet, until beef is well browned. Stir in tomato sauce, catsup, 1 teaspoon salt, lemon pepper, add chili powder. Put into 1 1/2-quart casserole. Stir flour, cornmeal, sweetener, baking powder, remaining salt and thyme together in a bowl; then add egg, milk, and rest of oil. Stir until smooth. Top the first mixture with the second and bake, uncovered, until cornbread is slightly brown and firm to touch (about 1/2 hour). Loosen cornbread with a knife around edges, turn on serving plate with top side down.

### ***MEAT CASSEROLE

Exchanges per serving: 1 4-ounce serving = 1 bread,
3 meat, 1 "A" vegetable.
Calories per serving: 280        Yield: 4 servings

| | |
|---|---|
| 3/4 cup noodles, uncooked | 2 cups meat, cooked and |
| 2 1/2 cups tomato juice | cubed |
| 2 cups celery, chopped fine | 1/8 teaspoon pepper |
| 1/2 cup green pepper, | 1 1/2 teaspoons salt |
| chopped fine | 1/2 teaspoon diet |
| | margarine |

Heat oven to 350°. Combine all ingredients. Turn into well-greased casserole; bake 2 hours and 15 minutes.

### ***SPAGHETTI AND SAUCE

Exchanges per serving: 1 serving = 1 bread, 3 meat,
1 "A" vegetable.
Calories per serving: 285        Yield: 8 servings

| | |
|---|---|
| 3 cups ground round | 2 tablespoons oil |
| 1 cup onion, chopped fine | 3/4 cup tomato paste |
| 1 1/2 cups celery, chopped fine | 1 1/2 cups tomato juice |
| 2 cloves garlic, minced very fine | 2 teaspoons salt |
| | 1/16 teaspoon pepper |
| 1/2 cup fresh mushrooms, sliced thin | 1/4 cup thin spaghetti |

Brown meat well; sauté onion, celery, garlic, and mushrooms in oil until onion is golden brown. Add tomato paste, tomato juice, salt, and pepper. Cover. Boil for 1 1/2 hours, gently. After cooling, refrigerate overnight. About 20 minutes before serving, cook spaghetti according to package instructions and thoroughly drain. Measure sauce and add enough water to make a total of 5 cups of sauce. Return sauce to pan, cover and boil gently about 10 minutes. Place 1/2 cup (cooked) spaghetti on plate and top with 2/3 cup meat sauce.

### ***CHILI CON CARNE

Exchanges per serving: 1 serving = 1 bread, 1/2 fat,
2 meat, 1 "A" vegetable.

Calories per serving: 250 Yield: 8 servings

| | |
|---|---|
| 2 cups ground beef | 1 1/4 cups condensed tomato soup, undiluted |
| 1 cup onion, chopped fine | |
| 1 clove garlic, crushed fine | 2 cups kidney beans |
| 2 tablespoons chili powder | 1 tablespoon malt vinegar |
| | 1/4 teaspoon salt |

Brown beef in hot pan; stir in onion, garlic, and chili powder. Cook, stirring often until onion is tender; add rest of ingredients; bring to boil. Reduce heat and simmer, uncovered, stirring occasionally, about 15 minutes.

### ***POLLY'S CHILI CON CARNE

Exchanges per serving: 1 serving = 1 bread, 1/2 fat,
2 meat, 1 "A" vegetable.

Calories per serving: 250 Yield: 5 servings

| 1 cup onion, chopped fine | 2 cups ground round |
| 1/2 cup green pepper, chopped fine | 2 cups kidney beans, thoroughly drained |
| 2 cups celery, chopped fine | 2 cups tomatoes |
| 1 clove garlic, sliced thin | 1 tablespoon chili powder |
| 1 tablespoon oil | 1/2 teaspoon salt |

Sauté onion, pepper, celery, and garlic in salad oil until onion is golden brown. Add beef and cook until well browned. Stir in kidney beans, tomatoes, chili powder, and salt; boil uncovered about 45-50 minutes. Just before serving taste to see if more chili is needed.

### ***CORNED BEEF DINNER

Exchanges per serving: 3-ounce slice = 1 bread, 1 "A" vegetable, 1 "B" vegetable, 3 meat.
Calories per serving: 300          Yield: 6 servings

| 1 4-pound corned-beef brisket | 6 parsnips, scraped |
| Water to cover brisket | 3 potatoes, peeled and halved |
| 6 onions | 1 head cabbage |
| 6 carrots | |

Cover brisket with cold water in Dutch oven and bring to a boil. Drain. Add water to cover and again bring to boil; reduce heat to low. Cover. Cook until nearly tender (about 3 hours), skimming off as much fat as possible from cooking water. Add vegetables. Cook until vegetables are done (about 10-15 minutes more). Remove fat and vegetables from water; drain vegetables and trim fat from meat.

### ***MEAT LOAF

Exchanges per serving: 1 serving = 1/2 bread, 3 meat.
Calories per serving: 250          Yield: 6 servings

| 1/4 cup (1 medium) egg | 2 tablespoons green pepper, chopped fine |
| 2 cups ground round | 1 teaspoon salt |
| 3 slices bread, cubed fine | 1/2 teaspoon dry mustard |
| 1/4 cup catsup | 1 tablespoon prepared horseradish, if desired |
| 1/3 cup onion, chopped fine | |

Preheat oven to 400°. Mix all ingredients well. Form into a loaf. Place in foil-lined baking pan and bake until done (15-20 minutes).

## ****MEATBALLS WITH CARAWAY SEEDS

Exchanges per serving: 4 meatballs = 1/2 bread, 4 meat.
Calories per serving: 335          Yield: 4 servings

| | |
|---|---|
| 2 cups ground round | 1 cup raw potato, coarsely |
| 1 onion, minced fine | grated |
| 1/4 cup (1 medium) egg | 2 1/2 cups water |
| 1 teaspoon lemon peel, | 4 beef bouillon cubes |
| grated fine | 1 teaspoon arrowroot |
| 1/4 teaspoon pepper | powder |
| 1/2 teaspoon salt | 1/2 teaspoon caraway |
| 1 tablespoon dried parsley | seeds |
| flakes | 1 tablespoon water |

Mix first eight ingredients. Form into sixteen meatballs. Bring water to boil, and in it dissolve the bouillon; then add meatballs and cover tightly. Gently boil about 1/2 hour. Remove meatballs from broth and stir arrowroot and caraway seeds, dissolved in water, into broth until thick and smooth. Pour a little gravy over meatballs, garnish with parsley, if desired. (Store remaining gravy in tightly covered jar in refrigerator for later use.)

## ****HAMBURGERS

Exchanges per serving: 1 4-ounce pattie = 1 bread,
                            4 meat.
Calories per serving: 370          Yield: 4 servings

| | |
|---|---|
| 2 cups ground round | 1/2 teaspoon celery seed |
| 1/4 cup (1 medium) egg | 1 tablespoon Worcester- |
| 1 onion, chopped fine | shire sauce |
| 1 tablespoon horseradish | 1/2 bun per person, or |
| 1 teaspoon salt | 1 slice bread |
| 1/2 teaspoon pepper | |

Mix all ingredients (except bun) and shape into patties. Broil about 6-7 minutes per side. Serve on bun (or 1 slice bread).

## ****MEATBALLS

Exchanges per serving: 4 meatballs = 1 bread, 2 meat, 1/2 milk.

Calories per serving: 310                    Yield: 6 servings

2 cups ground round
1/4 cup dried bread
  crumbs
1 teaspoon salt
1 1/2 cups buttermilk

3/4 cup minute rice
1 teaspoon diet margarine
1 cup water
1/2 tablespoon arrowroot
  powder

Mix beef, crumbs, salt, 1/2 cup buttermilk, and rice. Shape into two dozen meatballs (about 1″ round). In large skillet brown meatballs in margarine on all sides; pour water over and cover tightly. Boil until rice is tender and meat is cooked (about 30 minutes). Remove from skillet. Mix remaining 1 cup buttermilk with arrowroot to form smooth paste and stir this into liquid remaining in skillet. Stir constantly. Cook until gravy is thick (do not boil). Return meatballs to pan and gently heat. Serve with gravy.

## ****HEARTY HASH

Exchanges per serving: 1 serving = 1/2 bread, 3 meat, 1/4 skim milk, 1/2 "A" and 1/2 "B" vegetable.

Calories per serving: 325                    Yield: 4 servings

1/2 cup onion, ground
1/4 cup parsley, chopped
1 cup cooked potatoes,
  chopped
2 tablespoons green
  pepper, ground
1 teaspoon salt
1 1/2 cups leftover cooked
  beef, diced, chopped, or
  ground

2 teaspoons Worcester-
  shire sauce
1 tablespoon diet
  margarine
2/3 cup skim milk (or
  unsweetened tomato
  sauce)

Preheat oven to 350°. Mix all ingredients. Pour into a well-greased casserole. Bake about 1/2 hour.

## ****STUFFED FLANK STEAK

Exchanges per serving: 4 ounces = 1/2 bread, 1 fat,
4 meat.

Calories per serving: 340     Yield: 8 servings

2-pound flank steak
1/16 teaspoon salt
1/16 teaspoon lemon
 pepper
1 tablespoon flour
4 cups bread cubes
2 small onions, chopped
 fine

3/4 cup celery, chopped
 fine
1 1/2 teaspoons sage
1/2 teaspoon Mei Yen
 seasoning
3 tablespoons diet
 margarine
1/2 cup water

Preheat oven to 350°. Score steak lightly, crosswise.
Sprinkle with salt and pepper and dredge with flour (pound
it well into the steak). Combine next five ingredients and
spread over steak. Roll meat and tie, or fasten edge with
toothpicks. Brown in margarine, then add water; cover and
cook about 1 1/2 hours, until tender. Baste occasionally.

## ****MARGARET'S MEAT PIE

Exchanges per serving: 1 serving = 1 bread, 3 meat,
1/2 milk.

Calories per serving: 325     Yield: 6 servings

1/4 cup onion, chopped
 fine
1 clove garlic, minced fine
1 tablespoon oil
1 cup oat bread crumbs
1 whole egg plus 2 eggs
 separated
2 1/4 cups buttermilk
1/4 cup catsup
1 1/2 cups ground meat

2 1/2 teaspoons salt
1/8 teaspoon pepper
1/2 cup yellow cornmeal
1 teaspoon salt
1/2 teaspoon baking soda
Non-nutritive sweetener
 equivalent to 1 teaspoon
 sugar
1/4 cup Parmesan cheese,
 grated

Preheat oven to 350°. Sauté onion and garlic in oil until
onion is golden. Remove from heat and stir in oat crumbs,
whole egg (1/4 cup), 1/4 cup buttermilk, catsup, meat,
1 1/2 teaspoons salt, and pepper. Line bottom and sides

93

of 10″ pie tin with this mixture. Bake 15 minutes: pour off any excess liquid. Mix together rest of buttermilk, corn meal, remaining salt, baking soda, and sweetener in medium saucepan. Cook, stirring constantly until thick and smooth. Remove from heat. Stir in egg yolks. Beat egg whites until peaks form; fold into cornmeal mix. Fill meat pie shell. Top with cheese and bake until cheese is lightly brown (about 30 minutes). Let cool for five minutes before serving.

## ****MISSISSIPPI CASSEROLE

Exchanges per serving: 1 serving = 1/2 bread, 4 meat, 1 fruit.
Calories per serving: 410          Yield: 4 serving

| | |
|---|---|
| 4 large cooked sweet potatoes | 1/4 cup water |
| 2 cups pork sausage | Non-nutritive sweetener equivalent to 1/4 cup brown sugar |
| 4 large apples, sliced | |
| 1/16 teaspoon salt | |

Preheat oven to 350°. Peel potatoes. Cut in thin slices. Place half in bottom of greased casserole. Cover with sausage, shaped in 4 cakes. Add apples, sprinkle with salt, then cover with remaining potatoes. Brush with water, sprinkle with sweetener. Bake 1 hour.

## ***ROAST LEG OF LAMB

Exchanges per serving: 3 ounces = 3 meat.
Calories per serving: 225          Yield: 10-12 servings

| | |
|---|---|
| 5-6 pound leg of lamb | 1/8 cup flour |
| 1 clove garlic | 1 teaspoon ginger |
| 2-3 teaspoons Bouquet Garni | 1 teaspoon seasoned salt |
| | 1 teaspoon lemon pepper |

Preheat oven to 300°. Wipe meat with damp cloth. Do not remove the fell—the paperlike covering over the meat. Make gashes in roast with sharp knife; cut garlic into slivers and insert a piece in each gash. Rub meat with condiments and dredge with flour. Place, fat side up and

94

uncovered, in shallow roaster. Roast until tender (about 30-35 minutes per pound). Remove garlic and serve.

## ****VEAL A LA KING

Exchanges per serving: 3 ounces = 1/2 bread, 4 meat, 1/4 skim milk.
Calories per serving: 346          Yield: 16 servings

| | |
|---|---|
| 1/2 cup green pepper, chopped fine | 4 cups skim milk |
| 1/2 cup mushrooms | 1/16 teaspoon seasoned salt |
| 3 tablespoons diet margarine | 1/16 teaspoon pepper |
| 3 tablespoons arrowroot powder | 4 cups cooked veal, diced |
| | 1 pimiento, diced |
| | 8 slices toast |

Cook pepper and mushrooms in margarine for 8 minutes; remove vegetables. Add arrowroot to margarine and blend. Add skim milk and seasonings and cook until thickened, stirring constantly. Add green pepper, mushrooms, veal, and pimiento and heat. Serve on one-half slice toast.

## **SAUERKRAUT AND SPARERIBS

Exchanges per serving: 2 ounces = 2 meat.
Calories per serving: 150          Yield: 6 servings

| | |
|---|---|
| 1 quart sauerkraut | 4 pounds spareribs |
| Non-nutritive sweetener equivalent to 1/4 cup brown sugar | 1/16 teaspoon seasoned salt |
| | 1/16 teaspoon pepper |
| | 1/2 cup hot water |

Preheat oven to 350°. Place sauerkraut in greased baking dish. Sprinkle with sweetener. Brown spareribs under broiler. Season, place on sauerkraut, and add hot water. Cover. Bake 45 minutes to 1 hour.

## **HAM LOAF

Exchanges per serving: 1 serving = 1/2 bread, 2 meat.
Calories per serving: 200          Yield: 16 servings

| | |
|---|---|
| 1 1/2 pounds ham, ground well | Dash pepper |
| 1 pound beef, ground well | Non-nutritive sweetener equivalent to 3/4 cup sugar |
| 1/2 cup (2 medium) eggs, beaten | 1/4 teaspoon cinnamon |
| 1 1/4 cups milk | 1/4 teaspoon cloves |
| 4 slices soft bread, broken into small pieces | 1/4 teaspoon nutmeg |
| 1 1/2 teaspoons salt | 1/2 teaspoon dry mustard |
| | 1/2 teaspoon vegetable oil |

Preheat oven to 350°. Combine all ingredients except oil and mix well. Use oil to grease loaf pan and place mix in pan. Bake 1 1/2 hours.

### ***BAKED HAM OR HAM STEAK WITH PINEAPPLE

Exchanges per serving: 3 ounces = 1 fruit, 3 meat.
Calories per serving: 260          Yield: 24 servings

| | |
|---|---|
| 1 6-8 pound canned ham | 1/2 cup bread crumbs |
| Non-nutritive sweetener equivalent to 1/2 cup sugar | 3/4 cup pineapple juice |
| | 5-6 slices unsweetened pineapple |
| 1 teaspoon dry mustard | |

Preheat oven to 300°. Spread ham with mixture of sweetener, mustard, and bread crumbs. Add pineapple juice. Bake 15 minutes then add slices of pineapple and cook entire dish an additional 45 minutes.

### ****HAWAIIAN BAKED PORK

Exchanges per serving: 1 serving = 1 bread, 1 fat, 1/2 fruit, 3 meat.
Calories per serving: 344          Yield: 4 servings

| | |
|---|---|
| 2 cups crushed unsweetened pineapple | 4 shoulder pork steaks (3 ounces each) |
| 3 medium-sized sweet potatoes | 1/16 teaspoon salt |
| Non-nutritive sweetener equivalent to 3 3/4 cups brown sugar | 1/16 teaspoon pepper |
| | 4 bacon strips |

Preheat oven to 350°. Place pineapple in one large baking dish, or in 4 individual ones. Pare and slice sweet potatoes and place these over pineapple. Sprinkle with sweetener.

Season pork steaks with salt and pepper; place these on top of sweet potatoes; then arrange bacon strips on top of pork steaks. Cover and bake 1 hour, or until tender. Remove cover; increase temperature to 450° for the last 10 minutes to brown steak and bacon.

### ***PORK ROAST WITH SPICE SAUCE

Exchanges per serving: 3 ounces = 3 meat.
Calories per serving: 219                    Yield: 12 servings

| | |
|---|---|
| 1 4-5 pound fresh picnic shoulder of pork | Non-nutritive sweetener equivalent to 1 1/2 cups sugar |
| 1/16 teaspoon salt | |
| 1/16 teaspoon pepper | 1/2 teaspoon paprika |
| 2 small onions, minced | 1/2 cup vinegar |
| 1 tablespoon Worcestershire sauce | 1/2 cup water |
| | 2 tablespoons catsup |

Have butcher bone and roll roast. Salt, pepper, and place fat side up on rack in open roaster. Roast at 350° for 40-45 minutes per pound. Combine the other ingredients and cook together for 5 minutes. Pour over roast and serve.

### ***PORK PATTIES IN GRAVY

Exchanges per serving: 1 serving = 1/2 bread, 1/2 fat,
                              2 meat, 1 "B" vegetable.
Calories per serving: 220                    Yield: 8 servings

| | |
|---|---|
| 2 cups very lean pork shoulder, ground | 1/3 teaspoon pepper |
| | 3/4 teaspoon nutmeg |
| 1/2 cup (2 medium) eggs | 2 tablespoons salad oil |
| 1/2 cup skim milk | 1/2 cup water |
| 4 slices dry bread, cubed fine | 1 1/4 cups undiluted, condensed beef bouillon |
| 9 onions, one chopped fine, rest only peeled | 1 teaspoon oregano |
| | 1/4 teaspoon paprika |
| 1 1/2 teaspoons salt | |

Mix first eight ingredients well and let stand a few minutes. Then divide into patties. Brown these well in oil on both sides; then drain on brown paper or paper towel. Pour fat from pan and add the rest of ingredients. Return patties to mixture, cover, cook gently 1/2 hour.

### ***MAINE SUPPER

Exchanges per serving: 1 cup = 2 1/2 bread, 1/2 fat,
1 1/4 meat.

Calories per serving: 281                    Yield: 6 cups

1 tablespoon onion,
  chopped
2 tablespoons green
  pepper, chopped
2 tablespoons diet
  margarine
4 cups pork and beans

Non-nutritive sweetener
  equivalent to 1 1/2 cups
  brown sugar
1/2 cup chopped celery
1 cup Vienna sausage,
  sliced in half

Brown onion and pepper in margarine. Add pork and
beans, sweetener, and celery. Mix together and place in
individual casseroles. Place 3 sausages in each casserole
and bake at 350° until browned.

### ***CHICKEN LIVERS

Exchanges per serving: 1 serving = 1 fat, 3 meat, 1 "A"
and 1 "B" vegetable.

Calories per serving: 279                    Yield: 4 servings

2 onions, sliced thin
2 stalks celery, sliced thin
1 tablespoon diet margarine

1 pound chicken livers
1/2 teaspoon salt
1/2 teaspoon pepper

Sauté onions and celery in margarine until celery is wilted.
Remove and place to one side. Add chicken livers and turn
heat high; cook, turning once or twice until done (3-5 minutes). Top with onions and celery. Season with salt and
pepper.

### ***CHARLOTTE'S CURRIED CHICKEN

Exchanges per serving: 1/2 cup sauce over 1/2 cup rice =
1 bread, 1/4 fruit, 2 meat.

Calories per serving: 224                    Yield: 6 servings

1 cup long-grain white rice
2 chicken breasts, split,
  boned, and cut into 2"
  or 3" pieces

1 teaspoon salt
1 1/2 teaspoons curry
  powder

| | |
|---|---|
| 1 cup mushrooms, sliced thin | 1/2 tablespoon arrowroot powder |
| 1/3 cup onions, chopped fine | 3/4 cup skim milk |
| 1 tablespoon diet margarine | 1 cup water |
| 1 chicken bouillon cube | 1 cup apples, sliced |
| | 1 teaspoon parsley, chopped fine |

Cook rice as directed, but omit margarine. Sauté chicken, mushrooms, and onions in margarine until chicken is lightly browned on all sides (about 15 minutes). Make a smooth paste of bouillon cube, salt, curry powder, and arrowroot; then add milk, water, apple, and parsley. Cook until thick and smooth and apple is tender, stirring constantly. Stir chicken into sauce and pour onto the rice.

### ***CHICKEN SUPERB

Exchanges per serving: 1 serving = 1 fat, 1/4 fruit,
3 meat.

Calories per serving: 274            Yield: 4 servings

| | |
|---|---|
| 1/4 cup flour | 1/4 cup pimiento, diced fine |
| 1 1/16 teaspoons salt | 1/2 cup mushrooms, cut in quarters |
| 1/8 teaspoon pepper | 1/4 teaspoon ginger |
| 2 chicken breasts, split and skinned | 1 cup canned chicken broth |
| 2 tablespoons diet margarine | 1/4 cup orange juice |
| 1/2 green pepper, chopped fine | 1/2 orange, unpeeled and sliced thin |

Mix together flour, 1 teaspoon salt, half the pepper. Lightly coat chicken. Cook chicken in margarine until golden, using a tightly covered pan. Then turn breasts, meat side down, and add rest of ingredients. Cover. Stir occasionally while boiling gently, until tender (about 1/2 hour).

### ****BROILED SPRING CHICKEN

Exchanges per serving: 4 ounces = 4 meat.
Calories per serving: 300            Yield: 16 servings

| | |
|---|---|
| 1 4-pound broiling chicken, dressed | 1/16 teaspoon seasoned salt |

| 2 tablespoons diet margarine, melted | 1/16 teaspoon lemon pepper |
|---|---|

Preheat oven to 500°. Wash chicken inside and out. Brush with margarine. Rub with salt and pepper. Place in broiler; brown evenly, turn and brown other side. Allow 30 minutes or more to cook so the joints are not rare. Baste from time to time, adding water if needed.

## ****CHICKEN DELIGHT

Exchanges per serving: 1 serving = 1 bread, 1 1/2 fat,
3 meat, 1 "A," 1 "B" vegetable.
Calories per serving: 398                                    Yield: 5 servings

| | |
|---|---|
| 2 pounds chicken breasts, boned and split | 1/2 cup water chestnuts, drained and sliced thin |
| 1 cup long-grain rice | 1 teaspoon salt |
| 3 tablespoons oil | 1/4 teaspoon ginger |
| 1 green pepper, chopped fine | 3/4 cup water |
| 3 stalks celery, cut in 2" pieces | 1 teaspoon arrowroot powder |
| 1 small onion, chopped fine | 1 tablespoon soy sauce |
| 1 chicken bouillon cube | 1-pound can bean sprouts, drained thoroughly |

Remove any fat or gristle from chicken, split each piece into two thin layers, then cut layers into strips about 2" long and 1/4" wide. Cook rice according to directions on the package (omit margarine). Heat oil in skillet; add chicken. Cook, covered, over high heat. Stir constantly until chicken turns completely white and is slightly browned (about 2 minutes). Turn heat to medium and add green pepper, celery, onion, bouillon cube, water chestnuts, salt, ginger, and water. Make a smooth paste of arrowroot and soy sauce and stir this into chicken mixture until smooth. Boil gently 6-7 minutes, tightly covered. Add bean sprouts to cooked vegetables; cover and boil gently another 2 minutes. Each serving consists of 1/2 cup cooked rice with 1 cup chicken mixture.

# SAUCES

## Notes

### GRAVIES AND APPROXIMATE EXCHANGES

**Arrowroot:** 1 tablespoon = 1 slice bread. (May be used for fruit juices.)

**Cornstarch:** 2 tablespoons = 1 slice bread. (May be used for fruit juices.)

**Egg Yolk:** Used in place of 1 tablespoon flour = 1 fat exchange. (Yields 3 grams protein and 5 fat, no carbohydrate. *N. B.* This is of different food value than flour.)

**Flour:** 1 tablespoon = 1/3 bread exchange.
3 tablespoons = 1 bread exchange.
(Use all-purpose flour and sift.)

**Tapioca:** 1 teaspoon = None. (Use mostly for sweet sauces. In thickening power this is equivalent to 1 tablespoon flour.)

Nondairy whipping cream may be Dream Whip, Cool Whip, etc., any of your choice.

Imitation sour cream may be Imo, etc., any of your choice.

Granulated sweeteners are preferred for recipes for solids such as cake. Liquid sweeteners may be used for such things as drinks.

### SUBSTITUTE SUGAR SYRUPS AND GLAZES

Consult notes on Special Ingredients.

## *BERRY SAUCE

Exchanges per serving: 1 tablespoon = None.
Calories per serving: 0                         Yield: 1 1/2 cups

Non-nutritive sweetener
  equivalent to 1/2 cup
  sugar
1 teaspoon arrowroot
  powder
1/16 teaspoon salt

1/2 cup water
1 cup berries (blueberries,
  raspberries, etc.)
1 tablespoon lemon juice
1 teaspoon lemon rind,
  grated

Combine sweetener, arrowroot, and salt, then stir in water
and add berries. Bring to a boil, simmer until clear and
thick, about 5 minutes. Remove from heat and add lemon
juice and rind. Chill and use over ice creams, custards,
plain cakes, waffles, or pancakes.

## *BARB'S BARBECUE SAUCE

Exchanges per serving: 1/2 cup = 1/4 "A" and
                                 1/4 "B" vegetable.
Calories per serving: 0                         Yield: 2 cups

1/2 cup onions, chopped
  fine
2/3 cup tomato paste
1 cup water
1 teaspoon Worcestershire
  sauce
2 cups dietetic maple
  topping
2 tablespoons garlic-
  flavored vinegar

1/4 cup catsup (see next
  recipe)
1 teaspoon salt
1/8 teaspoon pepper
1/4 teaspoon dried
  oregano, crushed fine
1/4 teaspoon dried rose-
  mary, crushed fine

Blend all ingredients together in a saucepan. Simmer over
low heat about half an hour, or until onions are well
cooked. Use with any broiled meat such as lamb patties,
ground beef, beef, pork, or lamb chops.

## *CATSUP

Exchanges per serving: 1 tablespoon = None.
Calories per serving: 0                         Yield: 2 cups

4 tomatoes, quartered
1/3 cup green pepper, chopped fine
1/4 cup onions, chopped fine
1/8 cup red pepper, chopped very fine
1/2 cup malt vinegar
1/2 teaspoon salt
Non-nutritive sweetener equivalent to 1 cup sugar

1/4 teaspoon cinnamon
1/8 teaspoon allspice
1/8 teaspoon anise seed, crushed fine
1/4 teaspoon ground mustard
1/4 teaspoon powdered red pepper
1/4 teaspoon mace

If using blender, fill 3/4 full with first four ingredients and blend about 3-4 seconds at highest speed. If not using blender, mix until smoothness of a puree. Pour mixture into pan, adding vinegar, salt, and sweetener. Tie the spices loosely together in a bag of light cheesecloth and add. Simmer, uncovered, until only about 1/2 mixture remains. Remove bag of spices.

## *MINT SAUCE

Exchanges per serving: 1 tablespoon = None.
Calories per serving: 0               Yield: 1 3/4 cups

1/4 cup vinegar
1 cup water
1/2 cup mint leaves, chopped
1/4 cup lemon juice

Non-nutritive sweetener equivalent to 1 1/2 tablespoons sugar
1/2 teaspoon salt

Heat vinegar and 1/2 cup water to boiling. Pour over half the mint leaves. Let stand 15 minutes. Strain. Add remaining water, lemon juice, sweetener, and salt. Chill. Add remaining mint leaves. Serve with lamb.

## *SWEET AND TANGY TOMATO SAUCE FOR SPARERIBS AND LOIN OF PORK

Exchanges per serving: 1/2 cup = None.
Calories per serving: 0               Serves 2 1/2 cups

1/3 cup vinegar
Non-nutritive sweetener
    equivalent to 1 1/2 cups
    sugar
2 tablespoons Worcester-
    shire sauce

2 tablespoons prepared
    mustard
1/2 teaspoon Tabasco
    sauce
1/4 cup minced onion
2 cups tomato sauce

Combine all ingredients in a saucepan, bring to a boil. Use to baste spareribs or loin of pork.

## *GRAVY

Exchanges per serving: 1 tablespoon = None.
Calories per serving: 8                     Yield: 2 cups

1 onion, thinly sliced
2 stalks celery, diced
1 1/4 cups chicken broth
    (or condensed beef
    consommé)

1 1/4 cups water
1/4 teaspoon Gravy Master
1 tablespoon arrowroot
    powder

Combine onion, celery, broth, and water in a medium saucepan; cover and boil gently over low heat until onion is transparent. Strain. Reserve vegetables for later use. Return broth to pan. Use a little water, Gravy Master, and arrowroot to make smooth paste. Stir slowly into broth and heat to boiling.

## *HOT SHOYU (SOY) SAUCE

Exchanges per serving: 1 ounce = None.
Calories per serving: 8                     Yield: 1 2/3 cups

1 cup soy sauce
2/3 cup water
Non-nutritive sweetener
    equivalent to 1/2 cup
    brown sugar

1/4 teaspoon instant onion
1 teaspoon arrowroot
    powder

Blend all ingredients and heat to light boil. Serve as dip for Shrimp Tempura, "pupus," or as sauce for fish or chicken.

## *BARBECUE SAUCE

Exchanges per serving: 1 tablespoon = None.
Calories per serving: 10                     Yield: 2 cups

| 4 tablespoons lemon juice | 1/16 teaspoon lemon |
| 1/16 teaspoon red pepper | pepper |
| 2 tablespoons cider vinegar | 1 1/2 teaspoons mustard |
| 1 cup catsup (see catsup | Non-nutritive sweetener |
| recipe) | equivalent to 1/2 cup |
| 1/2 cup water | sugar |
| 3 tablespoons Worcester- | 1/2 teaspoon salt |
| shire sauce | |

Combine all ingredients and simmer over medium heat about 20-25 minutes.

## *COLD SHOYU (SOY) SAUCE

Exchanges per serving: 1 tablespoon = None.
Calories per serving: 0                     Serves: 3/4 cup

| 1/2 cup soy sauce | 2 tablespoons wine vinegar |
| Non-nutritive sweetener | |
| equivalent to 3 table- | |
| spoons brown sugar | |

Blend ingredients well. Serve in small bowls with hot fried foods, or cold meat, or fish "pupus."

## *TOMATO SAUCE

Exchanges per serving: 1/4 cup = None.
Calories per serving: 10                     Yield: 3 cups

| 1/2 onion, chopped fine | 1/4 teaspoon oregano |
| 1 tablespoon olive oil | 1/4 teaspoon basil |
| 1/2 clove garlic, minced | Non-nutritive sweetener |
| fine | equivalent to 1/4 tea- |
| 2 cups tomato sauce | spoon sugar |
| 1 cup water | 1/4 teaspoon salt |

Sauté onion in oil until lightly browned; add garlic and sauté this until lightly browned also. Stir in sauce, water, and condiments. Simmer 1 hour; if using for spaghetti, simmer 5 hours.

## *GOLDEN SHOYU DIP

Exchanges per serving: 1 ounce = 1/4 fat.
Calories per serving: 12                     Yield: 1 1/4 cups

| 1 cup safflower mayonnaise | 1/2 teaspoon instant onion |
| 1/4 cup soy sauce | 1/4 teaspoon arrowroot powder |

Blend all ingredients until smooth. Chill and restir before serving as dip for all fish "pupus" or with grilled or fried fish.

## *SWEET AND SOUR MARINADE
### For Shish Kabobs and Brochettes

Exchanges per serving: 1/2 cup = None.
Calories per serving: 0                    Yield: 2 cups

| 1 cup soy sauce | Non-nutritive sweetener |
| 1/2 cup vinegar | equivalent to 1 1/2 cups |
| 1/2 cup unsweetened | sugar |
| pineapple juice | 1/2 teaspon salt |
| | 1/2 teaspoon garlic powder |

Combine all ingredients and bring to a boil. Marinate beef or lamb cubes in mixture for at least four hours. Also useful for basting meat while cooking.

## *TANGY TONGUE SAUCE

(Not for diabetics without consent of doctor.)

Exchanges per serving: 1/4 cup = 1/2 fat, 1/2 fruit.
Calories per serving: 43 + alcohol        Yield: 3 1/4 cups
                content (about 90)

| 1/4 cup diet margarine | 2 tablespoons white vinegar |
| 1/8 cup arrowroot powder | Non-nutritive sweetener |
| 1 1/2 cups unsweetened | equivalent to 2 table- |
| apple juice | spoons brown sugar |
| 3/4 cup beer | 1/2 cup raisins |

Melt margarine, stir in arrowroot powder; gradually add apple juice and beer, stirring constantly. Add rest of the ingredients and cook over low heat, stirring until sauce is smooth and slightly thickened. Serve over hot or cold tongue.

## *RAISIN SAUCE

Exchanges per serving: 1 tablespoon = None.
Calories per serving: 16                Yield: 1 1/2 cups

Non-nutritive sweetener
   equivalent to 3/4 cup
   brown sugar
1 1/2 tablespoons arrow-
   root powder

1 1/2 cups broth
   (preferably tongue)
1 tablespoon fat
1/4 cup vinegar
1/2 cup golden raisins
1 lemon, sliced thin

Mix sweetener and arrowroot powder in top of double boiler. Add broth gradually, stirring constantly. Add remaining ingredients. Cook until raisins are plump and mixture thick. Stir occasionally. Serve hot with ham or tongue.

## *TARTAR SAUCE

Exchanges per serving: 2 tablespoons = 1/2 fat.
Calories per serving: 20                Yield: 1/2 cup

1/4 cup dietetic whipped
   dressing
2 tablespoons dill pickle,
   chopped

2 tablespoons parsley,
   minced
1 teaspoon lemon juice
1/4 teaspoon salt

Mix all ingredients together. Chill before serving. Store in refrigerator.

## *CELERY AND TOMATO SAUCE

Exchanges per serving: 1/2 cup = 1/2 fat,
              1 "A" vegetable.
Calories per serving: 23                Yield: 2 cups

1 tablespoon green pepper,
   minced fine
2 tablespoons dried onion
1 cup celery, sliced thin
1 tablespoon diet
   margarine
1 scant cup tomato sauce

1/2 teaspoon sesame seeds,
   crushed fine
1/4 teaspoon lemon
   pepper
1/16 teaspoon salt
1/16 teaspoon black
   pepper
1/4 teaspoon garlic salt

Sauté pepper, onion, and celery in margarine until golden and wilted. Add balance of ingredients. Boil gently about half an hour.

## *SPAGHETTI SAUCE

Exchanges per serving: 1 cup = 1/3 fat.
Calories per serving: 25                          Yield: 10 cups

| | |
|---|---|
| 1/2 cup celery, chopped fine | 1/2 teaspoon marjoram |
| | 1/8 teaspoon celery salt |
| 1 1/2 cups onion, chopped fine | 1/16 teaspoon garlic salt |
| | 1/4 teaspoon rosemary |
| 1/4 cup diet margarine | 1 teaspoon oregano |
| 8 cups tomatoes | 1/2 teaspoon basil |
| 1 cup tomato sauce | 1/4 teaspoon salt |
| 1/2 teaspoon thyme | 1/16 teaspoon pepper |

Sauté celery and onion in margarine until golden and wilted. Add remaining ingredients. Cover and bring to boil; uncover and boil gently until sauce is thick. Use for noodles, spaghetti, macaroni, or meat. This calorie count does not include calories for spaghetti, noodles, macaroni, or any complementary main course.

## *CHINESE MUSTARD

(Not for diabetics without consent of doctor.)

Exchanges per serving: 1 ounce = 1/4 fat.
Calories per serving: 15 + calories for          Yield: 1/2 cup
                          beer or wine

| | |
|---|---|
| 1/3 cup dry mustard | 1/2 teaspoon seasoned salt |
| 1 tablespoon safflower oil | 2 teaspoons flat beer or wine |
| Non-nutritive sweetener equivalent to 1 teaspoon sugar | |

Mix all ingredients until smoooth; serve in small dipping bowl.

# *APPLE CRANBERRY RELISH

Exchanges per serving: 1/4 cup = 1 fat, 1 fruit.
Calories per serving: 85                 Yield: 1 3/4 cups

1/2 cup apples, diced
2 cups fresh cranberries,
  chopped fine
1/4 cup white raisins,
  chopped fine

1/4 cup walnuts, chopped
  fine
Non-nutritive sweetener
  equivalent to 1 cup sugar
1/2 teaspoon lemon juice

Combine all ingredients, mixing well. Chill overnight in refrigerator.

# *LOW-CALORIE TOPPING WHIP

Exchanges per serving: 1/4 cup = 1/4 skim milk.
Calories per serving: 16                 Yield: 3 1/2 cups

1/2 cup nonfat dry milk
1/2 cup ice water
2 tablespoons fresh lemon
  juice

Non-nutritive sweetener
  equivalent to 1/4 cup
  sugar

Place bowl and egg beater in refrigerator for about two hours. Mix nonfat milk and ice water in chilled bowl, beat with mixer until soft peaks form. Add juice and sweetener and beat again until mixture forms stiff peaks.

# *CUSTARD SAUCE FOR SHORTCAKES

Exchanges per serving: 1 tablespoon = trace milk.
Calories per serving: 10                 Yield: 2 1/2 cups

2 cups skim milk
1/2 cup (2 medium) eggs
Non-nutritive sweetener
  equivalent to 1 1/2 cups
  sugar

1/2 tablespoon arrowroot
  powder
1/4 teaspoon salt
1 teaspoon vanilla extract
1 teaspoon almond extract

Scald milk in saucepan. Beat egg, sweetener, arrowroot, and salt in small bowl; gradually add in scalded milk. Return mixture to saucepan. Cook over low heat, stirring constantly until mixture coats a spoon and is slightly thickened. Remove from heat and beat in vanilla and almond extracts. Chill until ready to use.

## *CHERRY GLAZE

Exchanges per serving: 1/2 cup = 1 fruit.
Calories per serving: 40                          Yield: 3 cup

2 cups sour red cherries,
 water-packed and pitted
1/2 cup liquid from
 cherries
Non-nutritive sweetener
 equivalent to 2 table-
 spoons sugar

1 teaspoon arrowroot
 powder
1 tablespoon lemon juice
1/4 teaspoon almond
 extract
Drop of red vegetable food
 coloring (optional)

Mix liquid from cherries with sweetener and arrowroot and stir to make smooth paste. Cook, stirring constantly until thick and smooth. Add cherries, lemon juice and almond extract. Allow to cool at room temperature. May be used over dietetic ice cream, pineapple cheese pie, among other desserts.

## *LEMON SAUCE

Exchanges per serving: 1/4 cup = 1 fat.
Calories per serving: 50                          Yield: 1 cup

3/4 tablespoon arrowroot
 powder
Non-nutritive sweetener
 equivalent to 1/2 cup
 sugar
1/8 teaspoon salt
1 cup boiling water
2 tablespoons diet
 margarine

1 1/2 tablespoons lemon
 juice
1 1/2 teaspoons lemon
 rind, ground fine
1/16 teaspoon anise seed,
 crushed fine
1/16 teaspoon nutmeg
1/16 teaspoon cloves,
 ground fine

Combine arrowroot, sweetener, and salt in saucepan; add boiling water slowly, stirring to avoid lumps. Simmer and stir until thick; remove from heat. Stir in margarine and remaining ingredients. Use for cake fillings and over bread puddings and custards.

## *CUSTARD SAUCE

Exchanges per serving: 1/2 cup = 3/4 meat,
1/3 skim milk.

Calories per serving: 80            Yield: 4 servings

| | |
|---|---|
| 1 whole egg plus 2 egg yolks | 1/8 teaspoon salt |
| | 1 1/2 cups skim milk |
| Non-nutritive sweetener equivalent to 3 tablespoons sugar | 1 teaspoon vanilla extract |

Beat 1 egg and 2 yolks together in saucepan, reserving 2 whites, covered in refrigerator for use another time. Blend in sweetener and salt and gradually stir in skim milk. Place over low heat, stirring constantly until mixture slightly thickens and coats a metal spoon. Remove from heat. Stir in vanilla. Chill. (Sauce will thicken during chilling.)

## *POLLY'S CUSTARD SAUCE

Exchanges per serving: 1/2 cup = 1/2 meat,
1/2 skim milk.

Calories per serving: 75            Yield: 3 1/2 cups

| | |
|---|---|
| 3 cups skim milk | 1 tablespoon arrowroot powder |
| Non-nutritive sweetener equivalent to 1/2 cup sugar | 1/2 cup (3 medium) egg yolks |
| | 1 teaspoon almond extract |

Combine skim milk and sweetener in top of double boiler and heat. Mix arrowroot powder and egg yolks and beat well. Add small amount of hot milk mixture to egg mixture and blend. Return entire mixture to top of double boiler and cook over simmering water. Stir constantly (about 15 minutes) until mixture is slightly thickened. Remove from heat at once; pour into Pyrex bowl. Stir in

111

almond extract and place in refrigerator to chill. It will thicken as it chills.

## *ORANGE SAUCE

Exchanges per serving: 1/4 cup = 1 fruit.
Calories per serving: 40                    Yield: 2 cups

Non-nutritive sweetener equivalent to 1 cup sugar
1/4 teaspoon salt
1 tablespoon arrowroot powder
1 cup orange juice
1/4 cup lemon juice

3/4 cup boiling water
1 tablespoon diet margarine
1 teaspoon grated orange peel
1 teaspoon grated lemon peel

Combine sweetener, salt, and arrowroot. Stir in orange and lemon juices, and boiling water. Boil 1 minute, stirring constantly. Remove from heat and stir in margarine, orange and lemon peels. Serve over hot cake or pudding.

## *SAUCE ROYALE

Exchanges per serving: 1/2 cup = 1 fat.
Calories per serving: 52                    Yield: 4 servings

1 tablespoon arrowroot powder
1/2 teaspoon nutmeg
1/2 teaspoon cinnamon
1/8 teaspoon allspice
4 tablespoons cold water

2 cups boiling water
1/16 teaspoon salt
Non-nutritive sweetener equivalent to 1 cup sugar
2 tablespoons diet margarine

Dissolve arrowroot and spices in cold water; add to boiling water. Stir, bring to simmer, then add salt, sweetener, and margarine. Use hot for custards.

## *CITRUS FRUIT SAUCE

Exchanges per serving: 1/4 cup = 3/4 fat.
Calories per serving: 40                    Yield: 1 cup

Non-nutritive sweetener equivalent to 1/2 cup sugar
3/4 tablespoon arrowroot powder

2 tablespoons diet margarine, melted
1 1/2 tablespoons fruit juice (grapefruit, lemon, or orange)

1/8 teaspoon salt
1 cup boiling water

1 1/2 teaspoons grated
  fruit rind
1/16 teaspoon nutmeg

Combine sweetener, arrowroot, and salt in a saucepan. Stir in boiling water until smooth; stir and simmer until clear and thick; stir in balance of ingredients.

## *SAUCE CHERRIE

Exchanges per serving: 1/2 cup = 1 fruit.
Calories per serving: 40

Yield: 2 cups

1 teaspoon arrowroot
  powder
2 cups water-packed
  cherries
1/2 teaspoon almond
  extract

1/2 teaspoon vanilla
  extract
Non-nutritive sweetener
  equivalent to 1/2 cup
  sugar

Combine arrowroot and cherries; bring to boil and simmer 5-6 minutes. Remove from heat and add extracts and sweetener. Serve when slightly warm. Can be used over dietetic ice cream, custards, and the like.

## *CREAM SAUCE

Exchanges per serving: 1/2 cup = 1/4 milk.
Calories per serving: 45

Yield: 2 1/4 cups

4 tablespoons instant dry
  milk powder
1 tablespoon arrowroot
  powder

1/8 teaspoon lemon
  pepper
1/2 teaspoon seasoned salt
2 cups water

If using blender, blend all ingredients until completely blended; if not using blender, mix to puree smoothness. Cook over low heat.

## **CHOCOLATE SAUCE

Exchanges per serving: 1 tablespoon = 2 1/2 fat.
Calories per serving: 105

Yield: 1 cup

| 1 cup unsweetened choco-<br>late, shaved<br>1/4 cup water | Non-nutritive sweetener<br>equivalent to 1/4 cup<br>sugar<br>1/2 cup cream |
|---|---|

Combine chocolate, water, and sweetener. Melt over hot water in double boiler. Stir until smooth, remove from heat, and blend in cream. Serve either hot or cold.

## **MAPLE-FLAVORED SAUCE

Exchanges per serving: 1/4 cup = 1 fat, 1/2 milk.
Calories per serving: 130            Yield: 1 3/4 cups

| 1/4 cup diet margarine<br>1 tablespoon arrowroot<br>powder<br>Non-nutritive sweetener<br>equivalent to 1 cup sugar | 1/2 cup water<br>1 cup evaporated milk<br>1 1/2 teaspoons maple<br>flavoring |
|---|---|

Melt margarine. Blend in arrowroot powder; add sweetener, water, and milk. Cook over medium heat, stirring constantly until thick; remove from heat. Add maple flavoring and chill.

## **HAWAIIAN CURRY SAUCE

Exchanges per serving: 1/2 cup = 1 fat, 1/2 fruit,
                       1/2 skim milk.
Calories per serving: 105            Yield: 2 cups

| 1/4 cup safflower oil<br>1 onion, minced<br>2 apples, peeled and diced<br>2 1/2 teaspoons arrowroot<br>powder<br>2 cups coconut milk or<br>skim milk | 1 teaspoon garlic salt<br>1 teaspoon salt<br>1 teaspoon ground ginger<br>3 tablespoons soy sauce<br>1 to 3 teaspoons curry<br>powder |
|---|---|

Heat oil. Add onion and apples. Cover and cook 10 minutes, stirring occasionally. Add arrowroot and stir until smooth; add coconut or skim milk with garlic salt, salt, ginger, soy sauce, and curry powder, stirring constantly until mixture thickens and boils. Reduce heat to very low, cover and cook 20 minutes. Mix sauce with 2 cups cooked seafood, chicken, or meat and serve on steamed rice, or as called for in recipe.

# VEGETABLES

## PROXIMATE COMPOSITION OF CAMPBELL SOUP COMPANY PRODUCTS

(Contents of 100 grams, equivalent to one 3 1/2-ounce can. This makes one serving when prepared according to the directions.)

**JUICES**

|  | Calories | Protein | Fat | Carbohydrate | Sodium | Vitamin A |
|---|---|---|---|---|---|---|
|  |  | gm | gm | gm | mg | I. U. |
| Campbell's Tomato Juice | 20 | 0.8 | 0.1 | 4.0 | 365 | 620 |
| "V-8" Cocktail Vegetable Juice | 19 | 0.8 | 0.1 | 3.6 | 365 | 1260 |

## *EGGPLANT, PEPPER, AND MUSHROOMS

Exchanges per serving: 1 cup = 1/2 fat, 1 "A" vegetable.
Calories per serving: 23                           Yield: 12 cups

1 large eggplant, cut and
  diced into squares
1/3 cup oil
1/2 cup water
2 large green peppers, cut
  and diced
1 cup sliced mushrooms,
  drained

2 cups tomatoes, peeled
  and diced
1 clove garlic, minced
  very fine
1 teaspoon salt
Non-nutritive sweetener
  equivalent to 1 teaspoon
  sugar
1/2 teaspoon pepper

116

Place the squares of eggplant (unpeeled) into frying pan in which 3 tablespoons of oil have been heated. Sauté over medium heat 2 minutes, turning often. Add 2 tablespoons water. Cover and cook, adding water, 2 tablespoons at a time as it is absorbed. Turn eggplant until tender (about 10 minutes). Remove eggplant from pan into a bowl; add balance of oil to pan and sauté peppers about 10 minutes; heat mushrooms until soft. Add these to eggplant. Place tomato, garlic, salt, sweetener, and pepper in a pan. Simmer until it makes a thick sauce and pour over eggplant. Mix lightly.

## *EGGPLANT DELIGHT

Exchanges per serving: 1 cup = 1/2 fat, 1 "A" and
                                  1 "B" vegetable.

Calories per serving: 60                       Yield: 6 cups

| | |
|---|---|
| 1 onion, sliced thin | 3 cups eggplant, peeled, |
| 1/4 green pepper, chopped |    sliced, and cubed |
|    fine | 2 cups tomatoes |
| 2 tablespoons diet | 1/2 teaspoon salt |
|    margarine | 1/8 teaspoon pepper |

Sauté onion and pepper in margarine until soft, in medium skillet, tightly covered. Add eggplant cubes, tomatoes, salt and pepper, and cover. Boil until eggplant is tender (about 10 minutes).

## *DORIS' CREAMED MUSHROOMS

Exchanges per serving: 1/2 cup = 1 fat, 1 "B" vegetable.
Calories per serving: 80                     Yield: 6 cups

| | |
|---|---|
| 1 envelope dry cream of | 3 tablespoons diet |
|    mushroom soup mix |    margarine |
| 2 cups water | 1 tablespoon lemon juice |
| 4 cups fresh mushrooms | 1/16 teaspoon salt |
| | 1/16 teaspoon pepper |

Add soup mix to water, gently boil, stirring now and then, for about 10 minutes. In a large skillet sauté mushrooms in margarine until browned on all sides. Pour soup and lemon juice over mushrooms. Season.

## *CREAMED SPINACH

Exchanges per serving: 2/3 cup = 1/2 fat,
1 "A" vegetable.

Calories per serving: 40                    Yield: 2 cups

1 clove garlic, minced fine     1/2 teaspoon salt
1 tablespoon diet              1/8 teaspoon pepper
  margarine                    1/2 tablespoon arrowroot
1 1/4 cups frozen spinach,       powder
  chopped                      1/2 cup milk

Sauté garlic in margarine until brown, then discard garlic.
Add spinach, which has been thawed thoroughly, salt, and
pepper. Cover tightly and separate with fork occasionally.
Cook over low heat until spinach is tender and all liquid
evaporated (about 4-5 minutes). Form a smooth, thin
paste of arrowroot powder and milk and add to cooked
spinach. Heat, stirring constantly until thick and smooth.

## *GOURMET SPINACH

Exchanges per serving: 1 serving = 1 fat, 1 "B" vegetable.

Calories per serving: 80                    Yield: 6 servings

1 cup mushrooms, sliced       1 1/4 cups frozen spinach,
  thin                          chopped
1 onion, chopped fine         1/3 cup imitation sour
1 clove garlic, minced          cream
1 tablespoon diet             1 1/16 teaspoons salt
  margarine                   1/8 teaspoon pepper

Sauté mushrooms, onion, and garlic in margarine until
onion is golden. Place spinach on top of mushroom mixture and cover. Stir now and then. Cook until spinach is
heated through (8-9 minutes); then stir in sour cream,
salt, and pepper.

## *GREEN BEAN SPECIAL

Exchanges per serving: 1 serving = 1/2 fat,
1 "A" vegetable.

Calories per serving: 50                    Yield: 6 servings

1 teaspoon bacon chips          1 tomato, chopped
1 clove garlic, minced fine      2 1/2 cups green beans
1/4 cup onion, chopped          1 1/4 teaspoons salt
  fine                          1/8 teaspoon pepper
2 tablespoons green pepper,     1/2 teaspoon oregano
  chopped fine                  1/3 cup water

In skillet sauté bacon until lightly brown. Add garlic, onion, and pepper and sauté until onions are golden. Stir in tomato, green beans, salt, pepper, oregano, and water. Cover. Cook gently until beans are tender (about 15 minutes).

## *GREEN BEANS DE LUXE

Exchanges per serving: 1 serving = 1 fat, 1 "A" vegetable.
Calories per serving: 45                    Yield: 6 servings

4 cups green beans              2 tablespoons diet
1/4 cup mint flakes, dried        margarine
Non-nutritive sweetener         1/16 teaspoon salt
  equivalent to 1 table-        1/16 teaspoon pepper
  spoon sugar

Heat beans and mint flakes with sweetener to boiling point. Drain. Stir in rest of ingredients.

## *ASPARAGUS WITH HERBS

Exchanges per serving: 1 serving = 1 fat, 1 "A" vegetable.
Calories per serving: 45                    Yield: 3 servings

1 1/4 cups asparagus            2 tablespoons chives,
1 tablespoon diet                 chopped
  margarine                     1/16 teaspoon seasoned
1/2 teaspoon salt                 salt
1/4 cup water                   1/16 teaspoon pepper

Separate asparagus. Place margarine, salt, water, and chives in skillet and cover tightly. Bring to boil. Add asparagus and cover. Gently boil until asparagus is tender. Sprinkle with seasoned salt and pepper.

## *PEAS AND LETTUCE

Exchanges per serving: 1 serving = 1 fat, 1 "A" and
1 "B" vegetable.

Calories per serving: 75            Yield: 4 servings

1 1/4 cups frozen peas
1 cup lettuce, chopped
  coarsely

4 tablespoons diet marga-
  rine (or omit margarine
  and delete fat exchange)

Cook peas in boiling salted water until tender (5-6 minutes). Add lettuce and simmer until wilted and transparent.
Drain. Toss with margarine or butter.

## *BEETS WILLIAM-STYLE

Exchanges per serving: 1 serving = 1 "B" vegetable.
Calories per serving: 35            Yield: 4 servings

Non-nutritive sweetener
  equivalent to 2 table-
  spoons sugar
1/2 teaspoon salt
1/2 teaspoon pepper

3/4 teaspoon arrowroot
  powder
2 cups sliced beets
2 tablespoons lemon juice

Mix sweetener, salt, pepper, and arrowroot powder. Drain
liquid from beets, saving 1/3 cup. Stir the 1/3 cup liquid
with lemon juice and drained beets into sweetened mixture.
Boil until sauce thickens and beets are heated. Stir constantly.

## *TOMATOES WITH CHEESE TOPPING

Exchanges per serving: 1 serving = 1/4 meat,
1 "A" vegetable.

Calories per serving: 20            Yield: 4 servings

2 tomatoes, peeled and
  halved
1/2 teaspoon thyme
2 tablespoons American
  cheese, grated fine

2 tablespoons seasoned
  dried bread crumbs
1/2 teaspoon salt
1/8 teaspoon pepper

Preheat oven to 375°. Place tomatoes, cut side up, in
baking pan and top each half with a mixture of thyme,

cheese, bread crumbs, salt, and pepper. Bake until toma-
oes are tender and cheese melts (about 20 minutes). Put
aking pan under broiler for the last minute or so to brown
tops.

## *CELERY AND CARROTS (WITH HORSERADISH)

Exchanges per serving: 1 serving = 1/2 fat, 1 "A" and
                                  1 "B" vegetable.
Calories per serving: 55                Yield: 6 servings

| | |
|---|---|
| 2 cups carrots, cut into 1/2″ slices | 1 1/2 teaspoons prepared horseradish |
| 2/3 cup celery, cut into 1/2″ pieces | 1/2 teaspoon salt |
| 1 cup water | 2 tablespoons diet margarine |

Scrape carrots before slicing; remove any strings from
celery and slice. After slicing, place carrots and celery in
tightly covered saucepan and boil in water with horse-
radish and salt until tender (about 20 minutes). Drain and
add margarine.

## *SWEET CARROTS

Exchanges per serving: 2/3 cup = 1 fat, 1 "B" vegetable.
Calories per serving: 80                   Yield: 2 cups

| | |
|---|---|
| 1 tablespoon diet margarine | 2 tablespoons parsley, snipped fine |
| 2 tablespoons water | 2 cups carrots, scraped and sliced thin |
| 1/2 teaspoon salt | |
| 1/8 teaspoon pepper | |
| Non-nutritive sweetener equivalent to 1/2 tea-spoon sugar | |

Melt margarine; add rest of ingredients. Cover. Simmer
gently about 10 minutes. Stir occasionally.

## *GINGERED CARROTS

Exchanges per serving: 1 serving = 1/2 fat,
                                  1 "B" vegetable.

121

Calories per serving: 55
Yield: 2 1/2 cups

2 cups carrots, julienne
1/2 cup water
1/2 teaspoon Mei Yen Seasoning
1/2 teaspoon ginger

Non-nutritive sweetener equivalent to 1/2 teaspoon sugar
2 tablespoons diet margarine

Cook carrots in water seasoned with Mei Yen powder; add ginger, sweetener, and when tender, margarine. Continue to cook 3-4 minutes. Stir gently.

## *CARROTS WITH ORANGE

Exchanges per serving: 1/2 cup = 1/2 fat, 1 fruit, 1 "B" vegetable.

Calories per serving: 98
Yield: 6 servings

Water to cover carrots
3 teaspoons salt
3 cups carrots, scraped and sliced thin

Non-nutritive sweetener equivalent to 1 tablespoon sugar
2 tablespoons diet margarine
4 oranges, cut into sections

Place 2 teaspoons salt in water; gently boil carrots until tender; add remaining salt, sweetener, margarine, and oranges. Heat slowly and gently.

## **DELIGHTFUL CARROTS

Exchanges per serving: 1 serving = 1 1/2 fat, 1 "B" vegetable.

Calories per serving: 103
Yield: 4 servings

6 carrots, peeled and cut into 3" strips
4 tablespoons diet margarine

1 tablespoon lemon juice
1/8 teaspoon celery seed
1/2 teaspoon salt
2 tablespoons water

Preheat oven to 350°. Arrange carrots in small baking dish; melt margarine, then combine with remaining ingredients. Pour over carrots. Cover and bake about 3/4 hour (or until carrots are tender).

122

## **CARROTS WITH CHEESE**

Exchanges per serving: 1 cup = 1 meat, 1 "B" vegetable.
Calories per serving: 105          Yield: 2 cups

2 cups carrots, sliced          1/8 teaspoon pepper
1/2 cup cheese, grated          1/16 cup parsley flakes
1/8 teaspoon salt

Boil carrots gently about 5 minutes; turn off heat and drain thoroughly. Return to saucepan. Sprinkle with cheese, letting carrots stay on burner until cheese melts. Sprinkle with salt and pepper and top with parsley.

## **PINEAPPLE SWEET POTATOES**

Exchanges per serving: 1 serving = 1 bread, 1/2 fat,
                                             1 fruit.
Calories per serving: 135          Yield: 8 servings

8 sweet potatoes          2 cups artificially sweet-
1 1/2 teaspoons salt          ened pineapple tidbits
1/8 teaspoon pepper          2 tablespoons diet
                                             margarine

Boil potatoes until tender; cool slightly. Mash until smooth; stir in rest of ingredients, including syrup from pineapple tidbits. Return to stove and reheat.

## **BAKED POTATOES, STUFFED**

Exchanges per serving: 1 potato = 1 bread, 2 fat.
Calories per serving: 150          Yield: 8 servings

8 potatoes          1 1/2 teaspoons salt
1 tablespoon oil          1/8 teaspoon pepper
1 1/2 cups imitation sour          2 tablespoons chives,
   cream          snipped

Preheat oven to 450°. Prick skins of potatoes with fork, lightly oil your hands and rub the oil onto the potatoes. Place potatoes in oven and bake until done (about 35-40 minutes). Reduce heat to 325°. Remove potatoes from oven and cut a thin slice from each and hollow out, being sure to leave shell intact. Mash centers in electric mixer with sour cream, salt, pepper, and chives; refill shells, heaping high. Bake on aluminum foil until heated through and potato top is lightly browned (about 1/2 hour).

## **ANNE'S STUFFED BAKED POTATOES WITH CHEESE

Exchanges per serving: 1 potato = 1 bread, 1 fat, 1 meat.
Calories per serving: 186                     Yield: 8 servings

| | |
|---|---|
| 8 potatoes | 1/16 teaspoon salt |
| 5 tablespoons diet | 1/16 teaspoon pepper |
| margarine | 1 cup cheese, finely grated |
| 1/2 cup skim milk | |

Preheat oven to 400°. Bake potatoes in oven until done (approximately 1 hour); while hot, cut tops off and scoop insides into mixing bowl, keeping the 8 shells. Add margarine and skim milk and beat until smooth. Add rest of ingredients and continue beating until mixed thoroughly. Refill potato shells, place on baking dish for 20 minutes, then under broiler until delicately browned.

## **MARGE'S STUFFED POTATOES

Exchanges per serving: 1 potato = 1 bread, 1 fat.
Calories per serving: 115                     Yield: 6 servings

| | |
|---|---|
| 6 potatoes | 3 1/2 tablespoons Parmesan cheese, grated |
| 1 teaspoon salt | |
| 1 tablespoon chives, chopped fine | 1/2 teaspoon pepper |
| 2 tablespoons bacon bits | 1 tablespoon imitation sour cream |
| 1/2 cup diet margarine | 1/16 teaspoon paprika |

Preheat oven to 400°. Grease, then bake potatoes until soft. Cut in half lengthwise. Spoon out centers while hot, saving skins, and put centers in mixing bowl. Add rest of ingredients except paprika to bowl and mix about 3 minutes at medium speed with electric mixer. Place mixture in potato skins. Sprinkle lightly with paprika and brown in oven about 4 minutes.

## **POLLY'S CREAMED POTATOES**

Exchanges per serving: 1 serving = 1 bread, 1 fat,
1/2 milk, 1 "A" vegetable.
Calories per serving: 200          Yield: 8 servings

8 potatoes, pared and
  cubed
1 onion, sliced thin
1 cup celery, sliced thin
3/4 tablespoon chervil
2 teaspoons salt
1/8 teaspoon pepper

2 1/2 cups milk
2 tablespoons diet
  margarine
1/8 cup water
1/2 tablespoon arrowroot
  powder
2 tablespoons dried parsley

Mix everything except the water, arrowroot and parsley in
saucepan and cook until potatoes are tender (20-25 minutes). Mix arrowroot and water to make a thin paste and
stir into first mixture. Cover and cook until thick and
smooth, stirring occasionally. Garnish wih parsley.

## **SUPER RICE**

Exchanges per serving: 1 serving = 1 bread, 1 fat.
Calories per serving: 115          Yield: 8 servings

1 cup uncooked white rice
1/4 teaspoon lemon juice
1 cup + 2 tablespoons
  frozen peas

Non-nutritive sweetener
  equivalent to 1 table-
  spoon sugar
1 onion, diced fine
2 tablespoons salad oil
1/2 teaspoon parsley flakes

Cook rice according to the directions on the package, but
substitute lemon juice for butter. Cook peas, add sweetener. In a skillet sauté onion in oil until wilted and golden.
Add the peas and onion to rice. Garnish with parsley.

# BREADS

## *STUFFING
(For chicken, meat, or turkey)

Exchanges per serving: 1 cup = 1/2 bread, 1/2 fat.
Calories per serving: 57          Yield: 3 1/4 cups

1/2 cup celery, chopped
  fine
1/2 cup onion, chopped
  fine
1/2 cup mushrooms,
  chopped fine

1/4 cup diet margarine
1 cup herb-seasoned
  stuffing mix
1 cup boiling water

Sauté celery, onion, and mushrooms in margarine until onion is golden. Add stuffing mix to boiling water, then toss all together. Mix well.

## *BERRY MUFFINS

Exchanges per serving: 1 muffin = 1 bread.
Calories per serving: 68          Yield: 12 muffins

2 cups biscuit mix
Non-nutritive sweetener
  equivalent to 1/4 cup +
  2 tablespoons sugar
1 cup unflavored yogurt

1/4 cup (1 medium) egg
1 cup berries (blueberries,
  raspberries, etc.)
2 teaspoons lemon peel,
  grated

Preheat oven to 425°. Grease 12 muffin cups (2 1/2") and place in muffin pan. Combine mix and all but 2 tablespoons of sweetener in bowl; add yogurt. Add egg, beat with fork until well combined. Fold berries gently into batter with rubber spatula, then place about 1/4 cup batter into each cup. Combine lemon peel and remaining sweetener and mix well. Sprinkle over batter in each cup. Bake until golden brown (20-25 minutes). Serve hot.

# *EASY RAISIN BREAD

Exchanges per serving: 1 serving = 1 bread.
Calories per serving: 68        Yield: 15 servings

| | |
|---|---|
| 1/2 cup quick-cooking oatmeal | 1/4 cup (1 medium) egg, well beaten |
| 1 teaspoon baking powder | 1 1/4 cups skim milk |
| 2 cups biscuit mix | Non-nutritive sweetener equivalent to 4/5 cup sugar |
| 1/4 teaspoon salt | |
| 1/2 cup white raisins | |

Preheat oven to 350°. Combine dry ingredients, then mix rest of ingredients and add to dry ingredients. Blend well. Pour into 1 quart-round casserole, which has been well greased. Bake until done (about 1 hour). Cool ten minutes before turning out on rack.

# *PANCAKES

Exchanges per serving: 1 pancake = 1 bread.
Calories per serving: 70        Yield: 10 4-inch pancakes

| | |
|---|---|
| 1 1/4 cups flour | 3/4 teaspoon salt |
| 2 1/2 teaspoons baking powder | 1/4 cup (1 medium) egg |
| Non-nutritive sweetener equivalent to 2 tablespoons sugar | 1 1/4 cups skim milk |
| | 2 tablespoons diet margarine, melted |

Mix and sift flour, baking powder, sweetener, and salt in medium bowl. In another bowl beat egg, stir in skim milk and margarine; stir into flour mixture until dry ingredients are wet. Heat pan until water dropped on it "jumps" up and down. For each pancake put about 3 tablespoons of mixture on pan and cook over low heat until bubbles appear on top and underside is nicely browned. Turn with a spatula and brown other side.

# *SHORTBREAD

Exchanges per serving: 1" x 3" piece = 1/4 bread, 1 fat, 1/3 fruit.
Calories per serving: 73        Yield: 36 servings

1/2 cup diet margarine
Non-nutritive sweetener
    equivalent to 1 1/2 cups
    brown sugar
1 cup plus 2 tablespoons
    flour, sifted
1/2 cup (2 medium) eggs
1 teaspoon vanilla extract

1 teaspoon orange peel,
    grated
1/2 teaspoon salt
1 teaspoon baking powder
1 1/2 cups white raisins,
    chopped
1 cup nuts, chopped fine

Preheat oven to 375°. Mix margarine, 1/2 of the sweetener, and 1 cup of flour together to fine crumbs, then press firmly in the bottom of a 2″ x 9″ x 13″ pan. Bake 10 minutes. Meanwhile beat eggs until fluffy, beat in remaining sweetener, vanilla, and orange peel. Add remaining flour, salt, and baking powder. Mix well. Stir in raisins and nuts, then place over crust which has been slightly cooled. Place entire mixture in oven and bake another 30 minutes. Cool slightly, then cut.

## *JOAN'S BISCUITS

Exchanges per serving: 1 biscuit = 1 bread, 1/2 fat.
Calories per serving: 90                    Yield: 16 biscuits

2 cups flour
1 teaspoon salt
3 teaspoons baking powder

1/4 cup diet margarine
3/4 cup skim milk

Preheat oven to 450°. Sift flour, salt, and baking powder. Cut in margarine until well mixed with first ingredients, then add milk. Knead several times; roll out on lightly floured board until about 1/2″ thick. Cut with biscuit cutter or inverted glass, or drop by spoonsful. Place on heavy-duty aluminum foil or cookie sheet which has been well greased. Bake until browned (13-14 minutes).

## *BLINTZES WITH CHEESE FILLING

Exchanges per serving: 1 serving = 1/2 bread, 1/2 fat,
                                            1/2 meat.
Calories per serving: 95                    Yield: 12 servings

| | |
|---|---|
| 1 cup flour | 1 cup nonfat creamed |
| 1/2 teaspoon baking | cottage cheese, sieved |
| powder | Non-nutritive sweetener |
| 1/2 teaspoon salt | equivalent to 2 table- |
| 1 cup (4 medium) eggs | spoons sugar |
| 1 cup skim milk | 1/4 teaspoon cinnamon |
| 2 tablespoons diet | |
| margarine | |

Sift flour, baking powder, and salt together. Beat 1/2 cup eggs, skim milk, and half the margarine and slowly add to flour mixture. Stir to form smooth batter, which will be thin. Grease a pan with remaining margarine, lightly, then pour 1/8 cup batter into a 6" skillet. (Tilt pan so batter completely covers bottom.) Cook until top of pancake is dry and bubbly, then turn onto brown paper (or paper towel). Make another 11 pancakes. Grease skillet when necessary. Mix sieved cottage cheese, sweetener, cinnamon, and remaining 1/2 cup of eggs. Turn brown side of each pancake up and place 1 tablespoon of filling in center. Fold over sides, then ends, to seal; set to one side. Refrigerate until ready to serve. About 10 minutes before serving, melt some margarine in large skillet and, with flap side down, lightly brown each blintze; turn and brown other side. Serve warm.

## **MARY C'S MUFFINS

Exchanges per serving: 1 muffin = 1 bread, 1 fat.
Calories per serving: 115          Yield: 24 servings

| | |
|---|---|
| 1/2 cup diet margarine | 4 cups flour |
| Non-nutritive sweetener | 6 teaspoons baking powder |
| equivalent to 2/3 cup | 2 teaspoons salt |
| sugar | 1 1/2 cups milk |
| 3/4 cup (3 medium) eggs | |

Preheat oven to 400°. Cream margarine and sweetener well. Beat eggs and add. Sift flour, baking powder and salt together and add alternately with milk to creamed mixture. Fill well-greased muffin pans 2/3 full. Bake 45 minutes. Serve hot.

## **"SEEDED" STUFFING**
### (For chicken, meat, turkey)

Exchanges per serving: 1/2 cup = 1 bread, 1 fat.
Calories per serving: 115                    Yield: 6 cups

1 onion, chopped fine
2 stalks celery, chopped
   fine
1/4 pound mushrooms,
   chopped fine
2 tablespoons diet
   margarine

1 8-ounce package stuffing
   mix
1/4 teaspoon each, celery,
   sesame, and poppy seeds
1 cup boiling water

Sauté onion, celery, and mushrooms in margarine until
onion is golden. Add stuffing mix and seeds to boiling
water, then mix all ingredients together.

## **WAFFLES**

Exchanges per serving: 1 waffle = 1 bread, 1 fat.
Calories per serving: 115           Yield: 10 4-inch waffles

1 1/2 cups flour
2 teaspoons baking powder
1/2 teaspoon salt
1/2 cup (2 medium) eggs
1 1/4 cups skim milk

Non-nutritive sweetener
   equivalent to 1/4 cup
   sugar
3 tablespoons diet marga-
   rine, melted

Heat waffle iron. Sift dry ingredients into bowl. In another
bowl beat eggs, skim milk, sweetener, and margarine. Stir
mixtures together until flour is wet and batter nearly
smooth. Allow 4 tablespoons of batter for each 4" waffle.

## **"SEEDED" BREAD**

Exchanges per serving: 1 slice = 1 bread, 1 fat.
Calories per serving: 102                    Yield: 1 slice

1 slice bread
1 teaspoon diet margarine
1/4 teaspoon celery seeds

1/2 teaspoon poppy seeds
1/4 teaspoon sesame seeds
1/16 teaspoon garlic salt

Spread bread with margarine. Sprinkle with combination of
seeds, then garlic salt. Put under broiler until edges of
bread are brown and margarine melted. Serve hot or cold.

## **BARB'S POPOVERS**

Exchanges per serving: 1 popover = 1 bread, 1/2 fat.
Calories per serving: 104                Yield: 16 popovers

1 cup (4 medium) eggs
2 cups skim milk
2 cups flour, sifted

1/2 teaspoon salt
2 tablespoons diet marga-
rine, melted

Heat oven to 425°. Beat eggs, add milk while beating. Slowly add flour and salt. Continue to beat to prevent lumps, then add melted margarine. Pour batter into cups which have been well greased. Bake 3/4 hour.

## **SOUR CREAM MUFFINS**

Exchanges per serving: 1 muffin = 1 bread, 3 fat.
Calories per serving: 195                Yield: 8 muffins

1/4 cup diet margarine
3/4 cup imitation sour
cream
1 1/3 cups sifted all-
purpose flour
Non-nutritive sweetener
equivalent to 1/2 cup
sugar

1/2 teaspoon baking soda
1/4 teaspoon salt
1/16 teaspoon nutmeg
1/4 cup (1 medium) egg,
beaten

Preheat oven to 450°. Cream margarine; add sour cream. Mix well. Sift dry ingredients. Add alternately with egg to first mixture. Spoon into greased muffin tins and bake for 15 minutes.

## **CORNMEAL BERRY MUFFINS**

Exchanges per serving: 1 muffin = 1 bread, 1 fat.
Calories per serving: 113                Yield: 15 muffins

1/3 cup diet margarine,
melted
Non-nutritive sweetener
equivalent to 1/3 cup
sugar
1/4 cup water
1/2 cup (2 medium) eggs
1 1/4 cups cornmeal

3/4 cup flour
2 1/2 teaspoons baking
powder
1/4 teaspoon salt
3/4 cup milk
2/3 cup berries (blue-
berries, blackberries,
etc.)

Preheat oven to 400°. Beat together the margarine, sweetener, water, and eggs, then stir in cornmeal. Sift flour, baking powder, and salt. Stir 1/4 of this into first mixture with 1/4 of the milk. Repeat until used. Wash and drain berries and fold gently into batter. Place about 4 tablespoons in each muffin cup which has been well greased. Bake until brown and separated from edge of cups (about 20 minutes).

## **DATE BREAD

Exchanges per serving: 1 slice = 1 bread, 1/2 fat,
1/2 fruit.

Calories per serving: 113          Yield: 24 servings

- 3 cups flour, sifted
- 1 1/2 teaspoons salt
- 1/2 teaspoon ground cloves
- 1/2 teaspoon nutmeg
- 4 1/2 teaspoons baking powder
- 1 teaspoon mace
- 1/2 teaspoon allspice
- 2 dozen dates, chopped well
- 1 cup skim milk
- Non-nutritive sweetener equivalent to 1 1/2 cups sugar
- 1/2 cup (2 medium) eggs, well beaten
- 1/4 cup diet margarine, melted

Preheat oven to 350°. Sift first seven ingredients. Add dates; mix skim milk, sweetener, eggs, and margarine and add to first mixture. Place in 3" x 5" x 9" loaf pan which has been well greased. Bake 1 hour and 15 minutes.

## **CORNBREAD

Exchanges per serving: 1 square = 1 bread, 1 fat.
Calories per serving: 113          Yield: 9 servings

- 1 1/4 cups flour
- 3/4 cup yellow cornmeal
- Non-nutritive sweetener equivalent to 2 tablespoons sugar
- 4 1/2 teaspoons baking powder
- 1 teaspoon salt
- 1/4 cup (one medium) egg
- 2/3 cup milk
- 1/3 cup diet margarine, melted

132

Preheat oven to 425°. Sift everything except eggs, milk, and margarine into small bowl. Beat eggs well, stir in milk and margarine. Pour into flour mixture all at once; stir until flour is just moistened (mixture will be lumpy). Put into pan which has been well greased. Spread evenly and bake until bread comes away from edges of pan (about 1/2 hour). Cut into equal squares.

## **RAISIN BREAD

Exchanges per serving: 1 1/2" slice = 1 bread, 1 fat,
1/2 fruit, 1/2 meat.

Calories per serving: 168          Yield: 16 servings

3 cups flour
3 1/2 teaspoons baking
  powder
Non-nutritive sweetener
  equivalent to 3/4 cup
  sugar
1 1/2 teaspoons salt
1/3 cup diet margarine

2 teaspoons orange peel,
  grated
1/2 cup (2 medium) eggs
1 cup skim milk
1 cup white raisins,
  chopped
1/2 cup nuts, chopped fine

Preheat oven to 350°. Sift dry ingredients; add margarine, orange peel, egg, and skim milk. Mix until blended, then stir in raisins and nuts. Place in 3" x 5" x 9" loaf pan which has been well greased. Bake 1 hour and 15 minutes or until loaf tests done. Remove from pan. Cool and store 12 hours before slicing.

## **BARBARA'S BANANA BREAD

Exchanges per serving: 1 serving = 1 bread, 1 fat,
1/3 fruit.

Calories per serving: 130          Yield: 12 servings

1/4 teaspoon baking soda
1/2 teaspoon salt
1 3/4 cups flour
2 teaspoons baking powder
1/4 cup diet margarine,
  melted

1/4 cup (1 medium) egg,
  well-beaten
Non-nutritive sweetener
  equivalent to 1 cup sugar
1 teaspoon almond extract
2 bananas, mashed well

Preheat oven to 350°. Sift dry ingredients together. Combine margarine, eggs, sweetener, and almond extract; add to first mixture, stirring until flour is moistened. Fold in mashed bananas. Turn into loaf pan which has been well greased. Bake until done (about 1 hour).

## **BANANA BREAD

Exchanges per serving: 1 slice = 1 bread, 1 fat, 1/4 fruit.
Calories per serving: 135                    Yield: 30 servings

3 1/4 cups flour
4 teaspoons baking powder
1 teaspoon salt
1/2 teaspoon baking soda
1/2 cup diet margarine,
    melted

1 cup (4 medium) eggs,
    well beaten
Non-nutritive sweetener
    equivalent to 4 cups
    sugar
2 teaspoons vanilla extract
4 bananas, mashed well

Preheat oven to 350°. Sift flour, baking powder, salt, and baking soda. Mix margarine, eggs, sweetener, and vanilla. Add to flour mixture and stir until flour is moistened, then fold in mashed bananas. Place in 3″ x 4″ x 8″ loaf pan which has been well greased. Bake 1 hour and 10 minutes.

## **LEMON MUFFINS

Exchanges per serving: 1 muffin = 1 bread, 1 fat.
Calories per serving: 120                    Yield: 12 muffins

2 cups all-purpose flour,
    sifted
1/2 cup sugar
3 teaspoons baking powder
1/2 teaspoon salt
2/3 cup skim milk

1/3 cup lemon juice
1 teaspoon lemon rind,
    grated
1/3 cup salad oil
1/4 cup (1 medium) egg,
    slightly beaten

Preheat oven to 400°. Grease muffin tins. Sift flour, sugar, baking powder, and salt into a large bowl. Combine milk, lemon juice, lemon rind, oil, and egg and beat with a fork to mix well. Pour wet into dry ingredients; stir quickly with fork (do not beat—batter will be lumpy). Fill each muffin cup slightly more than half full. Bake 20-25 minutes or until golden (or until cake tester comes out clean). Remove from oven, loosen edge of muffins with spatula, and turn out.

## **AUNT JEANNE'S COFFEE CAKE

Exchanges per serving: 1 serving = 1 1/2 bread, 1 fat.
Calories per serving: 155 Yield: 8 servings

2 cups flour
3 teaspoons baking powder
1/4 teaspoon salt
1/3 cup diet marga-
rine, softened
3/4 cup skim milk
3 drops yellow food
coloring

Non-nutritive sweetener
equivalent to 1/2 cup
plus 4 teaspoons sugar
1/4 cup (1 medium) egg
1/2 teaspoon cinnamon
1/4 cup bread crumbs,
toasted

Preheat oven to 375°. Sift flour, baking powder, and salt into small bowl; with electric beater, cut in 3 tablespoons of margarine on lowest speed, then turn to medium speed for about 5 minutes until well blended and resembling small peas. Add 1/2 cup of skim milk mixed with coloring and all but 4 teaspoons of sweetener. Continue beating on medium speed for about one minute. Batter will be stiff. Add rest of skim milk and beat for a minute, then add unbeaten egg and beat one more minute. Pour into a greased 8" round cake pan. Mix remaining tablespoon of margarine, cinnamon, and toasted bread crumbs and sprinkle on top of dough. Bake until cake springs back when lightly touched (about 20 minutes).

## **MARVELOUS MARMALADE STUFFING

Exchanges per serving: 1/2 cup = 1 bread, 2 fat.
Calories per serving: 160 Yield: 3 cups

1 cup cornbread stuffing
1/2 cup diet margarine,
melted
1/2 cup celery, chopped
fine

1/4 cup onions, chopped
fine
1/4 cup almonds, slivered
and chopped
1/2 cup dietetic marmalade

135

Mix all ingredients. Toss lightly but thoroughly. Use to lightly stuff a 4-5 pound chicken.

## **PAULA'S POPOVERS

Exchanges per serving: 1 popover = 1 bread, 1 fat.
Calories per serving: 125          Yield: 8 popovers

2 cups flour
1 teaspoon salt
1 cup (4 medium) eggs

2 cups milk
6 tablespoons diet
margarine

Preheat oven to 350°. Sift flour and salt. Beat eggs slightly, add milk and margarine and beat until blended. Gradually add dry ingredients. Grease ramekin cups well and fill about 3/4 full. Bake 1 hour and 10 minutes, then remove from oven. Slit each side quickly to release steam. Return to oven until brown and crisp and tops are firm. Lift out of ramekins; serve hot.

## **DATE AND NUT BREAD

Exchanges per serving: 1/4" slice = 1 bread, 1 fat,
                        1/2 fruit.
Calories per serving: 133          Yield: 2 loaves

4 cups dates, pitted
2 cups nuts, coarsely
  chopped
2 cups boiling water
2 3/4 cups flour
1 1/2 teaspoons baking
  soda
1 teaspoon salt

1/2 cup diet margarine,
  softened
Non-nutritive sweetener
  equivalent to 1 1/4 cups
  brown sugar, firmly
  packed
1/2 cup (2 medium) eggs
1 teaspoon vanilla extract

Preheat oven to 350°. Cut dates into small pieces with scissors. Add nuts and boiling water. Allow to cool to room temperature (about 3/4 hour). Sift flour with the baking soda and salt. On high speed of mixer beat margarine with sweetener, eggs, and vanilla until smooth; then add date mixture and mix well. Add flour mixture. Beat with wooden spoon until well combined. Place in 2 well-greased loaf pans. Bake 70 minutes, or until tester inserted in center of bread comes out clean. Cool 10 minutes in pan, then on wire rack until room temperature.

## **BUTTERMILK BISCUITS WITH SEEDS

Exchanges per serving: 1 biscuit = 1 fat, 1 bread.
Calories per serving: 115          Yield: 24 servings

| | |
|---|---|
| 4 cups flour | 2 tablespoons seeds |
| 4 teaspoons baking powder | (sesame, caraway, etc.) |
| 1/2 teaspoon baking soda | 1 1/2 cups skim buttermilk |
| 2 teaspoons salt | 2/3 cup safflower oil |

Preheat oven to 350°. Sift the flour, baking powder, baking soda, and salt into bowl, then add seeds. Add buttermilk to oil but do not stir together; pour all at once over dry ingredients. Mix with fork to make soft dough. Turn dough onto floured board and knead lightly until smooth; flatten slightly, then cover with sheet of waxed paper; roll until about 1/4" thick, then remove paper. Cut a 6" x 8" rectangle into 2" squares. Bake until brown.

## ***PRUNE BREAD

Exchanges per serving: 1 slice = 2 bread, 1 fat,
                       1 fruit, 1/2 meat.
Calories per serving: 236          Yield: 12 slices

| | |
|---|---|
| 2 cups dried prunes | 1 teaspoon salt |
| 1 1/2 cups boiling water | 2 teaspoons baking soda |
| 3 cups flour | 1/2 cup (2 medium) eggs |
| Non-nutritive sweetener | 4 tablespoons salad oil |
| equivalent to 1 1/2 cups | |
| sugar | |

Preheat oven to 325°. Put prunes to soak in cold water for two hours. Drain and then pit and chop prunes. Add boiling water and let stand 5 minutes. Sift flour, sweetener, salt, and baking soda. Add prune mixture. Beat and add eggs, then add salad oil. Pour into 2 greased loaf pans 2 1/2" x 4 1/2" x 8 1/2" and bake for 1 hour. Remove from pans and cool on wire rack.

# ***COFFEE CAKE, CHOCOLATE STYLE

Exchanges per serving: 1 half-inch slice = 3 bread,
1/4 fat, 1/4 meat.

Calories per serving: 245                    Yield: 12 servings

2/3 cup diet margarine
Non-nutritive sweetener
  equivalent to 1 cup sugar
3/4 cup (3 medium) eggs
1 teaspoon orange peel,
  grated
1 cup artificial sour cream
1 teaspoon vanilla extract
1/4 teaspoon salt
1/2 teaspoon baking soda
2 cups + 2 tablespoons
  flour

1 1/2 teaspoons baking
  powder
1 ounce unsweetened
  chocolate
Non-nutritive sweetener
  equivalent to 1/2 cup
  brown sugar
1 teaspoon cinnamon
1 tablespoon diet
  margarine

Preheat oven to 350°. Cream margarine and sweetener
until light and fluffy; add eggs one at a time. Beat until
smooth. Mix orange peel, sour cream, and vanilla. Stir salt,
baking soda, baking powder, and two cups of flour together, then blend with creamed mixture thoroughly. Place
in a well-greased, 10" tube pan. Melt chocolate in aluminum foil and swirl over batter with spoon to form ripples
through batter. Mix sugar substitute, cinnamon, and softened margarine with remaining 2 tablespoons of flour and
sprinkle over batter. Bake until straw inserted in center
comes out clean (50-60 minutes).

# FRUITS AND FRUIT DESSERTS

## *LUCY'S LUSCIOUS APRICOT SOUFFLE DESSERT

Exchanges per serving: 1 serving = 1/2 fruit.
Calories per serving: 20                        Yield: 8 servings

1 cup dried apricots
Non-nutritive sweetener
   equivalent to 1 1/4
   cups sugar
Water to cover

2 cups (12 medium) egg
   whites
1/16 teaspoon salt
1 cup nondairy whipping
   cream

Preheat oven to 300°. Combine apricots and sweetener equivalent to 3/4 cup sugar in a saucepan; add sufficient water to cover. Cook slowly until sweetener dissolves, stirring occasionally, then cover pan and cook over low heat until apricots are tender and plump. Drain. Retain syrup; puree apricots. Beat egg whites, which should be at room temperature, with salt until egg whites are stiff; add rest of sweetener. Fold in pureed apricots, mixing thoroughly. Turn into buttered tube pan. Bake 3/4 hour. The soufflé will rise and become golden brown. Top with nondairy whip to which 2 tablespoons of apricot syrup have been added after whipping.

## *BAKED FRESH PEACHES

Exchanges per serving: 1 peach = 1 fruit.
Calories per serving: 40                         Yield: 4 servings

4 peaches
1 teaspoon diet margarine

Non-nutritive sweetener
   equivalent to 1/2 cup
   sugar
1 tablespoon lemon juice

Preheat oven to 350°. Cut about an inch of skin from each end of peach and set in a baking dish that has been well greased with the margarine. Sprinkle with sweetener and lemon juice. Bake about 20 minutes; serve cold or hot, with milk or cream if desired.

## *BANANA FREEZE

Exchanges per serving: 1 cup = 1 fruit.
Calories per serving: 40                    Yield: 6 cups

3 bananas, crushed
1 cup unsweetened orange
  juice

Non-nutritive sweetener
  equivalent to 2 table-
  spoons sugar
1 teaspoon lemon juice
1/4 cup water

Combine all ingredients, mixing well. Using paper cups, divide mixture evenly into 6 and freeze until firm. Let stand at room temperature a few minutes (5-6) and then peel paper cup as it is being eaten.

## *FRUIT COCKTAIL CAKE DESSERT

Exchanges per serving: 1 = 1/2 bread, 1/2 fruit,
                        1/2 skim milk.
Calories per serving: 95                    Yield: 10 servings

Non-nutritive sweetener
  equivalent to 1/2 cup
  sugar
1 tablespoon unflavored
  gelatin
1/4 teaspoon salt
1/2 cup water
4 cups dietetic fruit
  cocktail

1 tablespoon lemon juice
4-5 drops almond extract
1/4 cup (2 small) egg
  whites
1 cup nonfat dry milk,
  whipped
8 ladyfingers, split (these
  can be made from
  dietetic sponge cake)

Combine sweetener, gelatin, and salt. Add 1/2 cup water and cook, stirring over medium heat until gelatin dissolves. Chill until partially set; drain fruit cocktail, add lemon juice and almond extract. Put gelatin mixture, egg whites, and half the fruit cocktail in a large mixing bowl. Start mixer on low speed, then turn to high and beat 10 minutes, until fluffy. Chill until partially set. Fold in remaining fruit cocktail and whipped milk. Line sides of spring pan with ladyfingers. Pour filling in carefully. Chill overnight. Remove sides of pan.

## *APPLESAUCE, UNCOOKED

Exchanges per serving: 1 cup = 2 fruit.
Calories per serving: 80                         Yield: 4 cups

2 cups apples, washed,
  cored, and cubed, but
  not peeled
2 cups cold water
3 tablespoons lemon juice
1/16 teaspoon cloves
1/16 teaspoon ginger

1/4 teaspoon nutmeg
Non-nutritive sweetener
  equivalent to 3 tea-
  spoons sugar
2 drops red vegetable food
  coloring (optional)

Place apples in bowl which contains mixture of water and lemon juice. Remove 1/2 cup of the juice from bowl and to it add sweetener and spices and half the apple cubes. Blend, then add the additional cubes gradually until all smoothly blended. Add coloring.

## *SPICED FRUIT

Exchanges per serving: 1 cup = 2 fruit.
Calories per serving: 80                         Yield: 5 cups

1 cup dietetic pineapple
  juice
1/4 teaspoon cinnamon

2 cups dietetic pear halves
2 cups dietetic peach halves

Heat pineapple juice and cinnamon to boil; chill fruit, from which syrup has been drained, and place in a bowl. Pour pineapple juice over fruit, then serve at once.

## *DIETETIC SPICED PEACHES

Exchanges per serving: 1 serving = 1 fruit.
Calories per serving: 40                         Yield: 2 servings

4 dietetic peach halves
16 whole cloves

1 cup liquid from peaches

Preheat oven to 375°. Place peaches in small pan, pitted side up. Stick 4 cloves in each half, then pour liquid over fruit. Bake 20 minutes. Serve hot.

## *SUMMER FRUIT MIX

Exchanges per serving: 3/4 cup = 1 1/2 fruit.
Calories per serving: 60                          Yield: 5 cups

2 cups strawberries
1 cup grapes
1 cup melon balls
1 cup blueberries

Non-nutritive sweetener
    equivalent to 1/4 cup
    sugar

Wash and clean fruit, then combine with sweetener. Chill. This goes well topped with Custard Sauce for Shortcakes.

## *BAKED APPLES

Exchanges per serving: 1 apple = 1 fruit.
Calories per serving: 40                          Yield: 2 servings

2 medium apples
2 teaspoons lemon juice
1/16 teaspoon nutmeg
1/16 teaspoon cinnamon

1/16 teaspoon allspice
2 tablespoons dietetic
    maple topping for each
    apple

Preheat oven to 350°. Core apples and peel about 1/2 of each apple; sprinkle lemon juice over cut surfaces. Dust apple with mixture of nutmeg, cinnamon, and allspice. Fill cavity with dietetic maple topping; bake covered about 25 minutes. Remove cover and continue baking until apples are tender.

## *TASTY APPLESAUCE

Exchanges per serving: 1 serving = 1/4 fruit, 1/2 meat.
Calories per serving: 45                          Yield: 4 servings

4 teaspoons cinnamon
1 teaspoon salt
1 teaspoon vanilla
Non-nutritive sweetener
    equivalent to 1/4 cup
    sugar

1/2 cup unsweetened
    applesauce
1/3 cup (2 medium) egg
    whites
1/16 teaspoon allspice

142

Stir first five ingredients together. Place in refrigerator until chilled. Before serving beat whites to form stiff peaks. Fold applesauce mix into whites and sprinkle with allspice.

## *FRUIT WHIP

Exchanges per serving: 1 serving = 1/2 skim milk.
Calories per serving: 40          Yield: 6 servings

| | |
|---|---|
| 1 1/2 tablespoons un-<br>flavored gelatin<br>3 cups skim milk | Non-nutritive sweetener<br>equivalent to 1/4 cup<br>sugar<br>2 teaspoons any fruit<br>extract |

Sprinkle gelatin over skim milk in saucepan and cook over low heat until gelatin dissolves. Add sweetener and fruit extract. Chill in refrigerator until mixture is consistency of egg white. Remove from refrigerator and beat at highest speed of mixer until mixture is doubled in volume (this will be very fluffy). Pace in a mold and refrigerate until set. May be garnished with slice of favorite fruit, if desired.

## *OLGA'S FRUIT FESTIVAL

(Not for diabetics without consent of doctor.)

Exchanges per serving: 1 serving = 1/2 fat, 2 fruit.
Calories per serving: 100 + liqueur     Yield: 8 servings

| | |
|---|---|
| 2 cups strawberries, culled<br>and washed<br>3 cups fresh peaches,<br>peeled and sliced<br>2 cups seedless green<br>grapes<br>Non-nutritive sweetener<br>equivalent to 2/3 cup<br>sugar | 1/4 cup orange curaçao<br>1/2 cup low-calorie top-<br>ping whip (or artificial<br>whipping cream)<br>1 ounce unsweetened<br>chocolate, well grated |

Sprinkle strawberries over peaches, then add grapes, sweetener, and curaçao. Refrigerate overnight. Prior to serving heat broiler; place fruit in heatproof dessert dishes and top with topping whip or artificial whipping cream. Sprinkle top with grated chocolate and place under broiler about 1/2 minute, or just until chocolate melts. Serve at once.

## **WINE SAUCE WITH FRUIT

(Not for diabetics without consent of doctor.)

Exchanges per serving: 1 serving = 1 fat, 2 1/2 fruit.
Calories per serving: 165 + alcohol     Yield: 4 servings

| | |
|---|---|
| 4 cups apples, peeled and sliced (or substitute bananas, peaches, pears, etc.) | 1 cup red wine |
| | 1/2 tablespoon arrowroot powder |
| | Non-nutritive sweetener equivalent to 1 cup sugar |
| 2 tablespoons diet margarine | 1/16 teaspoon allspice |

Brown apples in margarine. Add wine to arrowroot powder a little at a time to make a smooth paste. Add sweetener and cook over medium heat. Stir constantly until clear and thick, then add allspice. Pour over fruit slices and simmer a few minutes. Serve immediately.

## ***HAWAIIAN FRUIT FRITTERS

Exchanges per serving: 1 fritter = 1/4 bread, 4 fat, 1/2 fruit, 1/4 meat.
Calories per serving: 235                    Yield: 7 servings

| | |
|---|---|
| 1/2 cup (2 medium) eggs | 2 cups fresh pineapple (or papaya or banana) |
| 1/2 cup skim milk | |
| 1/2 teaspoon seasoned salt | 2 cups cornflakes, finely crushed |
| | 1 1/2 cups safflower oil |

Beat eggs, skim milk, and salt together; cut fruit into inch-long pieces and dip in egg mixture. Roll in cornflakes. Deep fry in oil until golden brown. Serve with Hot Soy Sauce Dip.

## ***LEMON PUDDING

Exchanges per serving: 1 cup = 3 fat, 2 meat.
Calories per serving: 281                    Yield: 4 servings

| Non-nutritive sweetener equivalent to 1 1/2 cups sugar | 2 tablespoons lemon peel |
| 1/2 cup diet margarine | 2 cups (8-9 medium) eggs |
| | 1 cup lemon juice |

Combine all ingredients in top of double boiler. Cook over boiling water until thick; stir occasionally. Cover and store in refrigerator until cool.

### ****POLLY'S PEAR DISH

Exchanges per serving: 1 serving = 1 bread, 1 fat,
1 1/2 fruit.

Calories per serving: 310                    Yield: 8 servings

| 1/2 cup water | 1 pie shell, unbaked |
| Non-nutritive sweetener equivalent to 1 cup sugar | 1 cup low-calorie apricot preserves |
| 1 tablespoon fresh lemon juice | 1/16 teaspoon nutmeg |
| 8 fresh pears, pared, cored, and sliced thin | 1/16 teaspoon allspice |

Preheat oven to 425°. Combine water, sweetener, and lemon juice in saucepan, then add pear slices a few at a time; cook gently until tender (about 5-6 minutes). Cool a little, then drain and save 1/4 cup liquid. Place pear slices in circle in unbaked pie shell which has been rolled out to fit a 12″ pan. Bake until golden brown, then cool. Combine apricot preserves and reserved liquid in a saucepan, heat until bubbly, then force through sieve. Spoon this over pear slices to glaze, and sprinkle with nutmeg and allspice. Chill and serve.

# PUDDINGS AND SPECIAL DESSERTS

## *MOCHA SURPRISE

Exchanges per serving: 1 cup = None.
Calories per serving: 0                          Yield: 3 cups

2 envelopes unflavored
  gelatin
1/2 cup cold water
3 cups very strong coffee
Non-nutritive sweetener
  equivalent to 1/3 cup
  sugar

1/2 teaspoon vanilla
1/16 teaspoon salt
3 tablespoons nonfat
  whipping cream

Soften the gelatin in the water in a medium-size pan. Heat.
Stir constantly until dissolved, then stir in coffee, sweetener, vanilla, and salt. Pour into a 2″ x 8″ x 8″ pan and
chill 2 hours. Put gelatin through potato ricer (or sieve)
and place in 3 dessert dishes. Decorate each with 1 tablespoon nonfat whipping cream.

## *CHOCOLATE BISQUE CAPRI

Exchanges per serving: 1 = 1/2 fat, trace milk.
Calories per serving: 23 + ice cream   Yield: 16 servings

1/2 cup toasted almonds,
  chopped
1/3 cup toasted coconut,
  chopped

1/2 teaspoon almond
  extract
1 quart low-calorie chocolate ice cream

146

Combine almonds and coconut, but reserve 2 tablespoons or topping. Fold nuts and almond extract quickly into ice ream, which should be rather soft. Place in small paper essert cups and sprinkle with topping. Keep in freezer until ready to serve.

## *PEAR PUDDING DORIS

Exchanges per serving: 1 serving = 1/4 milk, 1/4 fruit.
Calories per serving: 50        Yield: 6 servings

6 tablespoons nonfat dry milk
1 cup water, ice cold
1 envelope unflavored gelatin

1 5-ounce jar low-calorie chocolate topping
1/3 cup (2 medium) egg whites
1 jar unsweetened pear halves

Dissolve dry milk in 3/4 water; on rest of water sprinkle gelatin to soften. Mix the milk with the gelatin. Stir over low heat until gelatin dissolves, then add chocolate topping. Cool until mixture thickens enough to mound on a spoon. Beat egg whites stiff. Fold in. Drain pears well and line dessert dishes. Add chocolate mixture and chill until firm.

## *APRICOT OR PRUNE FRUIT SNOW

Exchanges per serving: 1 = 1/3 fat, 1 fruit.
Calories per serving: 63        Yield: 6 servings

1 envelope lemon-flavored low-calorie gelatin
1 cup boiling water
1 cup low-calorie juice (apple or apricot nectar)

1/8 cup (1 medium) egg white
6 pieces of unsweetened fruit (apricots or prunes)
3 teaspoons almonds, slivered

Dissolve gelatin in boiling water. Add juice, cool. Chill until syrupy. Add white of egg and beat until frothy. Fill dessert glass with snow, chill until firm; decorate each with apricot or prune; sprinkle 1/2 teaspoon slivered almonds over fruit.

## *FRUIT CAKE PUDDING

Exchanges per serving: 1 = 1/3 bread, 1/2 meat,
                1/4 skim milk.

Calories per serving: 85           Yield: 6 servings

3/4 cup (3 medium) eggs,
separated
1 tablespoon fresh citrus
fruit peel, grated
1/4 cup fresh citrus fruit
juice

1 1/2 cups skim milk
Non-nutritive sweetener
equivalent to 6 table-
spoons sugar
1/4 cup flour, sifted
1/16 teaspoon salt

Preheat oven to 325°. Beat whites until stiff peaks form,
then set aside. Add peel and juice of fruit to yolk, beating
at medium speed until well blended. Add skim milk. Beat
about 1 minute at low speed, then add rest of dry ingredients and beat again at low speed until smooth. Fold into
egg whites. Place in custard cups; place cups in baking pan
filled with about 1" water. Bake until lightly browned on
top (about 3/4 hour). Serve hot or cold.


## *FRUIT MOUNTAIN

Exchanges per serving: 1 = 1 fruit, 1/4 milk.
Calories per serving: 100        Yield: 6 servings

1 envelope low-calorie
vanilla pudding and
pie-filling mix
1 teaspoon almond extract

1 jar low-calorie cherry or
apple pie filling
Cinnamon

Prepare pudding according to directions on the package
but using nonfat milk. Add almond extract. Divide into
dessert glasses. Cool. Top with pie filling and garnish with
cinnamon.


## *FRUIT SOUFFLE

Exchanges per serving: 1 = 1 1/2 fruit.
Calories per serving: 60        Yield: 6 servings

| 1 envelope unflavored | 1 teaspoon lemon rind, |
|---|---|
| gelatin | grated fine |
| 1 cup cold water | 2 cups unsweetened fruit |
| | (apples, pears, pineapple) |

Sprinkle gelatin on 1/2 cup water; soften a few minutes. Stir over low heat about 3 minutes until gelatin is dissolved. Add rest of water, rind, and fruit. Chill until thick enough to mound on spoon. Beat until very light, then pour into a souffle dish and chill until firm.

## *LOW-CALORIE COFFEE CREAM MOUSSE

Exchanges per serving: 1 serving = 1/4 meat.
Calories per serving: 100          Yield: 12 servings

| 2 envelopes unflavored | 1 ounce semisweet choco- |
|---|---|
| gelatin | late chips |
| 2 cups cold coffee, double | 3 tablespoons rum or |
| strength | brandy flavoring |
| 3/4 cup (3 medium) eggs, | 2 cups nondairy whipping |
| separated | cream |
| Non-nutritive sweetener | |
| equivalent to 3/4 cup | |
| sugar | |

Sprinkle gelatin over 1 cup coffee in small bowl and let soften about 5 minutes. Using a rotary beater, beat egg yolks with sweetener equivalent to 1/2 cup sugar until light, using the top of a double boiler in which to beat them. Once light, beat in rest of coffee, chocolate chips, and softened gelatin. Stir constantly over simmering water until chocolate is melted and coats a metal spoon (about 10 minutes). Remove from heat. Stir in flavoring. Set top of double boiler in ice and cool, stirring often, until mixture becomes as thick as unbeaten egg white. Beat 1 cup of nondairy cream until stiff, place in refrigerator until needed. When gelatin is nearly thick, beat the egg whites until soft peaks form when beaters are raised; gradually beat in rest of sweetener, until whites are stiff and glossy. Fold gelatin mixture into whipped cream; fold in whites gently, until well blended. Place in large mold which has been rinsed well with cold water. Place in refrigerator until firm, 5-6 hours. Beat 1 cup cream stiff and place on top of mold. To unmold: run knife around edge of mold; invert over serving platter. Place hot, damp cloth over mold and shake gently to release. Lift off mold.

# CAKES

## *DELIGHTFUL CHEESECAKE

Exchanges per serving: 1 = 1/8 bread, 1/4 fruit,
1/2 meat.

Calories per serving: 55                    Yield: 9 servings

4 tablespoons graham-
cracker crumbs
2 envelopes unflavored
gelatin
1/2 cup water
1 cup low-calorie pine-
apple tidbits
Juice from pineapple
tidbits plus water to
make 3/4 cup
1 1/2 cups nonfat cottage
cheese

3/4 cup (3 medium) eggs,
separated
1/4 cup skim milk
2 tablespoons unsweetened
lemon juice
Non-nutritive sweetener
equivalent to 1/2 cup
sugar
1 teaspoon vanilla extract
1/4 teaspoon salt

Sprinkle 3 tablespoons of the graham-cracker crumbs on
bottom of 9″ pan. Set aside. Soften gelatin in 1/2 cup
water. Bring the 3/4 cup juice to boil and stir in gelatin.
Beat cottage cheese until nearly smooth, at highest speed
on mixer (about 3-4 minutes). Add egg yolks, skim milk,
lemon juice, sweetener, vanilla extract, and salt. Beat well.
Blend in gelatin at low speed. Chill. Stir occasionally until
mixture is thick, but not set (about 1 hour). Beat whites
at highest speed until soft peaks form, then fold in gelatin
mixture by hand. Spoon over crumbs in pan and sprinkle
remaining tablespoon of crumbs over filling. Add pineapple
tidbits on top and chill overnight in refrigerator.

151

# *ORANGE CUPCAKES

Exchanges per serving: 1 cupcake = 1/2 bread, 1/2 fat.
Calories per serving: 58          Yield: 30 cupcake

1/2 cup diet margarine
Non-nutritive sweetener
  equivalent to 1 cup sugar
1/2 cup (2 medium) eggs,
  beaten

2/3 cup orange juice,
  strained
1/4 teaspoon salt
2 cups flour
2 teaspoons baking powder

Preheat oven to 325°. Cream margarine and sweetener
Add other ingredients and beat one minute or longer i
mixer at high speed. Pour into baking cups and set i
muffin tins. Bake until brown. Cool and frost, if desired.

# *MARY'S SPONGE CAKE

Exchanges per serving: 1 1/2" slice = 1/2 bread,
                   1/2 meat.
Calories per serving: 75        Yield: 12 serving

1 cup flour
1/4 cup nonfat dry milk
1 teaspoon baking powder
1/4 teaspoon salt
3/4 cup (3 medium) eggs
Non-nutritive sweetener
  equivalent to 8 tea-
  spoons sugar

2 tablespoons fresh orange
  juice
1 teaspoon orange rind,
  grated
1/2 teaspoon cream of
  tartar

Preheat oven to 325°. Sift flour, dry milk, baking powder
and salt together three times; beat 2 whole eggs and 3
yolks at top speed of mixer until quite thick and lemon-
colored (this takes about 10 minutes). Reduce speed, add
sweetener gradually, and orange juice; increase speed and
beat until very light and fluffy (about 5-6 minutes). Add
rind and beat a little more. Beat remaining egg white
slightly, add cream of tartar and continue beating until
whites hold a stiff peak. Let stand while completing next
step. Very carefully fold sifted dry ingredients, a small
amount at a time, into egg-sweetener mixture, using rubber spatula or wire whip. Then fold in egg-white mixture
very carefully. Pour at once into 9" tube pan. (If pan has

emovable bottom, no need to do anything to pan as a knife will help loosen cake from bottom. Otherwise line ust the bottom of pan with piece of thin waxed paper; noisten well with water to make it flat.) Bake about 35 minutes. Cake is done when it springs back when touched with finger. Cool in pan upside down and remove carefully.

## *POLLY'S DIETETIC JELLY ROLL

Exchanges per serving: 1 = 1/2 bread, 1/2 meat.
Calories per serving: 75          Yield: 12 servings

3/4 cup (3 medium) eggs, separated
Non-nutritive sweetener equivalent to 1/3 cup sugar
2 teaspoons orange juice
4 teaspoons liquid from any dietetic fruit
1/2 teaspoon lemon extract

1 cup flour
1/3 cup nonfat dry milk solids
1 teaspoon baking powder
1/4 teaspoon salt
1/2 teaspoon cream of tartar
1/2 cup dietetic jelly

Preheat oven to 325°. Mix eggs, sweetener, orange juice, liquid from fruit, and lemon extract. Beat about 10 minutes with electric beater until very light and fluffy. Sift flour, milk solids, baking powder, and salt together three times; very carefully fold sifted dry ingredients into whipped mixture. Beat remaining egg whites and cream of tartar together until mixture stands in soft peaks. Fold into cake mixture. Pour into jelly-roll pan (about 10" x 15") which has been lined with lightly greased wax paper. Bake about 20 minutes; cake will spring back when touched with finger. Remove from oven and run knife around edge. Turn out onto towel, remove paper carefully and roll up immediately. Let stand one minute, unroll to cool. Fill with jelly and reroll. Slice to serve. *NOTE:* Jelly roll must be kept in refrigerator. Any dietetic pudding mix may be used for filling. When pudding is set, beat and put in roll.

## *BANANA RAISIN CAKE

Exchanges per serving: 1 inch and a half cube =
                      1/2 bread, 1/2 fat, 1/4 fruit.
Calories per serving: 80          Yield: 36 servings

2 cups flour
1 1/2 teaspoons baking powder
Non-nutritive sweetener equivalent to 1 1/2 cups sugar
1 teaspoon baking soda
1 teaspoon salt
1/2 cup diet margarine
1 cup (about 3) mashed bananas
1/4 cup skim milk
1 teaspoon lemon peel, grated
1 teaspoon vanilla extract
1/2 cup (2 medium) eggs
1 cup white raisins, chopped
1/2 cup nuts, chopped fine

Preheat oven to 350°. Sift flour, baking powder, sweetener, baking soda and salt. Add margarine, bananas, skim milk, lemon peel, and vanilla. Beat 3 minutes on electric mixer at medium speed, scrape bowl constantly. Add eggs, beat 2 minutes more, continuing to scrape bowl frequently. Stir in raisins and nuts. Place batter in a 2" x 9" x 12" pan which has been well greased and lightly floured. Bake until cake tests done. Turn out on rack to cool after 5 minutes.

## *SPICE AND MAPLE CAKE

Exchanges per serving: 1 1/2" slice = 1/2 bread,
1/2 meat.
Calories per serving: 85          Yield: 10 servings

1 cup flour
1/4 cup nonfat dry milk solids
1 teaspoon baking powder
1 teaspoon cinnamon
1 teaspoon nutmeg
1/4 teaspoon salt
1/2 cup (2 medium) eggs, separated
1/4 cup (3 medium) egg yolks
1/2 cup maple-flavored topping
1/2 teaspoon cream of tartar

Preheat oven to 325°. Sift dry ingredients together three times. Mix eggs and egg yolks with the maple topping. Beat at top speed of mixer until light and fluffy (about 10 minutes). Beat remaining whites slightly; add cream of tartar and continue to beat until whites hold stiff peak. Fold sifted dry ingredients carefully, a small amount at a time, into egg and maple topping mixture. Fold in egg whites; pour into 9" tube cake pan at once. Bake about 35 minutes, or until cake springs back when lightly touched. Invert pan at once and let hang until cool.

## *AUNT JEANNE'S SPONGE CAKE

Exchanges per serving: 1/2″ thick slice = 1/2 bread, 1/2 meat.
Calories per serving: 70                    Yield: 20 servings

| | |
|---|---|
| 1 cup skim milk | Non-nutritive sweetener |
| 1 3/4 cups flour | equivalent to 2 cups |
| 2 teaspoons baking powder | sugar |
| 1/2 teaspoon salt | 2 teaspoons vanilla |
| 1 1/2 cups (6 medium) eggs | |

Preheat oven to 350°. Heat skim milk in a small saucepan just until bubbles form around edge of pan. Remove from heat and put aside until lukewarm. Sift flour, baking powder, and salt. Beat eggs until thick and lemon-colored; gradually add sweetener, beating until mixture is well blended and smooth (4-5 minutes). Blend in flour mixture at low speed of mixer until smooth, then add lukewarm milk and vanilla. Continue beating until well mixed. Place batter in an ungreased 10″ tube pan. Bake 50 minutes, or until tester inserted in center of cake comes out clean. Turn cake—and cake pan—upside down and place tube over the neck of a bottle. This allows air to circulate around top (upside down) of cake, cooling it. Serve with imitation strawberry ice cream.

## *VANILLA SPONGE ROLL

Exchanges per serving: 1 serving = 1/3 bread, 2/3 meat.
Calories per serving: 66                    Yield: 6 servings

| | |
|---|---|
| 1 cup (about 4 medium) eggs, separated | 1 teaspoon baking powder |
| Non-nutritive sweetener equivalent to 4 tablespoons sugar | 5 tablespoons potato flour |
| | 1 teaspoon vanilla |

Preheat oven to 325°. Add sweetener to stiffly beaten egg whites. Fold in the yolks and the rest of the ingredients. Bake in oblong pan 10″ x 15″ lined with paper greased on both sides; fill and bake 40 minutes. Spread cake with dietetic jelly, roll, and dust with granulated sugar substitute.

## *CHOCOLATE CAKE

Exchanges per serving: 1 = 3/4 bread, 3/4 fat.
Calories per serving: 70            Yield: 8 servings

| | |
|---|---|
| 3/4 cup flour, sifted | 1/4 cup (1 medium) egg |
| 1/4 teaspoon salt | Non-nutritive sweetener |
| 1 teaspoon baking powder |   equivalent to 1/2 cup |
| 1/4 teaspoon baking soda |   sugar |
| 3 tablespoons unsweetened | 1/4 cup water |
|   cocoa | 1 tablespoon salad oil |
| 1/4 cup cold coffee | 1 teaspoon vanilla extract |

Preheat oven to 350°. Line an 8" round layer cake pan with paper; grease with butter. Sift first four ingredients together; blend in cocoa and coffee. Beat egg, sweetener, water, oil, and vanilla. Stir into dry ingredients. Mix until smooth. Pour batter into pan, cover with foil, and place in shallow pan of water. Bake about 1/2 hour. Remove from pan and cool on cake rack. Cut crosswise, fill, and frost with desired frosting.

## *FRUIT SPONGE CAKE

Exchanges per serving: 1 serving = 1 bread, 1/2 meat.
Calories per serving: 100            Yield: 12 servings

| | |
|---|---|
| 1 tablespoon fresh orange | 2 tablespoons fresh lemon |
|   rind, grated |   juice |
| 1/2 cup fresh orange juice | 1/2 teaspoon vanilla |
| 1 cup (4 medium) eggs, |   extract |
|   separated | 1 1/2 cups flour |
| Non-nutritive sweetener | 1/4 teaspoon salt |
|   equivalent to 1/2 cup | 3/4 teaspoon cream of |
|   sugar |   tartar |

Preheat oven to 325°. Combine rind and juice. Beat egg yolks until thick and lemon-colored using highest speed of mixer. To juice and rind of orange, add sweetener, lemon juice, and vanilla extract. Sift flour and salt together and beat into egg yolks, alternating with liquid. Beat whites with cream of tartar until stiff peaks form. Fold the batter into the whites, being careful not to beat. Pour into 9″ ungreased tube pan. Bake until done (about 1 hour). Invert cake to cool.

## **CHARLOTTE'S CHOCOLATE CAKE

Exchanges per serving: 1 = 1 bread, 1 fat, 1/4 fruit.
Calories per serving: 130　　　　　　Yield: 9 servings

1/3 cup diet margarine, softened
Non-nutritive sweetener equivalent to 1/4 cup brown sugar
1/4 cup (1 medium) egg
Non-nutritive sweetener equivalent to 1/3 cup sugar
1 1/3 cups flour

3 tablespoons unsweetened cocoa
2 teaspoons baking powder
1/2 teaspoon baking soda
1/2 cup skim milk
1/2 teaspoon vanilla extract
1/2 teaspoon almond extract
2 tablespoons nuts, chopped fine

Preheat oven to 350°. Mix margarine, brown sugar substitute, egg and regular sugar substitute. Beat at high speed two minutes, scraping bowl occasionally. Add flour, cocoa, baking powder, baking soda, skim milk, and extracts and blend at low speed about 2 minutes (batter will be thick). Spread batter into an 8″ layer pan which has been well greased and sprinkle with nuts. Bake until tester inserted in center comes out clean.

## **GINGERBREAD

Exchanges per serving: 1 = 1 1/2 bread, 1/2 fat.
Calories per serving: 125　　　　　　Yield: 8 servings

4 tablespoons diet margarine
2 tablespoons molasses
1/2 teaspoon ginger
1/4 teaspoon cinnamon
1/4 teaspoon salt

1 1/2 cups plus 1 tablespoon boiling water
1 cup rye flour
1/8 teaspoon baking powder
4 teaspoons baking soda

157

Preheat oven to 400°. Measure margarine, molasses, ginger, cinnamon, and salt into bowl; add boiling water. Sift flour, baking powder, and baking soda into mixture and beat. Pour into greased oblong pan. Bake 30 minutes.

## **CHOCOLATE CHIFFON CAKE WITH RUM

Exchanges per serving: 1 1/2″ slice = 2 bread, 3 fat, 1/2 meat.

Calories per serving: 175                   Yield: 12 servings

2 cups (8 medium) eggs
1/2 cup cocoa
3/4 cup boiling water
Non-nutritive sweetener
    equivalent to 1 3/4 cups
    sugar

1 1/2 teaspoons baking
    soda
1 3/4 cups flour
1/2 cup soy oil
2 tablespoons rum extract
1/2 teaspoon cream of
    tartar

Preheat oven to 325°. Let eggs reach room temperature then separate them. Combine cocoa and water in small bowl. Stir until smooth; cool. Sift sweetener, baking soda, and flour into large bowl; make well in center and add oil, egg yolks, rum extract, and cocoa mixture. Beat until smooth. Add cream of tartar to the egg whites and beat very stiff. Pour batter over whites and gently fold into whites until just blended. Bake in ungreased bundt pan (or 10″ tube pan) until straw inserted comes out clean. Cool cake completely, then remove from pan. Serve either plain or top with nondairy whipping cream.

## **NO CRUST CHEESECAKE

Exchanges per serving: 1″ x 1/2″ = 2 fat, 1/2 meat.
Calories per serving: 140                   Yield: 24 servings

2 cups nonfat cottage
    cheese
2 cups creamed cheese
Non-nutritive sweetener
    equivalent to 1 1/2 cups
    sugar
3/4 cup (3 medium) eggs
1 1/2 tablespoons lemon
    juice

1 teaspoon vanilla extract
1/2 cup diet margarine,
    melted
1 1/2 tablespoons arrow-
    root powder
3 tablespoons flour
2 cups artificial sour cream

Preheat oven to 325°. Cream the cheeses together gradually adding sweetener, beating after each addition. Add eggs, beat well; add lemon juice, vanilla extract, and margarine. Mix arrowroot and flour with enough sour cream to make a smooth paste. Add paste and remaining sour cream; blend thoroughly. Pour into greased 9″ spring pan. Bake 1 hour or longer until firm, then turn off oven. Let cake remain in oven 2 hours or longer. Place in refrigerator overnight. Serve cold.

## **LORENE'S CHEESECAKE

Exchanges per serving: 1″ x 1/2″ piece = 1 1/2 fat, 3/4 meat.

Calories per serving: 141          Yield: 24 servings

| | |
|---|---|
| 3/4 cup diet margarine | 2 cups low-calorie cream |
| Non-nutritive sweetener | cheese (2 8-ounce |
| equivalent to 1 1/4 cups | packages) |
| sugar | 6 level tablespoons flour |
| 1 cup (4 medium) eggs | 1 cup imitation sour cream |
| 2 cups creamed low-calorie | 1/2 teaspoon vanilla |
| cottage cheese | extract |
| 3 tablespoons arrowroot | 1/2 teaspoon lemon juice |
| powder | 1 cup artificially sweetened |
| | crushed pineapple |

Preheat oven to 325°. Cream first two ingredients; add eggs, cottage cheese, arrowroot, cream cheese and beat well after each addition; add flour, sour cream, vanilla extract, lemon juice, and crushed pineapple, stirring well. Place in spring pan. Bake 2 hours. When baked, the dough will rise over edge but will not run out. Leave in oven for 2 hours with heat off, then leave in refrigerator overnight.

## **ORANGE CAKE

Exchanges per serving: 1 = 1 bread, 1 fat, 1/2 meat.
Calories per serving: 150          Yield: 10 servings

1 cup flour
1 1/2 teaspoons baking
  powder
1/2 teaspoon salt
1/4 cup oil
1 cup (4 medium) eggs,
  separated

1/2 cup unsweetened
  frozen orange juice
  concentrate
Non-nutritive sweetener
  equivalent to 1 1/2 cups
  sugar
1/4 teaspoon cream of
  tartar

Preheat oven to 350°. Sift flour, baking powder, and salt together. Set aside one yolk. Add, in order, oil, egg yolks, orange juice, and sweetener. Beat until smooth. Add cream of tartar to whites of eggs and beat until stiff. Add egg yolk mixture to whites and fold in gently until blended. Do not overmix. Pour into 9" tube pan and bake 35 minutes.

## **PAM'S QUICK LAYER CAKE

Exchanges per serving:   1 1/2" slice = 1 bread,
                         1 1/2 fat, 1/2 meat,
                         1/8 skim milk.

Calories per serving: 175                 Yield: 12 servings

Non-nutritive sweetener
  equivalent to 1 cup sugar
1/16 teaspoon salt
2 cups flour
3 teaspoons baking powder
1/3 cup diet margarine
1/4 cup (1 medium) egg

3/4 cup skim milk
1/2 teaspoon vanilla
  extract
1/2 teaspoon almond
  extract
1 cup pecans, chopped
  extra fine

Preheat oven to 375°. Sift sweetener, salt, flour, and baking powder three or four times. Cut in margarine with pastry blender or knife until mixture resembles cornmeal. Beat egg until lemon-colored and thick; then add skim milk and extracts. Add to first mixture gradually. Add nuts and stir well. Pour into two 8" layer pans which have been well greased. Bake about 25 minutes. Cool; remove cake from pans. Cool further on wire rack.

## **SOUTHERN HOSPITALITY CAKE

Exchanges per serving: 1 = 1 bread, 2 fat, 1/2 fruit.
Calories per serving: 175                 Yield: 9 servings

| 1/3 cup diet margarine, softened | 1/2 teaspoon baking soda |
|---|---|
| Non-nutritive sweetener equivalent to 3/4 cup sugar | 1/2 teaspoon orange extract |
| | 2/3 cup fresh orange juice |
| 1/4 cup (1 medium) egg | 1/3 cup raisins |
| 1 1/3 cups flour | 2 tablespoons nuts, chopped fine |
| 1 teaspoon baking powder | |

Preheat oven to 350°. Combine margarine, sweetener, and egg and beat 2 minutes on high speed of mixer. Scrape bowl occasionally. Add flour, baking powder, baking soda, orange extract, and juice. Blend at low speed about 2 minutes (batter will be fairly thick). Then stir in raisins and spread batter in an 8″ layer pan which has been well greased. Sprinkle nuts on top. Bake until golden brown (about 1/2 hour).

## **FAMILY FAVORITE CAKE

Exchanges per serving: 1 1/2″ slice = 1 bread, 1 1/2 fat, 1/4 meat, 1/8 skim milk.

Calories per serving: 195          Yield: 15 servings

| 3/4 cup diet margarine | 3 cups flour |
|---|---|
| Non-nutritive sweetener equivalent to 1 1/2 cups sugar | 1 cup skim milk |
| | 1 teaspoon almond extract |
| 4 teaspoons baking powder | 3/4 cup (4-5 medium) egg whites |
| 1/2 teaspoon salt | |

Preheat oven to 375°. Cream margarine and sweetener. Sift baking powder, salt, and flour, then add alternately with skim milk to creamed mixture. Add almond extract, and beat stiff and fold in whites. Pour into two well-greased 9″ layer pans. Bake about 30 minutes. Cool a few minutes, then remove cake from pans and cool further on wire rack.

## **ORANGE CHIFFON CAKE

Exchanges per serving:  1 1/2″ slice = 2 bread, 1 fat, 1/8 skim milk.

Calories per serving: 135          Yield: 16 servings

2 cups (about 8) eggs,
  separated
2 1/4 cups flour, sifted
3 teaspoons baking powder
1 teaspoon salt
3 tablespoons orange peel,
  grated fine
Non-nutritive sweetener
  equivalent to 1 1/2 cups
  sugar

Artificial sweetener equivalent to 1/4 cup sugar
  added to 3/4 cup orange
  juice
1/2 teaspoon cream of
  tartar
1/2 cup salad oil

Preheat over to 325°. Set aside 3 egg yolks and cover remaining eggs until they are room temperature. (Refrigerate the 3 yolks for other use.) Add cream of tartar to egg whites and beat until they stand in peaks (stiffer than for meringue). Sift dry ingredients, make a well in center, add salad oil, egg yolks, peel, and juice-sweetener mixture. Stir to blend. Beat one minute at medium speed. Add yolk-orange mixture to whites slowly, folding these together until smooth and completely mixed. Pour into a 2" x 9" x 9" cake pan which has first been rinsed and excess water shaken out. Bake until cake is pale golden brown and a cake tester comes out clean (about 1/2 hour or a little more). Invert pan and cool. When cake pan is cool enough to handle (but not cold) run a knife around edges of pan, then with fingertips carefully take cake away from edges, lifting slightly to loosen bottom. Cool on rack. Cut into serving pieces.

## **EASY SPONGE CAKE

Exchanges per serving: 1 = 1 bread, 1/2 meat.
Calories per serving: 110          Yield: 8 servings

1 cup (4 medium) eggs,
  separated
Non-nutritive sweetener
  equivalent to 1 cup sugar
1 cup flour

1 teaspoon baking powder
1/2 teaspoon vanilla
  or
1/2 teaspoon lemon juice

Preheat oven to 300°. Beat egg whites very stiff; beat yolks very lightly. Add half the sweetener to whites, the rest to yolks. Put together and beat hard; sift flour with

aking powder and fold in. Add vanilla or lemon juice.
lace in angel tin and bake 40 minutes.

## **CUPCAKES

Exchanges per serving: 1 cupcake = 3/4 bread, 1 1/2 fat.
Calories per serving: 140          Yield: 12 cupcakes

1 1/2 cups flour
1 1/2 teaspoons baking
  powder
1/2 teaspoon salt
1/4 teaspoon baking soda
1/2 teaspoon cinnamon
1/2 teaspoon allspice
1/2 teaspoon nutmeg

1/4 teaspoon ground
  cloves
1/2 cup diet margarine
1/2 cup (2 medium) eggs
Non-nutritive sweetener
  equivalent to 2/3 cup
  sugar
1/2 cup white raisins
1/2 cup cold water

Preheat oven to 350°. Combine flour, baking powder, salt,
baking soda, cinnamon, allspice, nutmeg, and cloves; cut
in margarine until size of small peas. Add remaining
ingredients and mix until all first mixture is moistened.
Fill 12 paper baking cups about 1/2 full and bake until
tester inserted in center comes out clean.

## **FRUIT CRISP

Exchanges per serving: 1 = 1/2 bread, 1/2 fat,
                           1 1/2 fruit.
Calories per serving: 115          Yield: 6 servings

4 cups fruit, peeled and
  sliced thin (apples,
  peaches, apricots)
Non-nutritive sweetener
  equivalent to 2/3 cup
  sugar
1 teaspoon fresh lemon
  juice
1/2 cup quick-cooking
  rolled oats

Non-nutritive sweetener
  equivalent to 2 table-
  spoons brown sugar
1 tablespoon arrowroot
  powder
1/4 teaspoon allspice
2 tablespoons diet
  margarine

Preheat oven to 350°. Combine fruit with sweetener
equivalent to 1/3 cup regular sugar and juice. Place in

casserole. Combine oats, brown sugar substitute, arrow-root, allspice and rest of regular sugar substitute. Cut in margarine until crumbly, then sprinkle evenly over fruit. Bake about 1 hour, or until tender. Serve hot or cold.

### ***LOU'S LIGHT CAKE

Exchanges per serving: 1 = 2 fat, 2 bread.
Calories per serving: 215                    Yield: 10 servings

| | |
|---|---|
| 2/3 cup diet margarine | 1 1/2 cups cold water |
| Non-nutritive sweetener equivalent to 2 cups sugar | 3 1/2 cups sifted flour |
| | 1/2 teaspoon salt |
| | 4 teaspoons baking powder |
| 2 teaspoons vanilla extract | 3/4 cup (4-5 medium) egg |
| 2 teaspoons boiling water | whites |

Preheat oven to 350°. Cream margarine and sweetener, add vanilla and boiling water and blend thoroughly. Add cold water and beat 1 minute. Sift flour and salt four times, then add bit by bit alternating with small amounts of the water mixture, beating well after each addition. Sift baking powder over top of batter and fold in gently with stiffly beaten egg whites. Bake in two 10-inch pans which have been well greased and floured, until done.

### ***LU'S CHIFFON CAKE

Exchanges per serving: 1 = 1 1/2 bread, 2 fat, 1/2 meat.
Calories per serving: 215                    Yield: 12 servings

| | |
|---|---|
| 1 teaspoon salt | Non-nutritive sweetener equivalent to 1 1/2 cups sugar |
| 2 1/4 cups flour, sifted | |
| 3 teaspoons baking powder | |
| 1/2 cup salad oil | 2 teaspoons lemon rind, grated |
| 1 cup (4 medium) eggs, separated | 1 teaspoon vanilla extract |
| 1/2 cup water | 1/2 teaspoon cream of tartar |

Preheat oven to 325°. Sift salt, flour, and baking powder. Add oil, well-beaten egg yolks, water, sweetener, rind, and vanilla extract. Beat until smooth. Beat egg whites until stiff, add cream of tartar and beat until very stiff peaks form. Gently fold the batter into egg whites until just blended (but do not stir). Place in ungreased 9″ tube pan. Bake until done (about 1 hour). Invert cake to cool.

## ****MARGARET'S POUND CAKE

Exchanges per serving: 1 1/2″ slice = 1 bread, 1 fat,
1/2 meat.

Calories per serving: 350          Yield: 15 servings

| | |
|---|---|
| 1 teaspoon salt | Non-nutritive sweetener |
| 4 cups flour | equivalent to 2 cups |
| 1/2 teaspoon cream of | sugar |
| tartar | 2 cups (8 medium) eggs |
| 2 cups diet margarine | 1 teaspoon vanilla extract |
| | 1/2 teaspoon allspice |

Preheat oven to 325°. Sift salt, flour, and cream of tartar, and set aside. Cream margarine until fluffy, then add sweetener gradually and continue to cream until very fluffy. Beat in eggs 1/4 cup at a time, add vanilla extract and allspice. Beat well, then add flour mixture a little at a time until well mixed. Turn batter into greased and lightly floured bundt pan (or 2 bread pans). Bake 1 1/4 to 1 1/2 hours for bundt cake or 1 hour for loaf cakes. Cool in pans; then turn out on wire rack and cool completely. May be sprinkled with substitute for confectioners' sugar.

## ***STRAWBERRY SHORTCAKE

Exchanges per serving: 1 cake = 2 bread, 2 fat.
1/2 cup berries = 1/2 fruit.

Calories per serving: 1 cake: 220          Yield: 6 servings
berries: 20

| | |
|---|---|
| 2 cups flour | 1/2 cup water |
| Non-nutritive sweetener | 1 quart strawberries (or |
| equivalent to 1 table- | other fruit) sweetened |
| spoon sugar | with equivalent to 1 |
| 1/2 teaspoon salt | teaspoon sugar |
| 3 teaspoons baking powder | 1 cup nonfat cream, |
| 4 tablespoons diet | whipped with equivalent |
| margarine | to 1 teaspoon sugar |

Preheat oven to 475°. Sift flour, sweetener, salt, and baking powder; add margarine and mix thoroughly with steel fork. Add water to make dough soft. Roll out on floured board until about 1/2" thick. Cut with large biscuit cutter dipped in flour, or half fill large greased muffin rings which have been placed on baking pan. Bake 10-12 minutes. Split while hot, butter, and fill with crushed sweetened berries. Put on tops and cover with strawberries and sweetened whipped cream. For nonfat whipping cream, check the label for calorie content of cream used.

## *CAKE FILLING

Exchanges per serving: 1 tablespoon = trace meat.
Calories per serving: 10 (plus calories   Yield: 1 1/2 cups
                          for frosting)

| | |
|---|---|
| 1 recipe Lemon Frosting (see recipe) | 1 1/2 teaspoons unflavored gelatin |
| 1 cup nonfat cottage cheese, drained and sieved | 2 tablespoons water |

To Lemon Frosting, add cottage cheese and beat until smooth. Add gelatin to water and dissolve over boiling water (about 5 minutes). Blend carefully and use at once.

## *CREAMY FROSTING

Exchanges per serving: 1 tablespoon = trace fat,
                              trace meat.
Calories per serving: 15                    Yield: 1/2 cup

| | |
|---|---|
| 1/2 cup nonfat cottage cheese, sieved | Non-nutritive sweetener equivalent to 1/2 cup sugar |
| 1/8 teaspoon salt | |
| 1/2 tablespoon diet margarine, melted | 1 teaspoon almond or vanilla extract |

Mix all ingredients. Beat until smooth. Spread on cake. (Frosts one 10" cake.)

# *LEMON FROSTING

Exchanges per serving: 1 tablespoon = 1/4 skim milk.
Calories per serving: 20                     Yield: 1/3 cup

2 tablespoons nonfat dry
  milk
1 1/2 teaspoons lemon
  juice
Non-nutritive sweetener
  equivalent to 2 table-
  spoons sugar

1 teaspoon vanilla
2 tablespoons water
1/2 teaspoon unflavored
  gelatin

Combine all ingredients except water and gelatin. Dissolve
1/2 teaspoon gelatin and 2 tablespoons water over hot
water. Beat rest of ingredients at high speed of electric
mixer about 15 minutes. Add gelatin gradually. Continue
beating until frosting stands in peaks. Use right away.

# *LOW-CALORIE FROSTING

Exchanges per serving: 1 tablespoon = 3/4 fat.
Calories per serving: 30               Yield: 3 tablespoons

2 tablespoons cream cheese
1 teaspoon skim milk
Non-nutritive sweetener
  equivalent to 2 table-
  spoons powdered sugar

1/8 teaspoon salt
1/4 teaspoon vanilla
  extract
1/16 teaspoon food
  coloring

Cream cheese and skim milk thoroughly. Add sweetener,
salt, and vanilla extract. Blend well. Add coloring last,
using green for St. Patrick's Day, red for Christmas, etc.

# COOKIES

## *BUTTERSCOTCH SQUARES

Exchanges per serving: 1 square = 1/2 fat.
Calories per serving: 25            Yield: 70 squares

1/2 cup diet margarine
Non-nutritive sweetener
  equivalent to 2 cups
  brown sugar
1/2 cup (2 medium) eggs

1 1/2 cups flour
2 teaspoons baking powder
1 teaspoon vanilla extract
1/2 cup walnuts, chopped

Preheat oven to 350°. Cook margarine and sweetener together until smooth. Cool to lukewarm. Add eggs and beat well. Add flour, baking powder, vanilla, and walnuts. Spread in 9" x 12" x 2" pan which has been lightly greased. Bake 1/2 hour. Cut in squares 1 1/4" x 1 1/4". Sprinkle with non-nutritive granulated sugar. Cool.

## *MARY'S CHOCOLATE CHIP COOKIES

Exchanges per serving: 1 cookie = 1/4 bread, 3/4 fat.
Calories per serving: 50         Yield: 3 dozen cookies

1/4 teaspoon salt
1/2 teaspoon baking soda
1 cup flour, sifted
1/2 cup diet margarine
Non-nutritive sweetener
  equivalent to 2/3 cup
  plus 4 teaspoons sugar

1/2 teaspoon vanilla
  extract
1/4 cup (1 medium) egg,
  beaten
1/2 cup semisweet chocolate, shaved fine

Preheat oven to 375°. Sift salt, baking soda, and flour together. Cream margarine and add sweetener, vanilla, and egg, blending well. Add flour mixture. Beat well; stir in chocolate. Drop by level spoonsful onto a baking sheet which has been lightly greased. Bake about 10 minutes.

## *ANGEL'S KISS

Exchanges per serving: 1 kiss = 1/8 fat, 1/8 meat.
Calories per serving: 15         Yield: 3 dozen kisses

Non-nutritive sweetener
   equivalent to 1 1/2 cups
   confectioners' sugar
1 1/2 cups (9 medium) egg
   yolks, lightly beaten

1/2 cup blanched almonds,
   finely cut
1 teaspoon instant diet tea
   mix
1 teaspoon almond extract

Preheat oven to 325°. Beat sweetener into yolks; add almonds, tea mix, and almond extract. (Mixture will be runny.) Line muffin pans with paper baking cups and fill each half full. Bake until golden brown; remove cups while warm. Cool on wire rack.

## *BUTTERMILK OAT COOKIES

Exchanges per serving: 1 square = 1/4 bread, 1/4 fat.
Calories per serving: 25      Yield: 2 1/2 dozen cookies

1 cup flour
1/2 cup rolled oats,
   uncooked
1/4 teaspoon baking soda
1/2 teaspoon salt

Non-nutritive sweetener
   equivalent to 3 table-
   spoons sugar
1/4 cup buttermilk
1/4 cup diet margarine,
   or butter, melted

Preheat oven to 400°. Sift flour, oats, baking soda, and salt. Add sweetener to buttermilk, then stir this and margarine into flour mixture until dry ingredients are moistened. Knead dough lightly on well-floured board for a few moments, then roll thin. Cut into 2" x 2" squares. Bake on ungreased cookie sheet until brown (10-12 minutes).

## *BROWNIES

Exchanges per serving: 1 brownie = 1/4 bread, 1 fat.
Calories per serving: 65      Yield: 5 dozen brownies

1 cup diet margarine
2 squares unsweetened
   chocolate

Non-nutritive sweetener
   equivalent to 5 cups
   sugar

2 cups flour
1 teaspoon salt
1 teaspoon baking soda

1 cup (4 medium) eggs,
  well beaten
4 teaspoons vanilla extract
1/2 cup chopped nuts

Preheat oven to 325°. Melt margarine and chocolate over low heat; then remove. Sift together flour, salt, and baking soda. Add sweetener, eggs, and vanilla extract and stir into dry ingredients until well blended; stir in nuts. Pour into 8″ square pan which has been well greased. Bake 20 minutes. Cool. Cut into squares.

## *TASTY DIET BROWNIES

Exchanges per serving: 1 brownie = 1/4 bread, 1 fat.
Calories per serving: 65                Yield: 16 brownies

2/3 cup flour, sifted
1/2 teaspoon baking
  powder
1/4 teaspoon salt
1 ounce unsweetened
  chocolate (1 square)
1/4 cup (1 medium) egg

1/2 cup dietetic maple
  topping
Non-nutritive sweetener
  equivalent to 2 teaspoons
  sugar
1/3 cup chopped walnuts
1/2 teaspoon vanilla
  extract

Preheat oven to 350°. Measure flour, add baking powder and salt and sift again. Melt chocolate over hot water. Beat egg one minute, add topping and sweetener and beat two more minutes, then add melted chocolate and blend. Add flour and stir (do not beat) until smooth. Add walnuts and vanilla extract. Spread batter 1/2″ to 3/4″ thick in 8″ square pan (or 9″ pie tin). Bake 40 minutes.

## *SPICY COOKIES

Exchanges per serving: 1 cookie = 1/8 bread, 1 fat.
Calories per serving: 55                Yield: 24 cookies

1/3 cup diet margarine
1 cup flour
1/4 teaspoon baking
  powder
1/4 teaspoon salt
2 tablespoons cocoa
1 tablespoon water

Non-nutritive sweetener
  equivalent to 1/3 cup
  sugar
1/2 teaspoon cinnamon
1/2 teaspoon nutmeg
1 teaspoon vanilla extract

Preheat oven to 375°. Cream margarine until light and nearly cream colored. Sift flour, baking powder, salt, and cocoa together and blend into margarine until smooth. Mix water, sweetener, cinnamon, nutmeg, and vanilla extract; add to flour-margarine mixture and mix until smooth (dough will be stiff). Shape into balls about 3/4" round. Place on cookie sheet; flatten with blade of knife dipped into cold water. Bake until done (about 15 minutes). Remove from tray and cool.

## *CHOCOLATE COOKIES

Exchanges per serving: 1 cookie, 2" diameter =
trace bread, trace meat.
Calories per serving: 22        Yield: 2 1/2 dozen cookies

| | |
|---|---|
| 1/4 cup (1 medium) egg, separated | 1 cup flour |
| Non-nutritive sweetener equivalent to 1/3 cup sugar | 1 teaspoon baking powder |
| | 1/4 teaspoon salt |
| | 1/2 cup unsweetened chocolate topping |
| 2 teaspoons unsweetened fruit liquid, any kind | 1/4 teaspoon cream of tartar |

Preheat oven to 325°. Mix egg yolks, sweetener, and fruit liquid together in large bowl. Beat with electric mixer until light and fluffy (about 10-12 minutes). Meanwhile sift flour, baking powder, and salt together 3 times. Add chocolate topping to first mixture and beat until mixed thoroughly. Beat egg whites with cream of tartar until they stand in soft peaks. Very carefully fold dry ingredients into chocolate topping mix. Fold beaten egg whites into this mixture and then drop by teaspoonsful onto lightly greased cookie sheet. Bake about 10 minutes or until cookie springs back when lightly touched. Remove cookies to wire rack to cool, with spatula.

## *MARY'S THUMBPRINTS

Exchanges per serving: 1 cookie = 1/4 fat.
Calories per serving: 20        Yield: 4 dozen cookies

1/2 cup diet margarine
Non-nutritive sweetener
    equivalent to 1/4 cup
    sugar
1/4 cup (1 medium) egg,
    separated
1 tablespoon orange rind
1 1/2 teaspoons lemon
    rind

1/2 teaspoon vanilla
    extract
1 tablespoon lemon juice
1 tablespoon orange juice
1 cup flour
1 teaspoon salt
1/2 cup nuts, finely
    chopped

Preheat oven to 350°. Mix together everything except the egg whites and nuts and roll into small balls. Beat the egg whites stiff and spread the nuts out on a piece of waxed paper. Roll each ball in egg white, then in the nuts, and make a thumbprint in each. Bake 12 minutes. Cool. When cooled, fill each thumbprint with diet jelly.

## *SPICY APPLESAUCE COOKIES

Exchanges per serving: 1 cookie, 2" diameter =
                1 bread, 1 fruit.
Calories per serving: 20          Yield: 3 1/2 dozen cookies

1 cup flour
1/3 cup nonfat dry milk
    solids
1 teaspoon baking powder
1/2 teaspoon cinnamon
1/4 teaspoon nutmeg
1/4 teaspoon cloves
1/8 teaspoon salt
1/2 cup (2 medium) eggs

Non-nutritive sweetener
    equivalent to 8 tea-
    spoons sugar
3 tablespoons unsweetened
    fruit liquid (any fruit)
1/2 cup unsweetened
    applesauce
10 almonds, blanched and
    cut in quarters

Preheat oven to 325°. Sift dry ingredients together three times; mix eggs, sweetener, and fruit liquid. Beat at top speed of mixer until fluffy and thick (about 10 minutes). Decrease speed. Add applesauce and beat three minutes; carefully fold in dry ingredients. Drop by teaspoonsful onto lightly greased cookie sheet. Place 1/4 almond on each cookie. Bake about 10 minutes. Cookie will spring back at light touch when done. (These may be placed under broiler to give deeper finish.)

# *COCONUT FRUIT COOKIES

Exchanges per serving: 1 cookie = 1/2 bread, 1/4 fat.
Calories per serving: 45          Yield: 3 dozen cookies

1 1/2 cups flour
1 teaspoon baking powder
1/4 teaspoon baking soda
1/4 teaspoon salt
1/3 cup diet margarine
1/3 cup flaked coconut
1/4 cup (1 medium) egg
1/2 cup unsweetened fruit
juice

2 teaspoons orange or
lemon peel, grated
Non-nutritive sweetener
equivalent to 1/3 cup
sugar
1 teaspoon almond (or
vanilla) extract

Preheat oven to 400°. Combine flour, baking powder, baking soda, and salt, then cut in margarine until consistency of peas. Stir in coconut then add remaining ingredients all at once. Stir with fork until dough holds together. Drop about 2 inches apart by teaspoonsful onto an ungreased cookie sheet. Bake until light golden brown (about 10 minutes).

# *YUMMY PEANUT BUTTER COOKIES

Exchanges per serving: 1 cookie = 1/4 bread, 1/4 meat.
Calories per serving: 34          Yield: 1 1/2 dozen cookies

1/3 cup flour
1/4 teaspoon baking soda
1/4 teaspoon baking
powder
1/4 cup diet margarine
4 tablespoons peanut butter
Non-nutritive sweetener
equivalent to 1 table-
spoon brown sugar

Non-nutritive sweetener
equivalent to 1/2 cup
regular sugar
1/4 cup (1 medium) egg,
well beaten

Preheat oven to 375°. Grease cookie sheet lightly. Sift flour, baking soda, and baking powder. Work margarine and peanut butter with spoon until creamy, then gradually add brown sugar substitute, continuing to work until light. Add regular sugar substitute and egg and beat well. Mix in dry ingredients thoroughly. Drop by teaspoonsful onto lightly greased heavy-duty aluminum foil, then flatten with tines of fork. Bake until done (about 8-10 minutes).

## *CHOCOLATE CHIP COOKIES

Exchanges per serving: 1 cookie = 1 fat.
Calories per serving: 45

1 1/2 cups diet margarine, softened
Non-nutritive sweetener equivalent to 3/4 cup sugar
2 tablespoons water
1/2 teaspoon vanilla extract
1/4 cup (1 medium) egg, beaten

1 cup, plus 2 tablespoons all-purpose flour
1/2 teaspoon baking soda
1/2 teaspoon salt
1/2 cup unsweetened chocolate bits
1/2 cup chopped nuts (optional)

Preheat oven to 375°. Cream margarine, mix in sweetener, water, and vanilla extract. To this mixture add the beaten egg. Sift flour, baking soda, and salt together; stir into mixture. Mix in chocolate bits and nuts. Drop by spoon onto greased cookie sheet. Bake from 10-12 minutes.

## *CREAM CHEESE-COCONUT DELIGHT

Exchanges per serving: 1 cookie = 2 fat.
Calories per serving: 90      Yield: 2 dozen cookies

2 ounces cream cheese
Non-nutritive sweetener equivalent to 1/2 cup sugar
1 teaspoon orange rind, grated

1 teaspoon lemon rind, grated
2 teaspoons walnuts, chopped fine
1/2 cup coconut, shredded and toasted

Work cream cheese with spoon until light and fluffy. Thoroughly mix sweetener, both grated rinds, and nuts. Add to cheese. Form in 1" balls. Roll in toasted coconut and refrigerate.

174

## **JOAN'S PEANUT BUTTER COOKIES

Exchanges per serving: 5 cookies = 1/2 bread, 1 fat,
1/2 meat.

Calories per serving: 116          Yield: 4 dozen cookies

1/4 cup diet margarine
Non-nutritive sweetener
    equivalent to 1 cup sugar
1/2 cup peanut butter,
    softened
1/4 cup (1 medium) egg

1/3 cup skim milk
1 teaspoon vanilla extract
1 cup flour
1/4 teaspoon salt
1 teaspoon baking powder

Preheat oven to 375°. Combine margarine, sweetener, peanut butter, and blend well. Combine egg, milk, and vanilla extract, and add to first mixture. Sift flour, salt, and baking powder together and add, blending well. Drop by spoonsful onto cookie sheet which has been greased (or onto heavy-duty aluminum foil). Flatten with tines of fork dipped in water. Bake 10 minutes.


## *REFRIGERATED COCONUT FRUIT COOKIES

Exchanges per serving: 1 cookie = 1/4 bread, 1/4 fat.

Calories per serving: 30          Yield: 2 1/2 dozen cookies

Non-nutritive sweetener
    equivalent to 1/2 cup
    sugar
1/4 cup unsweetened fruit
    juice
1 teaspoon vanilla extract

1/4 teaspoon baking
    powder
1/4 teaspoon salt
1 cup flour
1/4 cup diet margarine
2 tablespoons coconut

Combine sweetener, juice, and vanilla extract. Sift baking powder, salt, and flour and then cut the margarine into this. Add the liquid ingredients. After these are well mixed, work in coconut. Make dough into a roll about 2″ diameter and place in waxed paper in refrigerator until well chilled and firm. Slice into 2 1/2 dozen cookies and place on ungreased cookie sheet. Preheat oven to 400°. Bake 10 minutes.

175

# *CRISP APPLESAUCE COOKIES

Exchanges per serving: 1 cookie = 1/4 bread, 1/4 fat,
1/4 fruit.

Calories per cookie: 40          Yield: 4 dozen cookies

1 2/3 cups flour, sifted
1 teaspoon cinnamon
1/4 teaspoon nutmeg
1/4 teaspoon cloves
1/2 teaspoon allspice
1/2 teaspoon salt
1 teaspoon baking soda
1/2 cup diet margarine

Non-nutritive sweetener
   equivalent to 1 cup sugar
1/4 cup (1 medium) egg
1 cup unsweetened apple-
   sauce
1/3 cup white raisins
1 cup whole bran cereal

Preheat oven to 375°. Sift dry ingredients together. Mix
margarine, sweetener, and egg until light and fluffy; then
add flour mixture and applesauce alternately. Mix well
after each addition. Fold in raisins and cereal and drop by
teaspoonsful onto well-greased sheet of heavy-duty aluminum foil about 1" apart. Bake until golden brown (about
15 minutes).

# *CHOCOLATE BITES

Exchanges per serving: 1 cookie = 1/2 fat, 1/4 bread.
Calories per serving: 36          Yield: 2 1/2 dozen cookies

1/3 cup diet margarine
1/4 cup cocoa
2 tablespoons liquid
   sweetener
1/2 cup (2 medium) eggs,
   well beaten

2 teaspoons vanilla extract
1 cup flour
1/2 teaspoon baking soda
1/2 teaspoon salt

Preheat oven to 325°. Melt margarine, add cocoa, sweetener, eggs, and vanilla extract and stir until blended well.
Sift flour, baking soda, and salt together, add, and mix
well (batter will be quite dry). Spread on 8" square pan
which has been well greased. Bake about 20 minutes.
Cool and cut into bites.

# *ORANGE COOKIES WITH NUTS

Exchanges per serving: 1 cookie = 1/4 bread, 1/2 fat.
Calories per serving: 40          Yield: 2 1/2 dozen cookies

1/2 cup frozen unsweet-
ened orange juice
concentrate
1/4 cup (1 medium) egg
1/4 cup diet margarine
Non-nutritive sweetener
equivalent to 1 cup sugar

1 cup flour
1/4 teaspoon salt
1/4 teaspoon baking
powder
1 teaspoon vanilla extract
1/2 cup pecans, chopped
fine

Preheat oven to 375°. Cream first four ingredients and beat well. Sift flour, salt, and baking powder and add to creamed mixture. Mix gently, until just blended; add vanilla extract and nuts. Drop by teaspoonsful onto lightly greased heavy-duty aluminum foil, and bake until lightly browned (about 15 minutes).

## *RICE FLOUR COOKIES

Exchanges per serving: 1 cookie = 1/4 bread, 1/4 fat.
Calories per serving: 27          Yield: 2 dozen cookies

3/4 cup diet margarine
Non-nutritive sweetener
equivalent to 1 1/2 cups
sugar
1/2 cup (2 medium) eggs
1/2 teaspoon vanilla
extract

1/2 teaspoon almond
extract
1 teaspoon orange or
lemon extract
2 1/2 cups rice flour
1 teaspoon cream of tartar
1 teaspoon baking soda

Preheat oven to 375°. Cream margarine and sweetener; add eggs and extracts. Sift flour, cream of tartar, and baking soda; mix all ingredients well, then roll in small balls. Place on greased cookie sheet (or on heavy-duty aluminum foil) and flatten with tines of fork. Bake until brown (10 minutes).

## *ORANGE OR LEMON PEEL COOKIES

Exchanges per serving: 1 cookie = 1/2 bread, 1 fat.
Calories per serving: 79          Yield: 4 dozen cookies

1/2 cup diet margarine
Non-nutritive sweetener
equivalent to 1/2 cup
sugar

1/3 cup hot water
1 teaspoon orange extract
1 teaspoon vanilla extract
2 cups flour

1 teaspoon baking powder
1/2 teaspoon salt
3/4 cup pecans, chopped
    fine

1 tablespoon orange or
    lemon peel, finely grated

Cream first five ingredients, then sift together and add flour, baking powder, and salt. Blend in pecans and orange or lemon peel until mixture is smooth. Shape dough into roll about 2″ x 4″. Wrap in waxed paper; chill well in refrigerator. Cut roll into 48 cookies; place on lightly greased heavy-duty aluminum foil. Preheat oven to 400°; bake until brown around edges, about 12-15 minutes.

## *OATMEAL COOKIES

Exchanges per serving: 1 cookie = 1/4 bread, 1/4 fat,
                1/4 fruit.

Calories per serving: 35            Yield: 4 dozen cookies

1 1/2 cups quick-cooking
    oatmeal, uncooked
2/3 cup diet margarine,
    melted
1/2 cup (2 medium) eggs,
    beaten
Non-nutritive sweetener
    equivalent to 1 1/2 cups
    sugar

1 1/2 cups flour, sifted
2 teaspoons baking powder
1/2 teaspoon salt
1/2 cup skim milk
1 teaspoon vanilla extract
1/4 cup raisins

Preheat oven to 400°. Measure oatmeal into bowl, stir in melted margarine and mix well. Stir in eggs and sweetener, then add flour, baking powder, and salt, alternating with the combined milk and vanilla. Add raisins. Drop onto cookie sheet from level teaspoonsful and bake until golden brown (about 10-15 minutes).

## *FRUIT COOKIES

Exchanges per serving: 1 cookie = 1/3 bread, 1/2 fat,
                1/4 fruit.

Calories per serving: 56            Yield: 20 cookies

1/2 cup flour
1/8 teaspoon cloves
1/4 teaspoon nutmeg
1 teaspoon cinnamon
1/4 teaspoon salt
1/2 teaspoon baking soda
1/2 cup raisins

1/2 cup rolled oats,
   uncooked
1/2 cup unsweetened
   cranberry sauce
1/2 cup diet margarine,
   melted
1/4 cup (1 medium) egg
1 teaspoon vanilla extract

Preheat oven to 375°. Sift flour, cloves, nutmeg, cinnamon, salt, and baking soda together, then add raisins and oats. Combine cranberry sauce, margarine, egg, and vanilla extract. Stir into dry ingredients until they are moistened. Using lightly greased cookie sheet, drop by teaspoonsful and bake 10-12 minutes.

## *MACAROONS

Exchanges per serving: 1 macaroon = 1/2 fat.
Calories per serving: 24    Yield: 3 1/2 dozen macaroons

1/4 cup (1 medium) egg,
   separated
Non-nutritive sweetener
   equivalent to 1 cup sugar
2 cups cornflakes

1 cup shredded coconut
1/2 cup chopped pecans
   (optional)
1/2 teaspoon almond
   extract

Beat egg whites until stiff but not dry. Fold in sweetener, then add cornflakes, coconut, chopped pecans, and almond extract. Drop from teaspoon onto greased baking sheet and bake at 350° for about 12 minutes. Remove at once from baking sheet.

## *GRANDMA'S COOKIES

Exchanges per serving: 1 cookie = 1/2 bread, 1 fat.
Calories per serving: 85        Yield: 2 dozen cookies

2/3 cup diet margarine
Non-nutritive sweetener
   equivalent to 3/4 cup
   sugar
1 teaspoon vanilla extract
1/4 cup (1 medium) egg

4 teaspoons milk
2 cups all-purpose flour,
   sifted
1 1/2 teaspoons baking
   powder
1/4 teaspoon salt

Thoroughly cream margarine, sweetener, and vanilla extract. Add egg and beat until light and fluffy; then stir in milk. Sift flour, baking powder, and salt together; blend into creamed mixture. Divide dough in half and chill 1 hour. Roll half of the dough at a time. (Keep balance chilled for easier rolling.) On lightly floured surface, roll dough to about 1/2" thickness. Cut in desired shapes. Preheat oven to 375° and bake 6-8 minutes. Cool slightly, then remove from pan. Top with unsweetened fruit on each one, if desired.

## *PEANUT BUTTER COOKIES

Exchanges per serving: 1 cookie = 1/2 bread, 1/2 meat.
Calories per serving: 71                Yield: 8 cookies

| | |
|---|---|
| 8 graham crackers, crushed | 1 teaspoon baking powder |
| 2 tablespoons peanut butter | 1/4 cup (3 medium) egg |
| Non-nutritive sweetener | yolks |
| equivalent to 1/4 cup | 1 teaspoon milk |
| sugar | |

Preheat oven to 340°. Combine cracker crumbs and peanut butter, then add sweetener and baking powder. Add egg yolks and milk and mix well. Divide into eight 1" cookies and press with fork to flatten. Bake 10 minutes.

## **BROWNIES DIVINE

Exchanges per serving: 1 brownie = 1/2 bread, 2 fat.
Calories per serving: 120                Yield: 16 brownies

| | |
|---|---|
| 1/2 cup diet margarine | 1 teaspoon vanilla extract |
| Non-nutritive sweetener | 1/2 cup (2 medium) eggs |
| equivalent to 1 1/4 cups | 3/4 cup flour |
| sugar | 1 teaspoon baking powder |
| 1 square unsweetened | 1/2 cup nuts, chopped |
| chocolate | |

Preheat oven to 350°. Cream margarine and sweetener until light and fluffy. Place chocolate on aluminum foil and melt over boiling water. Stir chocolate into margarine mixture and beat until smooth. Then beat in vanilla and eggs. Sift and stir together flour and baking powder; add nuts, then stir this mixture into first mixture until smooth. Grease a 2″ x 8″ x 8″ pan; spread batter into this. Bake until brownies are shiny, about half an hour. Cool in pan. Cut into 16 pieces and serve cool.

# PIES AND PIE CRUST

## *DIETETIC APPLE CRUNCH

Exchanges per serving: 1 = 1/2 bread, 1/2 fat, 1 fruit.
Calories per serving: 86          Yield: 6 servings

2 slices dry bread
1 tablespoon diet
  margarine
1/2 teaspoon cinnamon
1/2 teaspoon allspice

3 cups apples, sliced
1 tablespoon lemon juice
3/4 cup dietetic maple
  topping

Preheat oven to 350°. Make crumbs from bread and toast in oven. Mix toasted crumbs with margarine, cinnamon, and 1/4 teaspoon allspice. Mix apples with lemon juice, maple topping, and rest of allspice. Spread in well-greased shallow baking dish (approximately 8″ round). Cover with crumb mixture and bake 45 minutes, or until apple slices are tender. Serve warm.

## *ICEBOX CHOCOLATE PIE

Exchanges per serving: 1 = 1/2 bread, 1/3 fat, 1/4 milk.
Calories per serving: 100          Yield: 8 servings

2 tablespoons cocoa
1/8 teaspoon salt
1 1/2 teaspoons arrowroot
  powder
1/2 cup skim milk, scalded
1/4 cup (1 medium) egg,
  separated

Non-nutritive sweetener
  equivalent to 3/4 cup
  sugar
1/2 cup evaporated milk,
  beaten
1 teaspoon vanilla
12 graham crackers

Mix cocoa, salt, and arrowroot, then blend in skim milk. Add slightly beaten egg yolk and sweetener. Cook in top of double boiler until thickened. Cool. Beat the egg white, evaporated milk, and vanilla until stiff and fold in. Roll raham crackers into crumbs and use half in 8" pie pan; our in filling. Use remaining crumbs on top. Put in reezer until firm.

## **PEACH PIE FILLING

Exchanges per serving: 1 filling = 1/2 fruit.
   1 pastry = 1 bread, 1 1/2 fat.
Calories per serving: filling: 20      Yield: 10 servings
   pastry: 135

| | |
|---|---|
| 2 cups firm, ripe peaches | 1/4 teaspoon lemon juice |
| 1/4 tablespoon salt | 2 tablespoons diet |
| 1 quart + 1/4 cup water | margarine |
| Non-nutritive sweetener | Pastry for one 10" pie |
| equivalent to 1/2 cup | crust |
| sugar | |

Remove peach skins and pits; slice peaches and drop into solution of salt and 1 quart hot water. Drain. Mix sweetener, 1/4 cup water, and lemon juice together; pour over peaches. Set in refrigerator until cool. Place in unbaked 10" crust and dot with margarine. Preheat oven to 325°. Bake peaches until they are tender to the touch of a fork (about 30-40 minutes).

## **MARGARET'S GLAZED BERRY TARTS

Exchanges per serving: 1 = 3/4 fruit.
   1 pastry = 1 bread, 1 1/2 fat.
Calories per serving: filling: 30      Yield: 6 servings
   pastry: 135

| | |
|---|---|
| 1 envelope unflavored | Non-nutritive sweetener |
| gelatin | equivalent to 1 1/2 cups |
| 1/4 cup cold water | sugar |
| 4 cups fresh berries, hulled | 3 drops food coloring |
| and washed (straw- | 2 tablespoons lemon juice |
| berries, boysenberries, | Pastry for 6 medium tarts |
| etc.) | |

Preheat oven to 425°. Bake tart shells until lightly browned. Remove from oven and let cool. Soften gelatin in cold water. Sweeten berries with sweetener and press through strainer until 1 1/2 cups are obtained. Add coloring and lemon juice and bring to a boil. Remove from heat. Add softened gelatin and stir to dissolve. Chill until mixture begins to thicken. Arrange rest of whole berries in baked shells. Cover with gelatin-berry mixture. May be topped with artificial cream or Low-Calorie Topping Whip.

## **FRUIT SHORTCAKE

Exchanges per serving: 1 shortcake = 1 bread, 1 fat,
1/2 fruit.

Calories per serving: 130          Yield: 6 shortcakes

| | |
|---|---|
| 1 cup flour | 1/2 cup skim milk |
| 2 teaspoons baking powder | Non-nutritive sweetener |
| 1/4 teaspoon salt | equivalent to 1 cup sugar |
| 2 tablespoons diet margarine | 3 cups fruit, cut up |

Preheat oven to 450°. Sift flour, baking powder, and salt together in a small mixing bowl. Cut in margarine until mixture resembles small peas. Combine skim milk and sweetener; add all at once to flour mixture, stirring lightly with a fork until all moistened. Drop by large spoonsful onto a greased sheet of heavy-duty aluminum foil. Bake until golden brown (about 15 minutes). Cool. Split and serve with fruit sweetened to taste with non-nutritive sweetener. Top with Custard Sauce for Shortcakes, if desired.

## **BERRY PIE

Exchanges per serving: 1 = 1/2 fruit.
1 crust = 1 bread, 1 1/2 fat.

Calories per serving: filling: 20          Yield: 8 servings
crust: 135

| | |
|---|---|
| 1 quart berries (blueberries, raspberries, etc.) | 1 tablespoon arrowroot powder |
| 2 teaspoons lemon juice | Non-nutritive sweetener |
| 1/4 teaspoon lemon peel, grated fine | equivalent to 3/4 cup sugar |
| 1/2 teaspoon cinnamon | Pastry for one-crust pie |

Preheat oven to 425°. Wash berries, mix with rest of ingredients. Put into unbaked pie crust and bake until tender (45-50 minutes). If a two-crust pie is desired, cover the pie before baking, cut vents in the top crust, flute edges, and cover fluting with foil to prevent excessive browning. *For a two-crust pie, adjust exchanges per serving to 2 bread, 3 fat, and add an additional 130 calories.*

## **BANANA CREAM PIE

Exchanges per serving: 1= 1/3 bread, 1/2 skim milk.
1 pastry= 1 bread, 1 1/2 fat.
Calories per serving: filling: 75          Yield: 6 servings
pastry: 135

| | |
|---|---|
| 1/4 cup flour | 1/8 teaspoon salt |
| 1 1/2 cups skim milk | 1 banana |
| 1/4 cup (1 medium) egg | Pastry for one-crust pie |
| 1 teaspoon lemon juice | Nondairy whipping cream |
| 1/2 teaspoon vanilla | (optional) |
| extract | |
| Non-nutritive sweetener | |
| equivalent to 1/2 cup | |
| sugar | |

Blend flour with 1/2 cup cold skim milk. Scald remaining 1 cup skim milk and add flour-milk mixture and egg, lemon juice, vanilla extract, sweetener, and salt. Cook in top of double boiler, stirring until thick. Slice banana into baked, cooled pie shell. Spread cream filling over top; cool. Cover with nondairy whipping cream, if desired. Use immediately.

## **OLGA'S PUMPKIN PIE

Exchanges per serving: 1 = 1 bread, 1/2 "B" vegetable.
Calories per serving: 100 (+ pudding     Yield: 6 servings
mix)

| | |
|---|---|
| 1 1/2 cups cornflakes | 1 cup skim milk |
| 1 teaspoon diet margarine, melted | 2 envelopes dietetic butterscotch or vanilla pudding |
| 1 tablespoon hot water | 1 cup pumpkin, canned or fresh cooked |
| 1/2 cup dietetic pancake and waffle topping | 1/4 cup (1 medium) egg |

185

Preheat oven to 325°. Crush cornflakes. Mix margarine and water, add to cornflakes and mix thoroughly. Spread mixture evenly in a 9″ pie pan; press firmly around edge with spatula. Bake 8-10 minutes. Cool. Blend rest of ingredients in saucepan; cook over medium heat, stirring constantly until mixture comes to a boil. Cool to room temperature; pour into previously prepared pie shell. Chill at least three hours before serving.

## **MARTI'S APPLE CRISP

Exchanges per serving: 1 = 1 fat, 1 fruit, 1/2 bread, 1/2 meat.

Calories per serving: 155          Yield: 6 servings

| | |
|---|---|
| 4 apples, cored, peeled, and sliced | 1/2 cup flour |
| 1/4 cup water | 1/2 teaspoon cinnamon |
| 1/2 teaspoon fresh lemon juice | 1/2 teaspoon allspice |
| Non-nutritive sweetener equivalent to 2/3 cup sugar | 1/2 teaspoon salt |
| | 3 tablespoons diet margarine |
| | 1/2 cup Parmesan cheese, grated (optional) |

Preheat oven to 325°. Grease a shallow baking dish and place apple slices on bottom. Combine water, lemon juice, and sweetener and pour over apples. Combine dry ingredients; cut in margarine until it is the consistency of large peas. Sprinkle over apples. If desired, cover with grated cheese.

## **DEEP DISH APPLE PIE

Exchanges per serving: 1 = 1 bread, 1 1/2 fat, 1 fruit.

Calories per serving: 165          Yield: 8 servings

| | |
|---|---|
| 4 apples, pared and sliced fine | Non-nutritive sweetener equivalent to 1 cup sugar |
| 2 teaspoons lemon juice | 1/2 tablespoon arrowroot powder |
| 1/2 teaspoon lemon rind, grated | 1 cup flour, sifted |
| 1 1/8 teaspoons salt | 1/3 cup diet margarine |
| 1/4 teaspoon nutmeg | 1/3 cup water |
| 1/2 teaspoon cinnamon | |

Preheat oven to 425°. Combine apples, lemon juice, lemon rind, nutmeg, cinnamon, sweetener, arrowroot and 1/8 teaspoon salt. Place in well-buttered 9″ deep-dish pie plate. Combine flour and 1 teaspoon salt; cut in margarine until consistency of cornmeal. Blend in water; roll out as for a pie crust; place this on top of filling. Bake until crust is brown (about 35 minutes).

## **FRUIT COBBLER

Exchanges per serving: 1 = 1 bread, 1 1/2 fruit,
 1/4 meat.

Calories per serving: 150                Yield: 4 servings

2 cups water-packed fruit
 (cherries, etc.),
 unsweetened
1/4 teaspoon lemon juice
1/8 teaspoon almond
 extract
1/2 teaspoon arrowroot
 powder
2/3 cup juice from fruit
1/2 cup flour, sifted

1/8 teaspoon salt
3/4 teaspoon baking
 powder
1 tablespoon diet
 margarine
1/4 cup (1 medium) egg
2 tablespoons skim milk
Non-nutritive sweetener
 equivalent to 1/4 cup
 sugar

Preheat oven to 425°. Using shallow cake pan, make a layer of drained fruit. Combine lemon juice, almond extract, arrowroot powder, and drained fruit juice. Pour over fruit. Mix flour, salt, and baking powder, cutting in margarine until mixture is like coarse sugar. Mix egg, skim milk, and sweetener. Stir into dry ingredients and spoon onto fruit. Bake until browned (25-30 minutes). Serve warm.

## **FRUIT FILLING FOR PIE

Exchanges per serving: 1 = 1 fruit.
 1 crust = 1 bread, 1 1/2 fat.

Calories per serving: filling: 40         Yield: 8 servings
 crust: 135

4 cups any fruit (apples,
  blueberries, fresh
  peaches, pears, orange
  sections, pineapple, seedless grapes, etc.)
Non-nutritive sweetener
  equivalent to 3/4 cup
  sugar

1 tablespoon arrowroot
  powder
1/4 teaspoon lemon peel,
  grated fine
2 teaspoons lemon juice
1/4 teaspoon nutmeg
1/2 teaspoon cinnamon
Pastry for one-crust pie

Preheat oven to 425°. Mix all ingredients together and place in uncooked pie crust. Bake until fruit is tender (about 45-50 minutes). If a two-crust pie is desired, cover unbaked pie with second crust, cut air vents in top, and flute edges. Cover fluted edges with foil to prevent excessive browning (remove foil after half an hour) and bake as before. *For a two-crust pie, adjust exchanges per serving to 2 bread, 3 fat, and add an additional 130 calories.*

## **PEACHY PIE

Exchanges per serving: 1 = 1/2 bread, 2 fruit.
Calories per serving: 113          Yield: 6 servings

1 1/2 cups cornflakes
1 tablespoon diet marga-
  rine, melted
1 teaspoon hot water
4 cups unsweetened or
  fresh peaches, sliced
2 envelopes dietetic cherry
  gelatin
3 teaspoons lemon juice

1 teaspoon lemon rind,
  grated
1/4 cup nonfat dry milk
  solids
1/4 cup cold water
Non-nutritive sweetener
  equivalent to 3 table-
  spoons sugar

Preheat oven to 325°. Crush cornflakes. Mix margarine and hot water; add to cornflakes and mix thoroughly. Spread mixture evenly in 8″ pie pan; press firmly around edge with spatula. Bake 8-10 minutes. Cool. Drain peaches, keeping the juice to dissolve the gelatin in, adding water to make 1 cup liquid. Heat almost to boiling. Add 2 tablespoons lemon juice and rind. Cool. Chop and add the peaches and chill until mixture begins to thicken. Mix nonfat dry milk solids, cold water, and rest of lemon juice; whip until mixture stands in peaks. Add sweetener and beat until mixture stands in very stiff peaks; very carefully fold gelatin-peach mixture into whipped milk; mix. Pour gently into pie shell above and serve chilled.

### ***YUMMY FRUIT TARTS

Exchanges per serving: 1 = 1 fat, 1/2 meat, 1 fruit.
                 1 pastry = 1 fat, 1/2 bread.
Calories per serving: filling: 145        Yield: 6 tarts
                pastry: 115

1 tablespoon arrowroot powder
1/8 teaspoon salt
Non-nutritive sweetener equivalent to 1 cup sugar
1 cup fresh orange juice
1 cup unsweetened pineapple chunks
1/2 cup (2 medium) eggs, beaten
1 banana, sliced thin
1/4 cup dried coconut, shredded
1 recipe Lorene's Graham Cracker Crust

Combine arrowroot, salt, sweetener, and orange juice. Drain pineapple and set fruit aside, using liquid and sufficient water to make 1 cup. Combine liquid, arrowroot mixture, and beaten eggs. Cook over medium heat, stirring constantly, until mixture boils and thickens. Remove from heat. Chill, then fold in pineapple chunks, sliced banana, and coconut. Place into crust and chill until ready to serve.

### ***APPLE TORTE

Exchanges per serving: 1 = 1 bread, 3 fat, 1 1/4 fruit.
Calories per serving: 245        Yield: 12 servings

2 cups flour
Non-nutritive sweetener equivalent to 1 1/3 cups sugar
3/4 cup diet margarine
1/4 cup (1 medium) egg
3 tablespoons lemon juice
1 cup water
10 apples, peeled, cored, and sliced
1/2 cup white raisins
1 teaspoon cinnamon

Preheat oven to 375°. Mix flour with 2/3 sweetener; crumble margarine into flour mixture with fingers until size of peas. Stir in egg with fork until well blended; work dough with hands until a smooth ball; divide into 3 sections. Wrap 1/3 dough in waxed paper and store in refrigerator until ready for top crust. Grease a 10" spring pan lightly and press remaining 2/3 of dough firmly and evenly over bottom and about 3/4 way up sides of pan. Set aside. Mix lemon juice and water; add apples a few at a time to the lemon-water to moisten each slice thoroughly. When apples are moistened, squeeze moisture out with hands and place apples in large bowl. Add raisins, balance of sweetener, and cinnamon. Stir and mix with apples. Place into crust. Roll refrigerated 1/3 dough on board which has been well floured, to 1" larger than pan. Fit dough over apples, pressing side and top together with wet fingers (so surface is flush with top). Prick pastry with fork several times. Bake 1 hour and 10 minutes. Cool 10 minutes; loosen but leave in pan until room temperature.

### ***PUMPKIN PIE

Exchanges per serving: 1 = 1/4 meat, 3/4 milk,
1/3 "B" vegetable.
Calories per serving: filling: 156       Yield: 8 servings
pastry: 135

| | |
|---|---|
| 1 1/2 cups canned or fresh cooked pumpkin | 1/4-1/2 teaspoon nutmeg |
| | 1/4-1/2 teaspoon cloves |
| Non-nutritive sweetener equivalent to 3/4 cup sugar | 1/2 cup (2 medium) eggs, slightly beaten |
| | 1 1/4 cups milk |
| 1/2 teaspoon salt | 2 cups evaporated milk |
| 1 1/4 teaspoons cinnamon | One 9" unbaked pastry |
| 1/2-1 teaspoon ginger | shell |

Preheat oven to 400°. Combine pumpkin, sweetener, salt, and spices thoroughly; blend in eggs, milk, and evaporated milk. Pour into unbaked pastry shell. Bake until knife inserted between center and outside comes out clean. Serve cool.

### ***POLLY'S PUMPKIN PIE

Exchanges per serving: 1 = 1/4 meat, 1/2 milk,
1 "B" vegetable.
1 pastry = 1 bread, 1 1/2 fat.

Calories per serving: filling: 135          Yield: 8 servings
                              pastry: 135

**Non-nutritive sweetener**          **1 3/4 cups evaporated**
  **equivalent to 1 cup sugar**  **milk, undiluted**
**1 1/2 teaspoons cinnamon**          **1/2 cup (2 medium) eggs,**
**1/2 teaspoon allspice**            **well beaten**
**1/2 teaspoon ginger**          **1 1/2 cups canned**
**1/2 teaspoon nutmeg**            **pumpkin**
**1/2 teaspoon cloves**          **Pastry for one 9" pie shell**

Preheat oven to 425°. Combine sweetener and spices, stir in evaporated milk and eggs and add pumpkin. Beat until smooth. Pour mixture into a chilled 9" pie shell (do not prick bottom of shell). Bake at 425° for 15 minutes, then reduce heat to 350° and bake until silver knife inserted at center of pie comes out clean (about 35-40 minutes). Cool.

### ***CHIFFON PUMPKIN PIE

Exchanges per serving: 1 = 1/2 meat, 1/4 milk,
                              1 "B" vegetable.
                              1 pastry = 1 bread, 1 1/2 fat.
Calories per serving: filling: 85          Yield: 8 servings
                              pastry: 135

**1 envelope unflavored**          **1/4 teaspoon ginger**
  **gelatin**          **1/2 teaspoon salt**
**1 cup evaporated milk,**          **Non-nutritive sweetener**
  **undiluted**            **equivalent to 3/4 cup**
**1/2 cup water**            **sugar**
**1 cup (4 medium) eggs,**          **1 1/4 cups canned pump-**
  **separated**            **kin, mashed**
**1/2 teaspoon nutmeg**          **Pastry for one 9" pie crust**
**1/2 teaspoon cinnamon**

Line a 9" pie plate with desired crust. Bake and cool. Combine first eight ingredients, reserving whites of eggs. Beat well. Stir and cook in top of double boiler until consistency of medium white sauce (about 10 minutes). Stir in sweetener. Place in refrigerator until cold. Beat whites until they form soft peaks. Fold pumpkin into gelatin mixture; add beaten egg whites carefully. Pour into pie shell and chill until set.

191

### ***CHIFFON EGGNOG PIE

Exchanges per serving: 1 = 1/2 fat, 1/4 skim milk.
1 pastry = 1 bread, 1 1/2 fat.
Calories per serving: filling: 70          Yield: 6 servings
pastry: 135

1 envelope unflavored
  gelatin
1/4 cup cold water
1 1/2 cups skim milk
Non-nutritive sweetener
  equivalent to 3/4 cup
  sugar
1/4 teaspoon salt

1/2 tablespoon arrowroot
  powder
1/4 cup (1 medium) egg,
  separated
1 teaspoon almond extract
1 tablespoon rum extract
Pastry for one 9" pie shell

Soften gelatin in cold water. Combine 1/2 of the skim milk, sweetener, and salt in top of double boiler. Make a paste from arrowroot powder and remaining milk; stir into first mixture. Cook over boiling water. Stir constantly until thick; beat egg yolks and add a little of the hot mixture to them; stir this into remaining hot liquid in double boiler. Cook another 2 minutes; remove from heat and stir in softened gelatin until dissolved. Chill until mixture begins to set, then stir in extracts. Beat egg whites very stiff and fold into gelatin mixture. Pour into baked pie shell and chill until firm. If desired, top with Low-Calorie Topping Whip or artificial whipped cream and sprinkle chocolate shavings over this.

### ***JIFFY BANANA CREAM PIE

Exchanges per serving: 1/8 filling = 1 fruit,
1/2 skim milk.
1/8 pastry = 1 bread, 1 1/2 fat.
Calories per serving: filling: 80          Yield: 1 pie
pastry: 135
pudding mix; consult package

2 packages dietetic vanilla
  pudding mix
2 cups skim milk

2 bananas, sliced (or other
  fruit such as peaches,
  strawberries, etc.)

192

Prepare pudding mix using the skim milk; cool slightly. Line 8″ pie pan with desired baked crust. Place banana slices to cover bottom of shell; fill with pudding and let stand until set.

### ***GREAT APPLE AND GRAPE PIE

Exchanges per serving: 1 = 1/2 fat, 2 fruit.
　　　　　　　　　　　1 pastry = 1 bread, 1 1/2 fat.
Calories per serving: filling: 105　　　　Yield: 6 servings
　　　　　　　　　　　pastry: 135

| | |
|---|---|
| 3 tablespoons tapioca | Non-nutritive sweetener |
| 1/16 teaspoon salt | equivalent to 1 cup sugar |
| 3 cups apples, cored, pared, and sliced | 2 tablespoons lemon juice |
| 2 cups seedless grapes, cut in halves | 1 tablespoon diet margarine, melted |
| 1/2 cup water | Pastry for one 9″ pie shell, unbaked |

Preheat oven to 425°. Mix tapioca and salt and toss with apples and grapes. Place into unbaked pie shell. Combine remaining ingredients and place over fruit. Cover top with aluminum foil and bake 15 minutes. Reduce heat to 325° and continue baking until apples are tender (about 50 minutes).

### ***MARY C'S PUMPKIN PIE

Exchanges per serving: 1 filling = 1/4 milk,
　　　　　　　　　　　1 "B" vegetable.
　　　　　　　　　　　1 pastry = 1 bread, 1 1/2 fat.
Calories per serving: filling: 100　　　　Yield: 6 servings
　　　　　　　　　　　pastry: 135

| | |
|---|---|
| 1/4 cup (1 medium) egg | 1/4 teaspoon cloves, finely grated |
| Non-nutritive sweetener equivalent to 1 cup sugar | 1 1/2 cups canned pumpkin |
| 3/4 teaspoon allspice | 3/4 cup evaporated milk |
| 3/4 teaspoon nutmeg | 3/4 cup fresh orange juice |
| 3/4 teaspoon cinnamon | One 9″ pastry shell, unbaked |
| 1/2 teaspoon ginger | |

Preheat oven to 425°. Combine egg, sweetener, spices, and pumpkin and blend well. Add milk and orange juice gradually; stir until well blended. Pour into unbaked pie shell. Bake 10-12 minutes, then reduce heat to 325° and bake until a knife inserted near center comes out clean (about 3/4 hour).

## ****APPLE PIE

Exchanges per serving: 1 filling = 1 fruit, 1/2 fat.
1 pastry = 2 bread, 3 fat.
Calories per serving: filling: 75      Yield: 8 servings
pastry: 265

| | |
|---|---|
| 3 cups tart apples | 1/16 teaspoon nutmeg |
| Non-nutritive sweetener equivalent to 3/4 cup sugar | 1/16 teaspoon salt |
| | Pastry for two-crust 9" pie |
| 2 tablespoons flour | 2 tablespoons diet margarine |
| 1/2 teaspoon cinnamon | |

Preheat oven to 400°. Pare apples and slice thin. Combine sweetener, flour, spices, and salt; mix with apples. Line pie plate with pastry; fill with apple mixture and dot with margarine. Place top crust on pie and sprinkle with sugar substitute, if desired. Bake about 50 minutes, or until done.

## ****QUICK APPLE PIE

Exchanges per serving: 1 = 1 fruit.
1 pastry = 2 bread, 3 fat.
Calories per serving: filling: 40      Yield: 8 servings
pastry: 265

| | |
|---|---|
| 4 cups apples, pared, and sliced very thin | 1 tablespoon arrowroot powder |
| 2 teaspoons lemon juice | Non-nutritive sweetener equivalent to 3/4 cup sugar |
| 1/4 teaspoon lemon peel, grated fine | |
| 1/4 teaspoon nutmeg | Pastry for two-crust Flaky Pie Crust |
| 1/2 teaspoon cinnamon | |

Preheat oven to 425°. Mix together everything except the pastry. Prepare crust, lining an 8″ pie plate. Fill with apple mix and top with second crust; flute edges. Make four or five cuts for air vents. Lightly cover fluted edges with aluminum foil to prevent excessive browning of crust. After about 30 minutes remove foil and continue baking until apples are tender (another 10-20 minutes). Cool.

## ****SHERRY'S APPLE PIE

Exchanges per serving: 1 = 1 fruit.
1 pastry = 2 bread, 3 fat.
Calories per serving: filling: 40      Yield: 6 servings
pastry: 265

| | |
|---|---|
| 5 apples, sliced | 1/16 teaspoon cinnamon |
| 2 teaspoons tapioca | Pastry for one-crust pie |
| Non-nutritive sweetener equivalent to 1/2 cup sugar | |

Preheat oven to 400°. Roll 1/2 of the crust recipe to fit a 9″ pie pan; arrange apple slices in crust; sprinkle tapioca, sweetener, and cinnamon over top. Roll out remaining crust and crimp edges securely over top (moisten edges between crusts with water if necessary), and perforate in about half dozen places. Bake until apples are tender (about 30 minutes). *If a one-crust pie is desired adjust exchange per serving to 1 bread, 1 1/2 fat, and subtract 130 calories per serving.*

## *RICE CEREAL PIE CRUST

Exchanges per serving: 1 serving = 1 fat.
Calories per serving: 50      Yield: 8 servings

| | |
|---|---|
| 1 cup crispy rice cereal, crushed | Non-nutritive sweetener equivalent to 4 tablespoons sugar |
| 2 tablespoons diet margarine, melted | |

Mix ingredients together and line bottom and sides of 8″ pan. Chill well before adding any desired filling.

## *CRUMBLY PIE CRUST

Exchanges per serving: 1″ slice = 1/2 fat.
Calories per serving: 35          Yield: One 10″ crust

3 tablespoons diet          3/4 cup cornflake crumbs
    margarine
Non-nutritive sweetener
    equivalent to 1 table-
    spoon sugar

Preheat oven to 375°. Mix margarine, sweetener, and crumbs; press into 9″ pie plate, with back of spoon. Press into bottom and up sides of plate (crust will be fairly thin).

## **RICH FLAKY CRUST

Exchanges per serving: 1 = 1 bread, 1 1/2 fat.
Calories per serving: 135          Yield: Two 8″ crusts

2 cups flour, sifted          1/2 cup oil
1 teaspoon salt               3 tablespoons cold water

Preheat oven to 450°. Sift flour and salt together, then dribble oil on surface. Stir with fork until completely mixed. Add cold water to form smooth ball. Divide dough in half. Place on waxed paper, cover with another piece of waxed paper, roll dough to 12″ circle. Peel off paper and fit into pie plate; flute edges with fork (or finger) which has been moistened. Bake until browned (12-15 minutes). Cool before filling. For two-crust pie, place one crust (unbaked) into pie plate, put in filling and top with other crust which has been slit in several places. Bake according to filling instructions. *For two-crust pie, allow 2 bread and 3 fat exchanges, and adjust calories to 265 per serving.*

## **PIE CRUST

Exchanges per serving: 1 = 1 1/4 bread, 2 fat.
Calories per serving: 190          Yield: 8 servings

| 1 1/3 cups flour, sifted | 1/2 cup diet margarine, |
| 1/2 teaspoon salt | melted |
| | 2 tablespoons cold water |

Sift flour and salt together, then dribble margarine over surface. Stir with fork until completely mixed. Add water over margarine and flour mixture and stir to smooth ball. Roll out dough to fit 8" pie plate. Flute edges with fork. Refrigerate if crust is to be filled prior to baking. If baked unfilled, make several cuts with sharp knife in bottom and sides of crust. Bake at 450° until golden brown (13-15 minutes).

## **LORENE'S GRAHAM CRACKER CRUST

Exchanges per serving: 1 = 1 bread, 1 fat.
Calories per serving: 115          Yield: 9 servings

| 1 cup graham crackers, | Non-nutritive sweetener |
| crushed fine | equivalent to 2 table- |
| 3 tablespoons diet marga- | spoons sugar |
| rine, melted | |

Preheat oven to 350°. Combine ingredients well and press firmly into a 9" pie plate. Bake about 10 minutes. Chill before filling.

## **PASTRY

Exchanges per serving: 1/8 crust = 1 bread, 1 1/2 fat.
Calories per serving: 135          Yield: One 8" crust

| 1 cup flour, sifted | 5 tablespoons diet |
| 1 teaspoon salt | margarine |
| | 4 tablespoons water |

Preheat oven to 425°. Combine flour and salt. Cut in margarine until consistency of peas. Add water slowly until the dough is moistened and holds together. Roll dough, pressing into a ball. Flour pastry board and rolling pin and roll gently, turning often. Roll thin, lay pastry over 8″ pie tin and press down gently, fluting edges. Slit bottom a few times with a sharp knife. Bake until golden brown (about 14-15 minutes). Fill with desired filling. Use extra dough for individual pastries.

# CANNING AND FREEZING
## and
# JAMS AND JELLIES

## Canning Fruits

To can fruits, use unsweetened fruit juice or water in place of the usual sugar-syrup. Be sure to adhere to processing time and other instructions, and when serving, count your fruit exchanges as you would for the commercially prepared sugar-free fruits.

Soak the fruit in lemon juice solution to keep it from darkening. Use sweetener equivalent to 2-4 cups of sugar for every 2-3 quarts of liquid; if this is not sweet enough (or yet too sweet) change it to suit your taste. The U. S. Department of Agriculture, Washington, D. C. 20402, has some excellent books on canning which you may wish to send for before trying any recipes. They cost about 20 cents each.

Use orange or pineapple juice, unsweetened, to obtain an unusual flavor. (These generally settle to the bottom of the jars, so shake well just before serving.) Another good variation is a half-and-half mixture of peaches and pears.

Raspberries and strawberries may be mashed and the juice saved; mixing this juice with water makes an excellent canning liquid.

Apples, grapes, peaches, pears, pineapple, and seedless oranges are fine to mix. Avoid fruits such as bananas, blueberries, cherries, plums, raspberries, and strawberries in fruit cocktail. (Bananas turn brown and become too soft, while the other fruits "weep" and become too liquid.)

Plums are fine for canning, but be sure you select the

proper varieties. Use half water and half plum juice for the canning liquid to help keep the color from being lost.

## Freezing Fruits Without Sugar

Wash and drain thoroughly blackberries, blueberries, cranberries, currants, gooseberries, grapes, pineapple chunks, plums, raspberries, or rhubarb. Leave about 1/2 inch at top of container when packing. Freeze.

Figs, peaches, and strawberries go into special containers, covered with the ascorbic acid water solution (1 teaspoon ascorbic acid—crystalline—to each quart of water). Package, leaving 1 inch at top of quarts and 1/2 inch for pints. Freeze. Thaw frozen fruits until all but a few ice crystals remain and sweeten as desired with non-nutritive sweetener.

## Jams and Jellies Without Sugar

Cover jars completely with water and bring water to boil. Boil 15-20 minutes. Then remove jars from water (hold tongs under boiling water 60-90 seconds before removing jars so jars do not break); drain jars upside down on aluminum foil paper until just before using, then turn to right side up.

Use your favorite non-nutritive sweetener, being careful to use proper amount needed. Stir until it is completely dissolved and mixed. (Do not reboil.)

In top of double boiler, over low heat, melt the paraffin. Pour jam or jellies into jars carefully, and pour on melted paraffin about 1/4 inch thickness. Cool. Place in refrigerator. Keep refrigerated, and after first opening, be sure to keep covered with tight lid or aluminum foil molded to top.

## Vegetables

Nearly any vegetable which can be cooked is recommended for freezing. Order the freezing booklet from the Department of Agriculture, Washington, D. C. 20402 (15-20¢).

# *CUCUMBER PICKLES

Exchanges per serving: 1 pint = None.
Calories per serving: 0                     Yield: 3 pints

6 cucumbers
1/4 cup salt
Non-nutritive sweetener
    equivalent to 3/4 cup
    sugar

1/4 cup water
2 cups white vinegar
2 tablespoons pickling
    spice

Wash and dry cucumbers, cut into strips about 4" long.
Place in large bowl and sprinkle with salt. Let stand overnight. In the morning rinse and drain well several times.
Combine sweetener, water, and vinegar in large pan and
bring to boil. Tie pickling spice in a cheesecloth bag and
add to boiling ingredients. Add cucumbers and reduce
heat; simmer about 15 minutes. Place cucumbers in clean
hot pint jars. Heat liquid once more to boiling point, and
pour over pickles in jars. Seal immediately.

# *APPLE BUTTER JELLY

Exchanges per serving: 1 tablespoon = 1/4 fruit.
Calories per serving: 10                Serves 5 3/4 cups

8 cups apples, washed and
    cut in quarters
2 cups unsweetened apple
    juice
1/4 cup lemon juice
1/4 cup cider vinegar
2 teaspoons lemon peel,
    ground fine

1/4 teaspoon nutmeg
1 teaspoon cloves
1/4 teaspoon anise seed,
    ground fine
Non-nutritive sweetener
    equivalent to 1/2 cup
    sugar

Prepare jelly jars. Mix all ingredients except sweetener.
Bring to a boil, stirring constantly; boil a few minutes.
Remove from heat, then stir in sweetener. Seal jars.

# *ANNE'S CHILI SAUCE

Exchanges per serving: 1 tablespoon = 1 "A" vegetable.
Calories per serving: 6                     Yield: 3 quarts

| | |
|---|---|
| 8 cups tomatoes, peeled and chopped | 1 tablespoon salt |
| | 1 1/2 cups cider vinegar |
| 1/4 cup red peppers, chopped fine | 1 tablespoon Tabasco sauce |
| | 1 whole stick cinnamon |
| 1/2 cup green peppers, chopped fine | 1 teaspoon cloves |
| | 1 1/2 teaspoons celery seed |
| 1 1/2 cups onion, chopped fine | 1 1/2 teaspoons mustard seed |
| 1 1/2 cups celery, chopped fine | 1 teaspoon Mei Yen seasoning |
| Non-nutritive sweetener equivalent to 1/2 cup sugar | |

In a large heavy pan combine first nine ingredients. Combine spices in a cheesecloth bag and add to first mixture. Bring to boil; reduce heat and simmer. Stir occasionally, simmering for about 5-6 hours. Remove bag of spices, pour remainder into clean, hot, pint jars and seal immediately.

## *RUTH'S RASPBERRY JAM

Exchanges per serving: 1 tablespoon = 1/8 fruit.
Calories per serving: 5                    Yield: 2 cups

| | |
|---|---|
| 1 1/2 teaspoons unflavored gelatin | Non-nutritive sweetener equivalent to 2/3 cup sugar |
| 1 1/2 tablespoons cold water | 1/4 teaspoon lemon juice |
| 3 cups fresh raspberries, crushed | 3 drops red food coloring (optional) |

Soften gelatin in cold water. Combine berries and sweetener in saucepan; place on high heat. Stir constantly until mixture boils, then remove from heat and add softened gelatin. Return to heat and cook for another minute. Remove and blend in lemon juice and food coloring. Place in pint jar. Seal and store in refrigerator.

## *ANNE'S APPLE JELLY

Exchanges per serving: 1 tablespoon = 1/4 fruit.
Calories per serving: 10                   Yield: 2 cups

| 2 teaspoons unflavored gelatin | 2 cups apple juice, unsweetened |
| 2 tablespoons lemon juice | Non-nutritive sweetener equivalent to 2 cups sugar |
| 1/8 teaspoon salt | |
| 1 teaspoon arrowroot powder | |

Prepare jelly jars. Mix the gelatin, lemon juice, salt, and arrowroot. Then stir in apple juice and boil, stirring constantly, for two minutes. Remove from heat. Stir in sweetener. Fill jelly jars, seal, and store.

## *BLUEBERRY JAM

Exchanges per serving: 1 tablespoon = 1/4 fruit.
Calories per serving: 10             Yield: 2 1/2 cups

| 2 tablespoons lemon juice | 2 1/2 cups frozen unsweetened blueberries, partially thawed |
| 3 teaspoons unflavored gelatin | |
| 1/8 teaspoon salt | Non-nutritive sweetener equivalent to 2 cups sugar |
| 1 1/2 teaspoons arrowroot powder | |

Prepare jelly jars. Mix lemon juice, gelatin, salt, and arrowroot, then stir in blueberries. Boil gently until mixture thickens, stirring constantly (about 3-4 minutes). Stir constantly, boiling at full boil for 2 minutes. Remove from heat; stir in sweetener. Fill jars.

## *PHYL'S APPLE JELLY

Exchanges per serving: 1 tablespoon = 1/4 fruit.
Calories per serving: 10             Yield: 2 cups

| 4 teaspoons unflavored gelatin | 1 1/2 teaspoons lemon juice |
| 2 cups unsweetened apple juice | 3 drops food coloring (yellow or green) |
| Non-nutritive sweetener equivalent to 1 cup sugar | |

Soften gelatin in 1/4 of the apple juice; bring rest of juice to boil. Remove from heat; add softened gelatin. Stir until dissolved; add sweetener, lemon juice, and food coloring. Bring to rolling boil. Place in clean pint jars; seal. Store in refrigerator.

## *APPLE-LEMON JELLY

Exchanges per serving: 1/2 cup = 1 fruit.
Calories per serving: 40                    Yield: 2 cups

1 package unflavored
  gelatin
2 tablespoons lemon juice
1/8 teaspoon salt
1 teaspoon arrowroot
  powder

2 cups apple juice,
  unsweetened
Non-nutritive sweetener
  equivalent to 2 cups
  sugar

Mix gelatin, lemon juice, salt, and arrowroot powder. Add apple juice and boil, stirring constantly, for two minutes. Remove from heat; add sweetener. Fill prepared jelly jars; seal.

## *STRAWBERRY JELLY

Exchanges per serving: 1 tablespoon = 1/4 fruit.
Calories per serving: 10                    Yield: 5 1/2 cups

2 envelopes unflavored
  gelatin
1/2 cup lemon juice
1/16 teaspoon salt
1 tablespoon arrowroot
  powder

4 cups strawberries, hulled,
  washed, and strained
Non-nutritive sweetener
  equivalent to 4 cups
  sugar

Mix gelatin, lemon juice, salt, and arrowroot, then add strawberries. Boil, stirring constantly, about 3 minutes. Remove from heat; stir in sweetener. Fill jars. Seal.

## *PINEAPPLE-APRICOT JAM

Exchanges per serving: 1 tablespoon = 1/2 fruit.
Calories per serving: 20                    Yield: 5 cups

| 2 cups dried apricots | 2 tablespoons lemon juice |
| 2 cups water | 1/16 teaspoon salt |
| 4 cups unsweetened pine- | Non-nutritive sweetener |
| apple tidbits | equivalent to 1 cup sugar |

Boil apricots in water until tender (about 25 minutes). Drain pineapple tidbits and cut each one in half. Puree apricots and water with lemon juice and salt. Return to saucepan and stir in pineapple. Boil a few minutes, stirring now and then. Remove from heat; add sweetener. Fill jelly jars, seal.

## *CONSERVE

Exchanges per serving: 1 tablespoon = 1/2 fat, 1/2 fruit.
Calories per serving: 42            Yield: 2 cups

| 1 cup dried apricots | 2 tablespoons lemon juice |
| 2 cups water | Non-nutritive sweetener |
| 2 1/4 cups unsweetened | equivalent to 1 cup sugar |
| pineapple tidbits | 1/2 cup nuts, finely |
| 1/8 teaspoon salt | chopped |

Boil apricots in water until tender. Puree. Drain pineapple tidbits, cut each piece into smaller pieces. Blend puree of apricots and water in saucepan; add pineapple, then salt and lemon juice. Boil slowly, stirring constantly, about 5 minutes. Remove from heat and stir in sweetener and nuts. Fill jars.

## *JOAN'S CHUTNEY

Exchanges per serving: 1/4 cup = 1 1/2 fruit.
Calories per serving: 60            Yield: 1 1/2 pints

| 3/4 cup white raisins | Non-nutritive sweetener |
| 1/4 cup bell peppers, | equivalent to 2 cups |
| chopped fine | sugar |
| 1 cup white vinegar | 1/2 teaspoon ginger |
| 4 pears, cored, pared, and | 1/4 teaspoon allspice |
| chopped | 1/4 teaspoon cloves |
| | 1/4 teaspoon salt |

Combine all the ingredients in large pan and bring to boil. Reduce heat to medium and cook until pears are tender and mixture is slightly thick (about an hour). Spoon into clean jars and seal immediately.

# TABLES AND CHARTS

# HEIGHT AND WEIGHT CHARTS

**DESIRABLE WEIGHT CHART FOR WOMEN, DRESSED**
(but minus coats, hats, purse, etc.)

| Height (with shoes) | Small Frame | Medium Frame | Large Frame | Calorie Intake |
|---|---|---|---|---|
| 4 ft. 10 in. | 92-98 | 96-107 | 104-119 | 1200-1500 |
| 4 ft. 11 in. | 94-101 | 98-110 | 106-122 | 1200-1500 |
| 5 ft. 0 in. | 96-104 | 98-110 | 109-125 | 1200-1500 |
| 5 ft. 1 in. | 99-107 | 104-116 | 112-128 | 1250-1575 |
| 5 ft. 2 in. | 102-110 | 107-119 | 115-131 | 1300-1650 |
| 5 ft. 3 in. | 105-113 | 110-122 | 118-134 | 1350-1725 |
| 5 ft. 4 in. | 108-116 | 113-126 | 121-138 | 1450-1800 |
| 5 ft. 5 in. | 111-119 | 116-130 | 125-142 | 1500-1850 |
| 5 ft. 6 in. | 114-123 | 120-135 | 129-146 | 1550-1950 |
| 5 ft. 7 in. | 118-127 | 124-139 | 133-150 | 1600-2000 |
| 5 ft. 8 in. | 122-131 | 128-143 | 137-154 | 1650-2100 |
| 5 ft. 9 in. | 126-135 | 132-147 | 141-158 | 1750-2200 |
| 5 ft. 10 in. | 130-140 | 136-151 | 145-163 | 1800-2300 |
| 5 ft. 11 in. | 134-144 | 140-155 | 149-168 | 1850-2300 |
| 6 ft. 0 in. | 138-148 | 144-159 | 153-173 | 1900-2400 |

## DESIRABLE WEIGHT CHART FOR MEN, DRESSED
(without outer garments, coat, hats., etc.)

| Height (with shoes) | Small Frame | Medium Frame | Large Frame | Calorie Intake |
|---|---|---|---|---|
| 5 ft.  2 in. | 112-120 | 118-129 | 126-141 | 1500-1850 |
| 5 ft.  3 in. | 115-123 | 121-133 | 129-144 | 1500-1900 |
| 5 ft.  4 in. | 118-126 | 124-136 | 132-148 | 1550-1950 |
| 5 ft.  5 in. | 121-129 | 127-139 | 135-152 | 1650-2050 |
| 5 ft.  6 in. | 124-133 | 130-143 | 138-156 | 1700-2150 |
| 5 ft.  7 in. | 128-137 | 134-147 | 142-161 | 1750-2200 |
| 5 ft.  8 in. | 132-141 | 138-152 | 147-166 | 1850-2300 |
| 5 ft.  9 in. | 136-145 | 142-156 | 151-170 | 1900-2400 |
| 5 ft. 10 in. | 140-150 | 146-160 | 155-174 | 1950-2500 |
| 5 ft. 11 in. | 144-154 | 150-165 | 159-179 | 2050-2550 |
| 6 ft.  0 in. | 148-158 | 154-170 | 164-184 | 2100-2650 |
| 6 ft.  1 in. | 152-162 | 158-175 | 168-189 | 2150-2800 |
| 6 ft.  2 in. | 156-167 | 162-180 | 173-194 | 2250-2850 |
| 6 ft.  3 in. | 160-171 | 167-185 | 178-199 | 2300-2900 |
| 6 ft.  4 in. | 164-175 | 172-190 | 182-204 | 2400-3000 |

*Courtesy Eli Lilly and Company, Indianapolis, Indiana*

## NUTRITIVE VALUES OF THE EDIBLE PART OF FOOD

| Food, approximate measure, and weight (In grams) | | Carbohydrate | Fat (total lipid) | Saturated (total) | Unsaturated Oleic | Linoleic | Food Energy | Protein | Water |
|---|---|---|---|---|---|---|---|---|---|
| | grams | grams | grams | grams | grams | grams | calories | grams | percent |
| **FATS, OILS** | | | | | | | | | |
| **Butter, 4 sticks per pound:** | | | | | | | | | |
| Sticks, 2 — 1 cup | 227 | 45 | 184 | 101 | 61 | 6 | 1,625 | 1 | 16 |
| Stick, ⅛ — 1 tablespoon | 14 | 3 | 11 | 6 | 4 | trace | 100 | trace | 16 |
| Pat or square (64 per lb.) — 1 pat | 7 | 1 | 6 | 3 | 2 | trace | 50 | trace | 16 |
| **Fats, cooking:** | | | | | | | | | |
| Lard — 1 cup | 200 | 0 | 220 | 84 | 101 | 22 | 1,985 | 0 | 0 |
| Lard — 1 tablespoon | 14 | 0 | 14 | 5 | 6 | 1 | 125 | 0 | 0 |
| Vegetable fats — 1 cup | 200 | 0 | 200 | 46 | 130 | 14 | 1,770 | 0 | 0 |
| Vegetable fats — 1 tablespoon | 12.5 | 0 | 12 | 3 | 8 | 1 | 110 | 0 | 0 |
| **Margarine, 4 sticks per pound:** | | | | | | | | | |
| Sticks, 2 — 1 cup | 227 | 1 | 184 | 37 | 105 | 33 | 1,635 | 1 | 16 |
| Stick, ⅛ — 1 tablespoon | 14 | trace | 11 | 2 | 6 | 2 | 100 | trace | 16 |
| Pat or square (64 per pound) — 1 pat | 7 | trace | 6 | 1 | 3 | 1 | 50 | trace | 16 |
| **Oils, salad or cooking:** | | | | | | | | | |
| Corn — 1 tablespoon | 14 | 0 | 14 | 1 | 4 | 7 | 125 | 0 | 0 |
| Cottonseed — 1 tablespoon | 14 | 0 | 14 | 4 | 3 | 7 | 125 | 0 | 0 |
| Olive — 1 tablespoon | 14 | 0 | 14 | 2 | 11 | 1 | 125 | 0 | 0 |
| Soybean — 1 tablespoon | 14 | 0 | 14 | 2 | 3 | 7 | 125 | 0 | 0 |

## Salad dressings:

| Food | Measure | | | | | | | | |
|---|---|---|---|---|---|---|---|---|---|
| Blue cheese | 1 tablespoon | 16 | 32 | 80 | 1 | 8 | 2 | 4 | 1 |
| Commercial, mayonnaise type | 1 tablespoon | 15 | 41 | 65 | trace | 6 | 1 | 3 | 2 |
| French | 1 tablespoon | 15 | 39 | 60 | trace | 6 | 1 | 3 | 3 |
| Home cooked, boiled | 1 tablespoon | 17 | 68 | 30 | 1 | 2 | 1 | trace | 3 |
| Mayonnaise | 1 tablespoon | 15 | 15 | 110 | trace | 12 | 3 | 6 | trace |
| Thousand Island | 1 tablespoon | 15 | 32 | 75 | trace | 8 | 2 | 4 | 2 |

## FRUITS AND FRUIT PRODUCTS

| Food | Measure | | | | | | | | |
|---|---|---|---|---|---|---|---|---|---|
| Apples, raw, medium 2½ inch. dia., about 3 per lb.[1] | 1 apple | 150 | 85 | 70 | trace | trace | | | 18 |
| Apple Brown Betty | 1 cup | 230 | 64 | 345 | 4 | 8 | 3 | 1 | 68 |
| Apple Juice, bottled or canned | 1 cup | 249 | 88 | 120 | trace | trace | | | 30 |
| Applesauce canned: Sweetened | 1 cup | 254 | 76 | 230 | 1 | trace | | | 60 |
| Unsweetened or artificially sweetened | 1 cup | 239 | 88 | 100 | trace | trace | | | 26 |
| Applesauce and apricots, canned, strained or junior (baby food) | 1 ounce | 28 | 77 | 25 | trace | trace | | | 6 |
| Apricots: Raw, about 12 per pound[1] | 3 apricots | 114 | 85 | 55 | 1 | trace | | | 14 |

1. Measure and weight apply to entire fruit including parts not usually eaten.

# NUTRITIVE VALUES OF THE EDIBLE PART OF FOOD

| Food, approximate measure, and weight (in grams) | | Carbohydrate | Fat (total lipid) | Saturated (total) | Unsaturated Oleic | Unsaturated Linoleic | Food Energy | Protein | Water |
|---|---|---|---|---|---|---|---|---|---|
| | grams | grams | grams | grams | grams | grams | calories | grams | percent |
| **Apricots (cont.)** | | | | | | | | | |
| Canned in heavy syrup: | | | | | | | | | |
| Halves and syrup 1 cup | 259 | 57 | trace | | | | 220 | 2 | 77 |
| Halves (medium) and syrup 4 halves; 2 tablespoons | 122 | 27 | trace | | | | 105 | 1 | 77 |
| Dried: | | | | | | | | | |
| Uncooked, 40 halves, small 1 cup | 150 | 100 | 1 | | | | 390 | 8 | 25 |
| Cooked, unsweetened, fruit and liquid 1 cup | 285 | 62 | 1 | | | | 240 | 5 | 76 |
| Apricot nectar, canned 1 cup | 250 | 36 | trace | | | | 140 | 1 | 85 |
| **Avocado, raw:** | | | | | | | | | |
| California varieties, mainly Fuerte: | | | | | | | | | |
| 10-ounce avocado, about 2½ inches by 4¼ inches, peeled and pitted ½ avocado | 108 | 6 | 18 | 4 | 8 | 2 | 185 | 2 | 74 |
| ½-inch cubes 1 cup | 152 | 9 | 26 | 5 | 12 | 3 | 260 | 3 | 74 |
| Florida varieties: | | | | | | | | | |
| 13-ounce avocado, | | | | | | | | | |

about 4 inches by 3 inches, peeled and pitted ½-inch cubes

| Food | Measure | | | | | | | | |
|---|---|---|---|---|---|---|---|---|---|
| ½ avocado | 123 | 11 | 14 | 3 | 6 | 2 | 160 | 2 | 78 |
| 1 cup | 152 | 13 | 17 | 3 | 8 | 2 | 195 | 2 | 78 |
| **Bananas,** raw, 6 by 1½ inches, about 3 per pound[1] — 1 banana | 150 | 23 | trace | | | | 85 | 1 | 76 |
| **Blackberries,** raw — 1 cup | 144 | 19 | 1 | | | | 85 | 2 | 84 |
| **Blueberries,** raw — 1 cup | 140 | 21 | 1 | | | | 85 | 1 | 83 |
| **Cantaloupes,** raw; medium, 5-inch dia., about 1⅔ pounds[1] — ½ melon | 385 | 14 | trace | | | | 60 | 1 | 91 |
| **Cherries:** Raw, sweet, with stems[1] — 1 cup | 130 | 20 | trace | | | | 80 | 2 | 80 |
| Canned, red, sour, pitted, heavy syrup — 1 cup | 260 | 59 | 1 | | | | 230 | 2 | 76 |
| **Cranberry** juice cocktail, canned — 1 cup | 250 | 41 | trace | | | | 160 | trace | 83 |
| Cranberry sauce, sweetened, canned, strained — 1 cup | 277 | 104 | 1 | | | | 405 | trace | 62 |

[1] Measure and weight apply to entire fruit including parts not usually eaten.

213

## NUTRITIVE VALUES OF THE EDIBLE PART OF FOOD

| Food, approximate measure, and weight (in grams) | | Carbohydrate | Fat (total lipid) | Fatty Acids | | | Food Energy | Protein | Water |
|---|---|---|---|---|---|---|---|---|---|
| | | | | Saturated (total) | Unsaturated Oleic | Linoleic | | | |
| | grams | grams | grams | grams | grams | grams | calories | grams | percent |
| **Dates,** domestic, natural and dry, pitted, cut | 1 cup | 178 | 130 | 1 | | | | 490 | 4 | 22 |
| **Figs:** | | | | | | | | | |
| Raw, small 1½ inch dia., about 12 per pound | 3 figs | 114 | 23 | trace | | | | 90 | 1 | 78 |
| Dried, large, 2 inch by 1 inch | 1 fig | 21 | 15 | trace | | | | 60 | 1 | 23 |
| **Fruit cocktail:** canned in heavy syrup, solids and liquid | 1 cup | 256 | 50 | 1 | | | | 195 | 1 | 80 |
| **Grapefruit:** | | | | | | | | | |
| Raw, medium, 4¼ inch diameter, size 64: | | | | | | | | | |
| White | ½ grapefruit | 285 | 14 | trace | | | | 55 | 1 | 89 |
| Pink or red¹ | ½ grapefruit | 285 | 15 | trace | | | | 60 | 1 | 89 |
| Raw sections, white | 1 cup | 194 | 20 | trace | | | | 75 | 1 | 89 |
| Canned, white: Syrup pack, solids and liquid | 1 cup | 249 | 44 | trace | | | | 175 | 1 | 81 |

214

| Food | Measure | | | | | | |
|---|---|---|---|---|---|---|---|
| Water pack, solids and liquid | 1 cup | 240 | 18 | trace | 70 | 1 | 91 |
| Grapefruit juice: | | | | | | | |
| Fresh | 1 cup | 246 | 23 | trace | 95 | 1 | 90 |
| Canned white: | | | | | | | |
| Unsweetened | 1 cup | 247 | 24 | trace | 100 | 1 | 89 |
| Sweetened | 1 cup | 250 | 32 | trace | 130 | 1 | 86 |
| Frozen, concentrate, unsweetened: | | | | | | | |
| Undiluted, can 6 fluid ounces | 1 can | 207 | 72 | 1 | 300 | 4 | 62 |
| Diluted with 3 parts water, by volume | 1 cup | 247 | 24 | trace | 100 | 1 | 89 |
| Frozen, concentrate, sweetened: | | | | | | | |
| Undiluted, can, 6 fluid ounces | 1 can | 211 | 85 | 1 | 350 | 3 | 57 |
| Diluted with 3 parts water, by volume | 1 cup | 249 | 28 | trace | 115 | 1 | 88 |
| Dehydrated: | | | | | | | |
| Crystals, can, net weight 4 ounces | 1 can | 114 | 103 | 1 | 430 | 5 | 1 |
| Prepared with water (1 pound yields about 1 gallon) | 1 cup | 247 | 24 | trace | 100 | 1 | 90 |
| Grapes, raw: | | | | | | | |
| American type (slip skin), such as Concord, Delaware, | | | | | | | |

215

1. Measure and weight apply to entire fruit including parts not usually eaten.

NUTRITIVE VALUES OF THE EDIBLE PART OF FOOD

| Food, approximate measure, and weight (in grams) | | Carbohydrate | Fat (total lipid) | Fatty Acids | | | Food Energy | Protein | Water |
|---|---|---|---|---|---|---|---|---|---|
| | | | | Saturated (total) | Unsaturated Oleic | Unsaturated Linoleic | | | |
| | grams | grams | grams | grams | grams | grams | calories | grams | percent |
| **Grapes** (cont.) | | | | | | | | | |
| Niagara, Catawba, and Scuppernong¹ 1 cup | | | | | | | | | |
| European type (adherent), such as Malaga, Muscat, Thompson Seedless, Emperor, and Flame | 153 | 15 | 1 | | | | 65 | 1 | 82 |
| Tokay 1 cup | 160 | 25 | trace | | | | 95 | 1 | 81 |
| Grape juice, bottled or canned 1 cup | 254 | 42 | trace | | | | 165 | 1 | 83 |
| **Lemons,** | | | | | | | | | |
| raw, medium, 2-1/5-inch diameter, size 150 1 lemon | 106 | 6 | trace | | | | 20 | 1 | 90 |
| Lemon juice: | | | | | | | | | |
| Fresh 1 cup | 246 | 20 | trace | | | | 60 | 1 | 91 |
| 1 tablespoon | 15 | 1 | trace | | | | 5 | trace | 91 |
| Canned, unsweetened 1 cup | 245 | 19 | trace | | | | 55 | 1 | 92 |
| Lemonade concentrate, frozen, sweetened: Undiluted, can, 6 fluid ounces 1 can | 220 | 112 | trace | | | | 430 | trace | 48 |

216

| Food | Measure | Weight | | | | | |
|---|---|---|---|---|---|---|---|
| Diluted with 4⅓ parts water, by volume | 1 cup | 248 | 28 | trace | 110 | trace | 88 |
| **Lime juice:** | | | | | | | |
| Fresh | 1 cup | 246 | 22 | trace | 65 | 1 | 90 |
| Canned | 1 cup | 246 | 22 | trace | 65 | 1 | 90 |
| **Limeade concentrate, frozen, sweetened:** | | | | | | | |
| Undiluted, can 6 fluid ounces | 1 can | 218 | 108 | trace | 410 | trace | 50 |
| Diluted with 4⅓ parts water, by volume | 1 cup | 248 | 27 | trace | 105 | trace | 90 |
| **Oranges, raw:** | | | | | | | |
| California, Navel (winter) 2-4/5-inch diameter, size 88[1] | 1 orange | 180 | 16 | trace | 60 | 2 | 85 |
| Florida, all varieties, 3-inch diameter | 1 orange | 210 | 19 | trace | 75 | 1 | 86 |
| **Orange juice:** | | | | | | | |
| Fresh: | | | | | | | |
| California, Valencia (summer) | 1 cup | 249 | 26 | 1 | 115 | 2 | 88 |
| Florida varieties: | | | | | | | |
| Early and mid-season | 1 cup | 247 | 23 | trace | 100 | 1 | 90 |
| Late season, Valencia | 1 cup | 248 | 26 | trace | 110 | 1 | 88 |

217

[1] Measure and weight apply to entire fruit including parts not usually eaten.

# NUTRITIVE VALUES OF THE EDIBLE PART OF FOOD

| Food, approximate measure, and weight (in grams) | | grams | Carbohydrate grams | Fat (total lipid) grams | Fatty Acids Saturated (total) grams | Unsaturated Oleic grams | Unsaturated Linoleic grams | Food Energy calories | Protein grams | Water percent |
|---|---|---|---|---|---|---|---|---|---|---|
| **Oranges (cont.)** | | | | | | | | | | |
| Canned, unsweetened | 1 cup | 249 | 28 | trace | | | | 120 | 2 | 87 |
| Frozen concentrate: | | | | | | | | | | |
| Undiluted, can, 6 fluid ounces | 1 can | 210 | 80 | trace | | | | 330 | 5 | 58 |
| Diluted with 3 parts water, by volume | 1 cup | 248 | 27 | trace | | | | 110 | 2 | 88 |
| Dehydrated: | | | | | | | | | | |
| Crystals, can, net weight 4 ounces | 1 can | 113 | 100 | 2 | | | | 430 | 6 | 1 |
| Prepared with water, 1 pound yields about 1 gallon | 1 cup | 248 | 27 | trace | | | | 115 | 1 | 88 |
| **Orange and grapefruit juice:** | | | | | | | | | | |
| Frozen concentrate: | | | | | | | | | | |
| Undiluted, can, 6 fluid ounces | 1 can | 209 | 78 | 1 | | | | 325 | 4 | 59 |
| Diluted with 3 parts water, by volume | 1 cup | 248 | 26 | trace | | | | 110 | 1 | 88 |
| **Papayas,** raw, ½-inch cubes | 1 cup | 182 | 18 | trace | | | | 70 | 1 | 89 |

## Peaches:

| | | | | | | | |
|---|---|---|---|---|---|---|---|
| **Raw:** | | | | | | | |
| Whole, medium, 2-inch diameter, about 4 per pound | 1 peach | 114 | 10 | trace | 35 | 1 | 89 |
| Sliced | 1 cup | 168 | 16 | trace | 65 | 1 | 89 |
| **Canned, yellow-fleshed, solids and liquid:** | | | | | | | |
| Syrup pack, heavy: | | | | | | | |
| Halves or Slices | 1 cup | 257 | 52 | trace | 200 | 1 | 79 |
| Halves (medium) Syrup | 2 halves, 2 tablespoons | 117 | 24 | trace | 90 | trace | 79 |
| Water pack | 1 cup | 245 | 20 | trace | 75 | 1 | 91 |
| Strained or chopped (baby food) | 1 ounce | 28 | 6 | trace | 25 | trace | 78 |
| **Dried:** | | | | | | | |
| Uncooked | 1 cup | 160 | 109 | 1 | 420 | 5 | 25 |
| Cooked, unsweetened, 10-12 halves and 6 tablespoons liquid | 1 cup | 270 | 58 | 1 | 220 | 3 | 77 |
| **Frozen:** | | | | | | | |
| Carton, 12 ounces, not thawed | 1 carton | 340 | 77 | trace | 300 | 1 | 76 |
| Can, 16 ounces, not thawed | 1 can | 454 | 103 | trace | 400 | 2 | 76 |
| Peach nectar, canned | 1 cup | 250 | 31 | trace | 120 | trace | 87 |

## NUTRITIVE VALUES OF THE EDIBLE PART OF FOOD

| Food, approximate measure, and weight (in grams) | | (grams) | Water (percent) | Protein (grams) | Food Energy (calories) | Fat (total lipid) (grams) | Fatty Acids Saturated (total) (grams) | Unsaturated Oleic (grams) | Unsaturated Linoleic (grams) | Carbohydrate (grams) |
|---|---|---|---|---|---|---|---|---|---|---|
| **Pears:** | | | | | | | | | | |
| Raw, 3-inch x 2½-inch diameter[1] | 1 pear | 182 | 83 | 1 | 100 | 1 | | | | 25 |
| Canned, solids and liquid: | | | | | | | | | | |
| Syrup pack, heavy: | | | | | | | | | | |
| Halves or Slices | 1 cup | 255 | 80 | 1 | 195 | 1 | | | | 50 |
| Halves (medium) Syrup | 2 halves, 2 tablespoons | 117 | 80 | trace | 90 | trace | | | | 23 |
| Water pack | 1 cup | 243 | 91 | trace | 80 | trace | | | | 20 |
| Strained or chopped (baby food) | 1 ounce | 28 | 82 | trace | 20 | trace | | | | 5 |
| Pear nectar, canned | 1 cup | 250 | 86 | 1 | 130 | trace | | | | 33 |
| **Persimmons,** | | | | | | | | | | |
| Japanese or kaki, raw, seedless, 2½-inch diameter[1] | 1 persimmon | 125 | 79 | 1 | 75 | trace | | | | 20 |
| **Pineapple:** | | | | | | | | | | |
| Raw, diced | 1 cup | 140 | 85 | 1 | 75 | trace | | | | 19 |
| Canned, heavy syrup pack, solids and liquid: | | | | | | | | | | |
| Crushed | 1 cup | 260 | 80 | 1 | 195 | trace | | | | 50 |

| | | | | | | | |
|---|---|---|---|---|---|---|---|
| Sliced, slices and juice | 2 small or 1 large / 2 tablespoons | 122 | 80 | 90 | trace | trace | 24 |
| Pineapple juice, canned | 1 cup | 249 | 86 | 135 | 1 | trace | 34 |
| **Plums, all except prunes:** Raw, 2-inch diameter, about 2 ounces[1] | 1 plum | 60 | 87 | 25 | trace | trace | 7 |
| Plums (without pits) and juice | 3 plums / 2 tablespoons | 122 | 77 | 100 | trace | trace | 26 |
| **Prunes, dried, "softenized," medium:** Uncooked[1] | 4 prunes | 32 | 28 | 70 | 1 | trace | 18 |
| Cooked, unsweetened, 17-18 prunes and 1/3 cup liquid[1] | 1 cup | 270 | 66 | 295 | 2 | 1 | 78 |
| Prunes with tapioca, canned, strained or junior (baby food) | 1 ounce | 28 | 80 | 200 | 1 | trace | 6 |
| Prune juice, canned | 1 cup | 256 | 80 | 200 | 1 | trace | 49 |
| **Raisins,** dried | 1 cup | 160 | 18 | 460 | 4 | trace | 124 |
| **Raspberries, red:** Raw | 1 cup | 123 | 84 | 70 | 1 | 1 | 17 |
| Frozen, 10-ounce carton, not thawed | 1 carton | 284 | 74 | 275 | 2 | 1 | 70 |

1.Measure and weight apply to entire fruit including parts not usually eaten.

# NUTRITIVE VALUES OF THE EDIBLE PART OF FOOD

| Food, approximate measure, and weight (in grams) | | Carbohydrate | Fat (total lipid) | Fatty Acids Saturated (total) | Fatty Acids Unsaturated Oleic | Fatty Acids Unsaturated Linoleic | Food Energy | Protein | Water |
|---|---|---|---|---|---|---|---|---|---|
| | grams | grams | grams | grams | grams | grams | calories | grams | percent |
| **Rhubarb,** | | | | | | | | | |
| cooked, sugar added | 1 cup | 272 | 98 | trace | | | | 385 | 1 | 63 |
| **Strawberries:** | | | | | | | | | |
| Raw, capped | 1 cup | 149 | 13 | 1 | | | | 55 | 1 | 90 |
| Frozen, 10-ounce carton, not thawed | 1 carton | 284 | 79 | 1 | | | | 310 | 1 | 71 |
| Frozen, 16-ounce can, not thawed | 1 can | 454 | 126 | 1 | | | | 495 | 2 | 71 |
| **Tangerines,** | | | | | | | | | |
| raw, medium, 2½-inch diameter, about 4 per pound[1] | 1 tangerine | 114 | 10 | trace | | | | 40 | 1 | 87 |
| **Tangerine juice:** | | | | | | | | | |
| Canned, unsweetened | 1 cup | 248 | 25 | trace | | | | 105 | 1 | 89 |
| Frozen concentrate: Undiluted, can, 6 fluid ounces | 1 can | 210 | 80 | 1 | | | | 340 | 4 | 58 |
| Diluted with 3 parts water, by volume | 1 cup | 248 | 27 | trace | | | | 115 | 1 | 88 |

222

## GRAIN PRODUCTS

| Food and description | Measure | Grams | Food energy (Cal.) | Protein (g) | Fat (g) | Saturated fatty acids (g) | Oleic (g) | Linoleic (g) | Carbohydrate (g) | Water (%) |
|---|---|---|---|---|---|---|---|---|---|---|
| Watermelon, raw, wedge, 4 inches by 8 inches (1/16 of 10 by 16-inch melon, about 2 pounds with rind)[1] | 1 wedge | 925 | 115 | 2 | 1 | trace | 1 | 1 | 27 | 93 |
| **Barley,** pearled, light, uncooked | 1 cup | 203 | 710 | 17 | 2 | 2 | 3 | 1 | 160 | 11 |
| **Biscuits,** baking powder with enriched flour, 2½-inch diameter | 1 biscuit | 38 | 140 | 3 | 6 |  | 3 | 1 | 17 | 27 |
| **Bran flakes** (40 percent bran) added thiamine | 1 ounce | 28 | 85 | 3 | 1 | 2 |  |  | 23 | 3 |
| **Breads:** Boston brown bread, Slice, 3 inches x ¾ inch | 1 slice | 48 | 100 | 3 | 1 |  | 5 |  | 22 | 45 |
| Cracked-wheat bread: Loaf, 1-pound (20 slices) | 1 loaf | 454 | 1,190 | 39 | 10 |  | 8 | 2 | 236 | 35 |
| Slice | 1 slice | 23 | 60 | 2 | 1 |  |  |  | 12 | 35 |
| French or Vienna bread: Enriched, 1-pound loaf | 1 loaf | 454 | 1,315 | 41 | 14 | 3 | 8 | 2 | 251 | 31 |
| Unenriched, 1-pound loaf | 1 loaf | 454 | 1,315 | 41 | 14 | 3 | 8 | 2 | 251 | 31 |

[1] Measure and weight apply to entire fruit including parts not usually eaten.

# NUTRITIVE VALUES OF THE EDIBLE PART OF FOOD

| Food, approximate measure, and weight (in grams) | | Carbohydrate | Fat (total lipid) | Fatty Acids Saturated (total) | Unsaturated – Oleic | Unsaturated – Linoleic | Food Energy | Protein | Water |
|---|---|---|---|---|---|---|---|---|---|
| | grams | grams | grams | grams | grams | grams | calories | grams | percent |
| **Breads (cont.)** | | | | | | | | | |
| Italian bread: | | | | | | | | | |
| Enriched, 1-pound loaf    1 loaf | 454 | 256 | 4 | trace | 1 | 2 | 1,250 | 41 | 32 |
| Unenriched, 1-pound loaf    1 loaf | 454 | 256 | 4 | trace | 1 | 2 | 1,250 | 41 | 32 |
| Raisin bread: | | | | | | | | | |
| Loaf, 1-pound    1 loaf | 454 | 243 | 13 | 3 | 8 | 2 | 1,190 | 30 | 35 |
| Slice    1 slice | 23 | 12 | 1 | | | | 60 | 2 | 35 |
| Rye bread: | | | | | | | | | |
| American, light (⅓ rye, ⅔ wheat): | | | | | | | | | |
| Loaf, 1 pound,    1 loaf | 454 | 236 | 5 | | | | 1,100 | 41 | 36 |
| 20 slices    1 slice | 23 | 12 | trace | | | | 55 | 2 | 36 |
| Pumpernickel, loaf, 1 pound    1 loaf | 454 | 241 | 5 | | | | 1,115 | 41 | 34 |
| White bread, enriched; 1 to 2 percent nonfat dry milk: | | | | | | | | | |
| Loaf, 1-pound    1 loaf | 454 | 229 | 15 | 3 | 8 | 2 | 1,225 | 39 | 36 |
| 20 slices    1 slice | 23 | 12 | 1 | trace | trace | trace | 60 | 2 | 36 |

3 to 4 percent nonfat dry milk:[2]

| | | | | | | | | | |
|---|---|---|---|---|---|---|---|---|---|
| Loaf, 1-pound | 1 loaf | 454 | 229 | 15 | 3 | 8 | 2 | 1,225 | 39 | 36 |
| Slice, 20 per loaf | 1 slice | 23 | 12 | 1 | trace | trace | trace | 60 | 2 | 36 |
| Slice, toasted | 1 slice | 20 | 12 | 1 | trace | trace | trace | 60 | 2 | 25 |
| Slice, 26 per loaf | 1 slice | 17 | 9 | 1 | trace | trace | trace | 45 | 1 | 36 |

5 to 6 percent nonfat dry milk:

| | | | | | | | | | |
|---|---|---|---|---|---|---|---|---|---|
| Loaf, 1-pound, 20 slices | 1 loaf | 454 | 228 | 17 | 4 | 10 | 2 | 1,245 | 41 | 35 |
| Slice | 1 slice | 23 | 12 | 1 | trace | trace | trace | 65 | 2 | 35 |

White bread, unenriched:

1 to 2 percent nonfat dry milk:

| | | | | | | | | | |
|---|---|---|---|---|---|---|---|---|---|
| Loaf, 1-pound, 20 slices | 1 loaf | 454 | 229 | 15 | 3 | 8 | 2 | 1,225 | 39 | 36 |
| Slice | 1 slice | 23 | 12 | 1 | trace | trace | trace | 60 | 2 | 36 |

3 to 4 percent nonfat dry milk:[2]

| | | | | | | | | | |
|---|---|---|---|---|---|---|---|---|---|
| Loaf, 1-pound, 20 per loaf | 1 loaf | 454 | 229 | 15 | 3 | 8 | 2 | 1,225 | 39 | 36 |
| Slice | 1 slice | 23 | 12 | 1 | trace | trace | trace | 60 | 2 | 36 |
| Slice, toasted | 1 slice | 20 | 12 | 1 | trace | trace | trace | 60 | 2 | 25 |

[2] When the amount of nonfat dry milk in commercial white bread is unknown, values for bread with 3 or 4 percent nonfat dry milk are suggested.

## NUTRITIVE VALUES OF THE EDIBLE PART OF FOOD

| Food, approximate measure, and weight (in grams) | | Carbohydrate | Fat (total lipid) | Fatty Acids | | | Food Energy | Protein | Water |
|---|---|---|---|---|---|---|---|---|---|
| | | | | Saturated (total) | Unsaturated Oleic | Unsaturated Linoleic | | | |
| | grams | grams | grams | grams | grams | grams | calories | grams | percent |
| **Breads** (cont.) | | | | | | | | | |
| Slice, 26 per loaf | | | | | | | | | |
| 5 to 6 percent nonfat dry milk: | | | | | | | | | |
| Slice, 1 slice | 17 | 9 | 1 | trace | trace | trace | 45 | 1 | 36 |
| Loaf, 1-pound, 20 slices | 454 | 228 | 17 | 4 | 10 | 2 | 1,245 | 41 | 35 |
| Slice, 1 slice | 23 | 12 | 1 | trace | trace | trace | 65 | 2 | 35 |
| Whole-wheat bread, made with 2 percent nonfat dry milk: | | | | | | | | | |
| Loaf, 1-pound, 20 slices | 454 | 216 | 14 | 3 | 6 | 3 | 1,105 | 48 | 36 |
| Slice, 1 slice | 23 | 11 | 1 | trace | trace | trace | 55 | 2 | 36 |
| Slice, toasted, 1 slice | 19 | 11 | 1 | trace | trace | trace | 55 | 2 | 24 |
| Bread crumbs, dry grated, 1 cup | 88 | 65 | 4 | 1 | 2 | 1 | 345 | 11 | 6 |
| **Cakes:[3]** | | | | | | | | | |
| Angel food cake; sector, 2-inch (1/12 of 8-inch diameter cake) 1 sector | 40 | 24 | trace | | | | 110 | 3 | 32 |
| Chocolate cake, chocolate | | | | | | | | | |

| Food | Measure | | | | | | | | |
|---|---|---|---|---|---|---|---|---|---|
| icing; sector, 2-inch (1/16 of 10-inch diameter layer cake) | 1 sector | 120 | 67 | 20 | 8 | 10 | 1 | 445 | 5 | 22 |
| Fruitcake, dark (made with enriched flour); piece, 2 inches by 2 inches by ½ inch | 1 piece | 30 | 18 | 5 | 1 | 3 | 1 | 115 | 1 | 18 |
| Gingerbread (made with enriched flour); piece, 2 inches by 2 inches by 2 inches | 1 piece | 55 | 29 | 6 | 1 | 4 | trace | 175 | 2 | 31 |
| Plain cake and cupcakes without icing: Piece, 3 inches by 2 inches by 1½ inches | 1 piece | 55 | 31 | 8 | 2 | 5 | 1 | 200 | 2 | 24 |
| Cupcake, 2¾-inch diameter | 1 cupcake | 40 | 22 | 6 | 1 | 3 | trace | 145 | 2 | 24 |
| Plain cake and cupcakes, with chocolate icing: Sector, 2-inch (1/16 of 10-inch layer cake) | 1 sector | 100 | 59 | 14 | 5 | 7 | 1 | 370 | 4 | 21 |
| Cupcake, 2¾-inch diameter | 1 cupcake | 50 | 30 | 7 | 2 | 4 | trace | 185 | 2 | 21 |
| Pound cake, old-fashioned (equal weights flour, sugar, fat, eggs); Slice, 2¾ inches by 3 inches by ⅝ inch | 1 slice | 30 | 14 | 9 | 2 | 5 | 1 | 140 | 2 | 17 |

a. Unenriched cake flour and vegetable cooking fat used unless otherwise specified.

227

# NUTRITIVE VALUES OF THE EDIBLE PART OF FOOD

| Food, approximate measure, and weight (in grams) | | | Carbohydrate | Fat (total lipid) | Fatty Acids Saturated (total) | Unsaturated Oleic | Unsaturated Linoleic | Food Energy | Protein | Water |
|---|---|---|---|---|---|---|---|---|---|---|
| | | grams | grams | grams | grams | grams | grams | calories | grams | percent |
| **Cakes (cont.)** | | | | | | | | | | |
| Sponge cake; sector, 2-inch (1/12 of 8-inch diameter cake) | 1 sector | 40 | 22 | 2 | 1 | 1 | trace | 120 | 3 | 32 |
| **Cookies:** | | | | | | | | | | |
| Plain and assorted, 3-inch diameter | 1 cookie | 25 | 18 | 5 | | | | 120 | 1 | 3 |
| Fig bars, small | 1 fig bar | 16 | 12 | 1 | | | | 55 | 1 | 14 |
| Corn, rice and wheat flakes, mixed, added nutrients | 1 ounce | 28 | 24 | trace | | | | 110 | 2 | 3 |
| **Cornflakes, added nutrients:** | | | | | | | | | | |
| Plain | 1 ounce | 28 | 24 | trace | | | | 110 | 2 | 4 |
| Sugar-covered | 1 ounce | 28 | 26 | trace | | | | 110 | 1 | 2 |
| **Corn grits, degermed, cooked:** | | | | | | | | | | |
| Enriched | 1 cup | 242 | 27 | trace | | | | 120 | 3 | 87 |
| Unenriched | 1 cup | 242 | 27 | trace | | | | 120 | 3 | 87 |
| **Cornmeal, white or yellow, dry:** | | | | | | | | | | |
| Whole ground, unbolted | 1 cup | 118 | 87 | 5 | 1 | 2 | 2 | 420 | 11 | 12 |
| Degermed, enriched | 1 cup | 145 | 114 | 2 | trace | 1 | 1 | 525 | 11 | 12 |

| Food | Measure | | | | | | | | | |
|---|---|---|---|---|---|---|---|---|---|---|
| Corn muffins, made with enriched degermed cornmeal and enriched flour; muffin 2¾-inch diameter | 1 muffin | 48 | 23 | 5 | 2 | 2 | trace | 150 | 3 | 33 |
| Corn, puffed, presweetened, added nutrients | 1 ounce | 28 | 26 | trace | | | | 110 | 1 | 5 |
| Corn, shredded, added nutrients | 1 ounce | 28 | 25 | trace | | | | 110 | 2 | 3 |
| Crackers: | | | | | | | | | | |
| Graham, plain | 4 small or 2 medium | 14 | 10 | 1 | | | | 55 | 1 | 6 |
| Saltines, 2 inches square | 2 crackers | 8 | 6 | 1 | | | | 35 | 1 | 4 |
| Soda: | | | | | | | | | | |
| Cracker, 2½ inches square | 2 crackers | 11 | 8 | 1 | trace | 1 | trace | 50 | 1 | 4 |
| Oyster crackers | 10 crackers | 10 | 7 | 1 | trace | 1 | trace | 45 | 1 | 4 |
| Cracker meal | 1 tablespoon | 10 | 7 | 1 | trace | 1 | trace | 45 | 1 | 6 |
| Doughnuts, cake type | 1 doughnut | 32 | 16 | 6 | 1 | 4 | trace | 125 | 1 | 24 |
| Farina, regular, enriched, cooked | 1 cup | 238 | 21 | trace | | | | 100 | 3 | 90 |
| Macaroni, cooked: | | | | | | | | | | |
| Enriched: | | | | | | | | | | |
| Cooked, firm stage (8 to 10 minutes; undergoes additional cooking in a food mixture) | 1 cup | 130 | 39 | 1 | | | | 190 | 6 | 64 |
| Cooked until tender | 1 cup | 140 | 32 | 1 | | | | 155 | 5 | 72 |

## NUTRITIVE VALUES OF THE EDIBLE PART OF FOOD

| Food, approximate measure, and weight (in grams) | | Carbohydrate | Fat (total lipid) | Fatty Acids Saturated (total) | Unsaturated Oleic | Linoleic | Food Energy | Protein | Water |
|---|---|---|---|---|---|---|---|---|---|
| | grams | grams | grams | grams | grams | grams | calories | grams | percent |
| **Macaroni** (cont.) | | | | | | | | | |
| Unenriched: | | | | | | | | | |
| Cooked, firm stage (8 to 10 minutes; undergoes additional cooking in a food mixture) 1 cup | 130 | 39 | 1 | | | | 190 | 6 | 64 |
| Cooked until tender 1 cup | 140 | 32 | 1 | | | | 155 | 5 | 72 |
| Macaroni (enriched) and cheese, baked 1 cup | 220 | 44 | 24 | 11 | 10 | 1 | 470 | 18 | 58 |
| **Muffins,** with enriched white flour; muffin 2¾-inch diameter 1 muffin | 48 | 20 | 5 | 1 | 3 | trace | 140 | 4 | 38 |
| **Noodles** (egg noodles), cooked: | | | | | | | | | |
| Enriched 1 cup | 160 | 37 | 2 | 1 | 1 | trace | 200 | 7 | 70 |
| Unenriched 1 cup | 160 | 37 | 2 | 1 | 1 | trace | 200 | 7 | 70 |
| **Oats** (with or without corn) puffed, added nutrient 1 ounce | 28 | 21 | 2 | trace | 1 | 1 | 115 | 3 | 3 |
| Oatmeal or rolled oats, regular or quick-cooking, cooked 1 cup | 236 | 23 | 2 | trace | 1 | 1 | 130 | 5 | 86 |
| **Pancakes** (griddlecakes), 4-inch diameter: | | | | | | | | | |

| Food | Measure | | | | | | | | | |
|---|---|--|--|--|--|--|--|--|--|--|
| Wheat, enriched flour (home recipe) | 1 cake | 27 | 9 | 2 | trace | 1 | trace | 60 | 2 | 50 |
| Buckwheat (buckwheat pancake mix, made with egg and milk) | 1 cake | 27 | 6 | 2 | 1 | 1 | trace | 55 | 2 | 58 |
| **Piecrust, plain, baked:** Enriched flour: | | | | | | | | | | |
| Lower crust, 9-inch shell | 1 crust | 135 | 59 | 45 | 10 | 29 | 3 | 675 | 8 | 15 |
| Double crust, 9-inch pie | 1 double crust | 270 | 118 | 90 | 21 | 58 | 7 | 1,350 | 16 | 15 |
| **Pies** (piecrust made with unenriched flour); sector, 4-inch, 1/7 of 9-inch pie: | | | | | | | | | | |
| Apple | 1 sector | 135 | 51 | 15 | 4 | 9 | 1 | 345 | 3 | 48 |
| Cherry | 1 sector | 135 | 52 | 15 | 4 | 10 | 1 | 355 | 4 | 47 |
| Custard | 1 sector | 130 | 30 | 14 | 5 | 8 | 1 | 280 | 8 | 58 |
| Lemon Meringue | 1 sector | 120 | 45 | 12 | 4 | 7 | 1 | 305 | 4 | 47 |
| Mince | 1 sector | 135 | 56 | 16 | 4 | 10 | 1 | 365 | 3 | 43 |
| Pumpkin | 1 sector | 130 | 32 | 15 | 5 | 7 | 1 | 275 | 5 | 59 |
| **Pizza** (cheese); 5½-inch sector; ⅛ of 14-inch diameter pie | 1 sector | 75 | 27 | 6 | 2 | 3 | trace | 185 | 7 | 45 |
| **Popcorn,** popped, with added oil and salt | 1 cup | 14 | 8 | 3 | 2 | trace | trace | 65 | 1 | 3 |
| **Pretzels,** small stick | 5 sticks | 4 | 4 | trace | 2 | trace | | 20 | trace | 8 |

NUTRITIVE VALUES OF THE EDIBLE PART OF FOOD

| Food, approximate measure, and weight (in grams) | | Carbohydrate | Fat (total lipid) | Fatty Acids Saturated (total) | Unsaturated Oleic | Unsaturated Linoleic | Food Energy | Protein | Water |
|---|---|---|---|---|---|---|---|---|---|
| | grams | grams | grams | grams | grams | grams | calories | grams | percent |
| Rice, white (fully milled or polished), enriched, cooked: | | | | | | | | | |
| Common commercial varieties, all types  1 cup | 168 | 41 | trace | | | | 185 | 3 | 73 |
| Long grain, parboiled  1 cup | 176 | 41 | trace | | | | 185 | 4 | 73 |
| Rice, puffed, added nutrients (without salt)  1 cup | 14 | 13 | trace | | | | 55 | 1 | 4 |
| Rice flakes, added nutrients  1 cup | 30 | 26 | trace | | | | 115 | 2 | 3 |
| Rolls: | | | | | | | | | |
| Plain, pan; 12 per 16 ounces: | | | | | | | | | |
| Enriched  1 roll | 38 | 20 | 2 | trace | 1 | trace | 115 | 3 | 31 |
| Unenriched  1 roll | 38 | 20 | 2 | trace | 1 | trace | 115 | 3 | 31 |
| Hard, round; 12 per 22 ounces  1 roll | 52 | 31 | 2 | trace | 1 | trace | 160 | 5 | 25 |
| Sweet, pan; 12 per 18 ounces  1 roll | 43 | 21 | 4 | 1 | 2 | trace | 135 | 4 | 32 |
| Rye wafers, whole-grain, 1⅞ inches by 3½ inches  2 wafers | 13 | 10 | trace | | | | 45 | 2 | 6 |

| Food | Amount | g | g | g | g | g | | | |
|---|---|---|---|---|---|---|---|---|---|
| **Spaghetti** with meatballs in tomato sauce (home recipe) | 1 cup | 250 | 37 | 9 | 2 | 5 | 1 | 260 | 9 | 77 |
| **Waffles,** with enriched flour, ½ inch by 4½ inches by 5½ inches | 1 waffle | 75 | 28 | 7 | 2 | 4 | 1 | 210 | 7 | 41 |
| **Wheat, puffed:** | | | | | | | | | | |
| With added nutrients (without salt) | 1 ounce | 28 | 22 | trace | | | | 105 | 4 | 3 |
| With added nutrients, with sugar and honey | 1 ounce | 28 | 25 | 1 | | | | 105 | 2 | 3 |
| Wheat, rolled: cooked | 1 cup | 235 | 40 | 1 | | | | 100 | 3 | 7 |
| Wheat, shredded, plain (long, round, or bite-size) | 1 ounce | 28 | 23 | 1 | | | | 100 | 3 | 7 |
| Wheat and malted barley flakes, with added nutrients | 1 ounce | 28 | 23 | trace | | | | 100 | 3 | 4 |
| **Wheat flours:** | | | | | | | | | | |
| Whole-wheat, from hard wheats, stirred | 1 cup | 120 | 85 | 2 | trace | 1 | 1 | 400 | 16 | 12 |
| All-purpose or family flour: | | | | | | | | | | |
| Enriched, sifted | 1 cup | 110 | 84 | 1 | trace | trace | trace | 400 | 12 | 12 |
| Unenriched, sifted | 1 cup | 110 | 84 | 1 | trace | trace | trace | 400 | 12 | 12 |

NUTRITIVE VALUES OF THE EDIBLE PART OF FOOD

| Food, approximate measure, and weight (in grams) | | | Carbohydrate | Fat (total lipid) | Fatty Acids | | | Food Energy | Protein | Water |
| --- | --- | --- | --- | --- | --- | --- | --- | --- | --- | --- |
| | | | | | Saturated (total) | Unsaturated | | | | |
| | | | | | | Oleic | Linoleic | | | |
| | | grams | grams | grams | grams | grams | grams | calories | grams | percent |
| **Wheat (cont.)** | | | | | | | | | | |
| Self-rising, enriched | 1 cup | 110 | 82 | 1 | trace | trace | trace | 385 | 1 | 11 |
| Cake or pastry flour, sifted | 1 cup | 100 | 79 | 1 | trace | trace | trace | 365 | 8 | 12 |
| **Wheat germ,** crude, commercially milled | 1 cup | 68 | 32 | 7 | 1 | 2 | 4 | 245 | 18 | 11 |
| **MATURE DRY BEANS AND PEAS, NUTS, PEANUTS: RELATED PRODUCTS** | | | | | | | | | | |
| **Almonds,** shelled | 1 cup | 142 | 28 | 77 | 6 | 52 | 15 | 850 | 26 | 5 |
| **Beans, dry:** | | | | | | | | | | |
| Common varieties, such as Great Northern, navy, and others, canned: | | | | | | | | | | |
| Red | 1 cup | 256 | 42 | 1 | | | | 230 | 15 | 76 |
| White, with tomato sauce: | | | | | | | | | | |
| with pork | 1 cup | 261 | 50 | 7 | 3 | 3 | 1 | 320 | 16 | 71 |
| without pork | 1 cup | 261 | 60 | 1 | | | | 310 | 16 | 68 |
| Lima, cooked | 1 cup | 192 | 48 | 1 | | | | 260 | 16 | 64 |

234

| | | | | | | | | | |
|---|---|---|---|---|---|---|---|---|---|
| Brazil nuts | 1 cup | 140 | 24 | 94 | 19 | 45 | 24 | 915 | 20 | 5 |
| Cashew nuts, roasted | 1 cup | 135 | 40 | 62 | 10 | 43 | 4 | 760 | 23 | 5 |
| **Coconut:** | | | | | | | | | | |
| Fresh, shredded | 1 cup | 97 | 9 | 34 | 29 | 2 | trace | 335 | 3 | 51 |
| Dried, shredded, sweetened | 1 cup | 62 | 33 | 24 | 21 | 2 | trace | 340 | 2 | 3 |
| **Cowpeas** or blackeye peas, dried, cooked | 1 cup | 248 | 34 | 1 | | | | 190 | 13 | 80 |
| **Peanuts,** roasted, salted: | | | | | | | | | | |
| Halves | 1 cup | 144 | 27 | 72 | 16 | 31 | 21 | 840 | 37 | 2 |
| Chopped | 1 tablespoon | 9 | 2 | 4 | 1 | 2 | 1 | 55 | 2 | 2 |
| Peanut butter | 1 tablespoon | 16 | 3 | 8 | 2 | 4 | 2 | 95 | 4 | 2 |
| **Peas,** split, dry, cooked | 1 cup | 250 | 52 | 1 | | | | 290 | 20 | 70 |
| **Pecans:** | | | | | | | | | | |
| Halves | 1 cup | 108 | 16 | 77 | 5 | 48 | 15 | 740 | 10 | 3 |
| Chopped | 1 tablespoon | 7.5 | 1 | 5 | trace | 3 | 1 | 50 | 1 | 3 |
| **Walnuts,** shelled: | | | | | | | | | | |
| Black or native, chopped | 1 cup | 126 | 19 | 75 | 4 | 26 | 36 | 790 | 26 | 3 |
| English or Persian: | | | | | | | | | | |
| Halves | 1 cup | 100 | 16 | 64 | 4 | 10 | 40 | 650 | 15 | 4 |
| Chopped | 1 tablespoon | 8 | 1 | 5 | trace | 1 | 3 | 50 | 1 | 4 |

235

# NUTRITIVE VALUES OF THE EDIBLE PART OF FOOD

| Food, approximate measure, and weight (in grams) | | Carbohydrate | Fat (total lipid) | Fatty Acids | | | Food Energy | Protein | Water |
| | | | | Saturated (total) | Unsaturated | | | | |
| | | | | | Oleic | Linoleic | | | |
| | grams | grams | grams | grams | grams | grams | calories | grams | percent |
|---|---|---|---|---|---|---|---|---|---|
| **MEAT, POULTRY, FISH, SHELLFISH: RELATED PRODUCTS** | | | | | | | | | |
| Bacon, | | | | | | | | | |
| broiled or fried, crisp    2 slices | 16 | 1 | 8 | 3 | 4 | 1 | 100 | 5 | 8 |
| Beef, trimmed to retail basis,[4] cooked: | | | | | | | | | |
| Cuts braised, simmered, or pot-roasted: | | | | | | | | | |
|    Lean and fat    3 ounces | 85 | 0 | 16 | 8 | 7 | trace | 245 | 23 | 53 |
|    Lean only    2.5 ounces | 72 | 0 | 5 | 2 | 2 | trace | 140 | 22 | 62 |
| Hamburger (ground beef), broiled: | | | | | | | | | |
|    Lean    3 ounces | 85 | 0 | 10 | 5 | 4 | trace | 185 | 23 | 60 |
|    Regular    3 ounces | 85 | 0 | 17 | 8 | 8 | trace | 245 | 21 | 54 |
| Roast, oven-cooked, no liquid added: | | | | | | | | | |
| Relatively fat, such as rib: | | | | | | | | | |
|    Lean and fat    3 ounces | 85 | 0 | 34 | 15 | 16 | 1 | 375 | 17 | 40 |
|    Lean only    1.8 ounces | 51 | 0 | 7 | 3 | 3 | trace | 125 | 14 | 57 |
| Relatively lean, such as heel of round: | | | | | | | | | |
|    Lean and fat    3 ounces | 85 | 0 | 7 | 3 | 3 | trace | 165 | 25 | 62 |
|    Lean only    2.7 ounces | 78 | 0 | 3 | 1 | 1 | trace | 125 | 24 | 65 |

236

| Item | Amount | | | | | | | | | |
|---|---|---|---|---|---|---|---|---|---|---|
| **Steak, broiled:** | | | | | | | | | | |
| Relatively fat, such as sirloin: | | | | | | | | | | |
| Lean and fat | 3 ounces | 85 | 0 | 27 | 13 | 12 | 1 | 330 | 20 | 44 |
| Lean only | 2 ounces | 56 | 0 | 4 | 2 | 2 | trace | 115 | 18 | 59 |
| Relatively lean, such as round: | | | | | | | | | | |
| Lean and fat | 3 ounces | 85 | 0 | 13 | 6 | 6 | trace | 220 | 24 | 55 |
| Lean only | 2.4 ounces | 68 | 0 | 4 | 2 | 2 | trace | 130 | 21 | 61 |
| **Beef, canned:** | | | | | | | | | | |
| Corned beef | 3 ounces | 85 | 0 | 10 | 5 | 4 | trace | 185 | 22 | 59 |
| Corned beef hash | 3 ounces | 85 | 9 | 10 | 5 | 4 | trace | 155 | 7 | 67 |
| Beef, dried or chipped | 2 ounces | 57 | 0 | 4 | 2 | 2 | trace | 115 | 19 | 48 |
| Beef and vegetable stew | 1 cup | 235 | 15 | 10 | 5 | 4 | trace | 210 | 15 | 82 |
| Beef potpie, baked; Individual pie, 4¼-inch diameter, weight before baking about 8 ounces | 1 pie | 227 | 43 | 33 | 9 | 20 | 2 | 560 | 23 | 55 |
| **Chicken, cooked:** | | | | | | | | | | |
| Flesh only, broiled | 3 ounces | 85 | 0 | 3 | 1 | 1 | 1 | 115 | 20 | 71 |
| Breast, fried, ½ breast: | | | | | | | | | | |
| With bone | 3.3 ounces | 94 | 1 | 5 | 1 | 2 | 1 | 155 | 25 | 58 |
| Flesh and skin only | 2.7 ounces | 76 | 1 | 5 | 1 | 2 | 1 | 155 | 25 | 58 |
| Drumstick, fried: | | | | | | | | | | |
| With bone | 2.1 ounces | 59 | trace | 4 | 1 | 1 | 1 | 90 | 12 | 55 |
| Flesh and skin only | 1.3 ounces | 38 | trace | 4 | 1 | 1 | 1 | 90 | 12 | 55 |

[4] Outer layer of fat on the cut was removed to within approximately ½ inch of the lean. Deposits of fat within the cut were not removed.

# NUTRITIVE VALUES OF THE EDIBLE PART OF FOOD

| Food, approximate measure, and weight (in grams) | | Carbohydrate | Fat (total lipid) | Saturated (total) | Fatty Acids Unsaturated Oleic | Linoleic | Food Energy | Protein | Water |
|---|---|---|---|---|---|---|---|---|---|
| | grams | grams | grams | grams | grams | grams | calories | grams | percent |
| **Chicken (cont.)** | | | | | | | | | |
| Chicken, canned; boneless | 3 ounces | 85 | 0 | 10 | 3 | 4 | 2 | 170 | 18 | 65 |
| Chicken potpie. SEE Poultry potpie. | | | | | | | | | | |
| Chili con carne, canned: | | | | | | | | | | |
| With beans | 1 cup | 250 | 30 | 15 | 7 | 7 | trace | 335 | 19 | 72 |
| Without beans | 1 cup | 255 | 15 | 38 | 18 | 17 | 1 | 510 | 26 | 67 |
| Heart, beef, lean, braised | 3 ounces | 85 | 1 | 5 | | | | 160 | 27 | 61 |
| Lamb, trimmed to retail basis,[4] cooked: | | | | | | | | | | |
| Chop, thick, with bone, broiled | 1 chop | 137 | 0 | 33 | 18 | 12 | 1 | 400 | 25 | 47 |
| Lean and fat | 4.0 ounces | 112 | 0 | 33 | 18 | 12 | 1 | 400 | 25 | 47 |
| Lean only | 2.6 ounces | 74 | 0 | 6 | 3 | 2 | trace | 140 | 21 | 62 |
| Leg roasted: | | | | | | | | | | |
| Lean and fat | 3 ounces | 85 | 0 | 16 | 9 | 6 | trace | 235 | 22 | 54 |
| Lean only | 2.5 ounces | 71 | 0 | 5 | 3 | 2 | trace | 130 | 20 | 62 |
| Shoulder, roasted: | | | | | | | | | | |
| Lean and fat | 3 ounces | 85 | 0 | 23 | 13 | 8 | 1 | 285 | 18 | 50 |
| Lean only | 2.3 ounces | 64 | 0 | 6 | 3 | 2 | trace | 130 | 17 | 61 |

| | | | | | | | | | | |
|---|---|---|---|---|---|---|---|---|---|---|
| Liver, beef, fried | 2 ounces | 57 | 3 | 6 | 7 | 8 | 2 | 130 | 15 | 57 |
| **Pork, cured, cooked:** | | | | | | | | | | |
| Ham, light cure, lean and fat, roasted | 3 ounces | 85 | 0 | 19 | 7 | 8 | 2 | 245 | 18 | 54 |
| **Luncheon meat:** | | | | | | | | | | |
| Boiled ham, sliced | 2 ounces | 57 | 0 | 10 | 4 | 4 | 1 | 135 | 11 | 59 |
| Canned, spiced or unspiced | 2 ounces | 57 | 1 | 14 | 5 | 6 | 1 | 165 | 8 | 55 |
| **Pork, fresh trimmed to retail basis,[4] cooked:** | | | | | | | | | | |
| Chop, thick, with bone | 1 chop, 3.5 ounces | 98 | 0 | 21 | 8 | 9 | 2 | 260 | 16 | 42 |
| Lean and fat | 2.3 ounces | 66 | 0 | 21 | 8 | 9 | 2 | 260 | 16 | 42 |
| Lean only | 1.7 ounces | 48 | 0 | 7 | 2 | 3 | 1 | 130 | 15 | 53 |
| Roast, oven-cooked, no liquid added: | | | | | | | | | | |
| Lean and fat | 3 ounces | 85 | 0 | 24 | 9 | 10 | 2 | 310 | 21 | 46 |
| Lean only | 2.4 ounces | 68 | 0 | 10 | 3 | 4 | 1 | 175 | 20 | 55 |
| Cuts, simmered: | | | | | | | | | | |
| Lean and fat | 3 ounces | 85 | 0 | 26 | 9 | 11 | 2 | 320 | 20 | 46 |
| Lean only | 2.2 ounces | 63 | 0 | 6 | 2 | 3 | 1 | 135 | 18 | 60 |
| **Poultry potpie** (based on chicken potpie) Individual pie, 4¼-inch diameter, weight before | | | | | | | | | | |

[4] Outer layer of fat on the cut was removed to within approximately ½ inch of the lean. Deposits of fat within the cut were not removed.

## NUTRITIVE VALUES OF THE EDIBLE PART OF FOOD

| Food, approximate measure, and weight (in grams) | | | Carbohydrate | Fat (total lipid) | Fatty Acids | | | Food Energy | Protein | Water |
|---|---|---|---|---|---|---|---|---|---|---|
| | | | | | Saturated (total) | Unsaturated – Oleic | Linoleic | | | |
| | | grams | grams | grams | grams | grams | grams | calories | grams | percent |
| Poultry potpie (cont.) baking about 8 ounces | 1 pie | 227 | 42 | 31 | 10 | 15 | 3 | 535 | 23 | 57 |
| Sausage: | | | | | | | | | | |
| Bologna, slice, 4.1 inch by 0.1 inch | 8 slices | 227 | 2 | 62 | | | | 690 | 27 | 56 |
| Frankfurter, cooked | 1 frankfurter | 51 | 1 | 14 | | | | 155 | 6 | 58 |
| Pork, links or patty, cooked | 4 ounces | 113 | trace | 50 | 18 | 21 | 5 | 540 | 21 | 35 |
| Tongue, beef, braised | 3 ounces | 85 | trace | 14 | | | | 210 | 18 | 61 |
| Turkey potpie. SEE poultry potpie. | | | | | | | | | | |
| Veal, cooked: | | | | | | | | | | |
| Cutlet, without bone, broiled | 3 ounces | 85 | 0 | 9 | 5 | 4 | trace | 185 | 23 | 60 |
| Roast, medium fat, medium done; lean and fat | 3 ounces | 85 | 0 | 14 | 7 | 6 | trace | 230 | 23 | 55 |
| Fish and shellfish: | | | | | | | | | | |
| Bluefish, baked or broiled | 3 ounces | 85 | 0 | 4 | | | | 135 | 22 | 68 |
| Clams: | | | | | | | | | | |
| Raw, meat only | 3 ounces | 85 | 2 | 1 | | | | 65 | 11 | 82 |

| Food | Approximate measure | Grams | | | | | | | | |
|---|---|---|---|---|---|---|---|---|---|---|
| Canned, solids and liquid | 3 ounces | 85 | 2 | 1 | 5 | 4 | 10 | 45 | 7 | 86 |
| Crabmeat, canned | 3 ounces | 85 | 1 | 2 | 1 | 3 | trace | 85 | 15 | 77 |
| Fish sticks, breaded, cooked, frozen; stick 3.8 inches x 1.0 inch x 0.5 inch | 10 sticks or 8-ounce package | 227 | 15 | 20 | | | | 400 | 38 | 66 |
| Haddock, fried | 3 ounces | 85 | 5 | 5 | | | | 140 | 17 | 66 |
| Mackerel: Broiled, Atlantic | 3 ounces | 85 | 0 | 13 | | | | 200 | 19 | 62 |
| Canned, Pacific, solids and liquid[5] | 3 ounces | 85 | 0 | 9 | | | | 155 | 18 | 66 |
| Ocean perch, breaded (egg and bread crumbs), fried | 3 ounces | 85 | 6 | 11 | | | | 195 | 16 | 59 |
| Oysters, meat only: Raw, 13-19 medium selects | 1 cup | 240 | 8 | 4 | | | | 160 | 20 | 85 |
| Stew, 1 part oysters to 3 parts milk by volume, 3-4 oysters | 1 cup | 230 | 11 | 12 | | | | 200 | 11 | 84 |
| Salmon, pink, canned | 3 ounces | 85 | 0 | 5 | | | | 120 | 17 | 71 |
| Sardines, Atlantic, canned in oil, drained solids | 3 ounces | 85 | 0 | 9 | 1 | 1 | trace | 175 | 20 | 62 |
| Shad, baked | 3 ounces | 85 | 0 | 10 | | | | 170 | 20 | 64 |

[a] Vitamin values based on drained solids.

## NUTRITIVE VALUES OF THE EDIBLE PART OF FOOD

| Food, approximate measure, and weight (in grams) | | | Carbohydrate | Fat (total lipid) | Fatty Acids | | | Food Energy | Protein | Water |
|---|---|---|---|---|---|---|---|---|---|---|
| | | | | | Saturated (total) | Unsaturated Oleic | Linoleic | | | |
| | | grams | grams | grams | grams | grams | grams | calories | grams | percent |
| **Fish and shellfish (cont.)** | | | | | | | | | | |
| Swordfish, broiled with butter or margarine | 3 ounces | 85 | 0 | 5 | | | | 150 | 24 | 65 |
| Tuna, canned in oil, drained solids | 3 ounces | 85 | 0 | 7 | | | | 170 | 24 | 61 |
| **MILK, CREAM, CHEESE: RELATED PRODUCTS** | | | | | | | | | | |
| Milk, cow's: | | | | | | | | | | |
| Fluid, whole (3.5% fat) | 1 cup | 244 | 12 | 9 | 5 | 3 | trace | 160 | 9 | 87 |
| Fluid, nonfat (skim) | 1 cup | 246 | 13 | trace | | | | 90 | 9 | 90 |
| Buttermilk, cultured, from skim milk | 1 cup | 246 | 13 | trace | | | | 90 | 9 | 90 |
| Evaporated, unsweetened, undiluted | 1 cup | 252 | 24 | 20 | 11 | 7 | 1 | 245 | 18 | 74 |
| Condensed, sweetened, undiluted | 1 cup | 306 | 166 | 27 | 15 | 9 | 1 | 980 | 25 | 27 |
| Dry, whole | 1 cup | 103 | 39 | 28 | 16 | 9 | 1 | 515 | 27 | 2 |
| Dry, nonfat, instant | 1 cup | 70 | 36 | trace | | | | 250 | 25 | 3 |
| Milk, goat's: | | | | | | | | | | |
| Fluid, whole | 1 cup | 244 | 11 | 10 | 6 | 2 | trace | 165 | 8 | 88 |

242

| Food | Amount | Grams | Water (%) | Food energy (cal) | Protein (g) | Fat (g) | Saturated fat (g) | Oleic (g) | Linoleic (g) | Carbohydrate (g) |
|---|---|---|---|---|---|---|---|---|---|---|
| **Cream:** | | | | | | | | | | |
| Half-and-half (cream and milk) | 1 cup | 242 | 80 | 325 | 8 | 28 | 16 | 9 | 1 | 11 |
| | 1 tablespoon | 15 | 80 | 20 | trace | 2 | 1 | 1 | trace | 1 |
| Light, coffee or table | 1 cup | 240 | 72 | 505 | 7 | 49 | 27 | 16 | 1 | 10 |
| | 1 tablespoon | 15 | 72 | 30 | trace | 3 | 2 | 1 | trace | 1 |
| Whipping, unwhipped (volume about double when whipped): | | | | | | | | | | |
| Light | 1 cup | 239 | 62 | 715 | 6 | 75 | 41 | 25 | 2 | 9 |
| | 1 tablespoon | 15 | 62 | 45 | trace | 5 | 3 | 2 | trace | 1 |
| Heavy | 1 cup | 238 | 57 | 840 | 5 | 89 | 49 | 29 | 3 | 7 |
| | 1 tablespoon | 15 | 57 | 55 | trace | 6 | 3 | 2 | trace | trace |
| **Cheese:** | | | | | | | | | | |
| Blue or Roquefort type | 1 ounce | 28 | 40 | 105 | 6 | 9 | 5 | 3 | trace | 1 |
| Cheddar or American: | | | | | | | | | | |
| Ungrated | 1-inch cube | 17 | 37 | 70 | 4 | 6 | 3 | 2 | trace | trace |
| Grated | 1 cup | 112 | 37 | 445 | 28 | 36 | 20 | 12 | 1 | 2 |
| | 1 tablespoon | 7 | 37 | 30 | 2 | 2 | 1 | 1 | trace | trace |
| | 1 ounce | 28 | 37 | 105 | 7 | 9 | 5 | 3 | trace | 1 |
| Cheddar, process | 1 ounce | 28 | 40 | 105 | 7 | 9 | 5 | 3 | trace | 1 |
| Cheese foods, Cheddar | 1 ounce | 28 | 43 | 90 | 6 | 7 | 4 | 2 | trace | 2 |
| Cottage cheese, from skim milk: | | | | | | | | | | |
| Creamed | 1 cup | 225 | 78 | 240 | 31 | 9 | 5 | 3 | trace | 6 |
| | 1 ounce | 28 | 78 | 30 | 4 | 1 | 1 | trace | trace | 1 |
| Uncreamed | 1 cup | 225 | 79 | 195 | 38 | 1 | trace | trace | trace | 6 |
| | 1 ounce | 28 | 79 | 25 | 5 | trace | trace | trace | trace | 1 |
| Cream cheese | 1 ounce | 28 | 51 | 105 | 2 | 11 | 6 | 4 | trace | 1 |
| | 1 tablespoon | 15 | 51 | 55 | 1 | 6 | 3 | 2 | trace | trace |
| Swiss (domestic) | 1 ounce | 28 | 39 | 105 | 8 | 8 | 4 | 3 | trace | 1 |

## NUTRITIVE VALUES OF THE EDIBLE PART OF FOOD

| Food, approximate measure, and weight (in grams) | | | Carbohydrate | Fat (total lipid) | Fatty Acids | | | Food Energy | Protein | Water |
|---|---|---|---|---|---|---|---|---|---|---|
| | | | | | Saturated (total) | Unsaturated Oleic | Unsaturated Linoleic | | | |
| | | grams | grams | grams | grams | grams | grams | calories | grams | percent |
| **Milk beverages:** | | | | | | | | | | |
| Cocoa | 1 cup | 242 | 26 | 11 | 6 | 4 | trace | 235 | 9 | 79 |
| Chocolate-flavored milk drink (made with skim milk) | 1 cup | 250 | 27 | 6 | 3 | 2 | trace | 190 | 8 | 83 |
| Malted milk | 1 cup | 270 | 32 | 12 | | | | 280 | 13 | 78 |
| **Milk desserts:** | | | | | | | | | | |
| Cornstarch pudding, plain (blanc mange) | 1 cup | 248 | 39 | 10 | 5 | 3 | trace | 275 | 9 | 76 |
| Custard, baked | 1 cup | 248 | 28 | 14 | 6 | 5 | 1 | 285 | 13 | 77 |
| Ice cream, plain, factory packed: | | | | | | | | | | |
| Slice or cut brick, ⅛ of quart brick | 1 slice or cut brick | 71 | 15 | 9 | 5 | 3 | trace | 145 | 3 | 62 |
| Container | 3½ fluid ounces | 62 | 13 | 8 | 4 | 3 | trace | 130 | 2 | 62 |
| Container | 8 fluid ounces | 142 | 29 | 18 | 10 | 6 | 1 | 295 | 6 | 62 |
| Ice milk | 1 cup | 187 | 42 | 10 | 6 | 3 | trace | 285 | 9 | 67 |
| Yogurt, from partially skim milk | 1 cup | 246 | 13 | 4 | 2 | 1 | trace | 120 | 8 | 89 |

244

# EGGS

Eggs, large, 24 ounces per dozen:

| Food | Measure | | | | | | | | | |
|---|---|---|---|---|---|---|---|---|---|---|
| **Raw:** | | | | | | | | | | |
| Whole, without shell | 1 egg | 50 | trace | 6 | 2 | 3 | trace | 80 | 6 | 74 |
| White of egg | 1 white | 33 | trace | trace | 2 | 2 | trace | 15 | 4 | 88 |
| Yolk of egg | 1 yolk | 17 | trace | 5 | 2 | 2 | trace | 60 | 3 | 51 |
| **Cooked:** | | | | | | | | | | |
| Boiled, shell removed | 2 eggs | 100 | 1 | 12 | 4 | 5 | 1 | 160 | 12 | 74 |
| Scrambled with milk and fat | 1 egg | 64 | 1 | 8 | 3 | 3 | trace | 110 | 7 | 72 |

# SUGARS, SWEETS

| Food | Measure | | | | | | | | | |
|---|---|---|---|---|---|---|---|---|---|---|
| **Candy:** | | | | | | | | | | |
| Caramels | 1 ounce | 28 | 22 | 3 | 2 | 1 | trace | 115 | 1 | 8 |
| Chocolate, milk, plain | 1 ounce | 28 | 16 | 9 | 5 | 3 | trace | 150 | 2 | 1 |
| Fudge, plain | 1 ounce | 28 | 21 | 3 | 2 | 1 | trace | 115 | 1 | 8 |
| Hard candy | 1 ounce | 28 | 28 | trace | | | | 110 | 0 | 1 |
| Marshmallows | 1 ounce | 28 | 23 | trace | | | | 90 | 1 | 17 |
| **Chocolate syrup,** thin type | 1 tablespoon | 20 | 13 | trace | trace | trace | trace | 50 | trace | 32 |
| **Honey,** strained or extracted | 1 tablespoon | 21 | 17 | 0 | | | | 65 | trace | 17 |
| **Jams and preserves** | 1 tablespoon | 20 | 14 | trace | | | | 55 | trace | 29 |
| **Jellies** | 1 tablespoon | 20 | 14 | trace | | | | 55 | trace | 29 |
| **Molasses,** cane: Light (first extraction) | 1 tablespoon | 20 | 13 | | | | | 50 | | 24 |
| Blackstrap (third extraction) | 1 tablespoon | 20 | 11 | | | | | 45 | | 24 |

## NUTRITIVE VALUES OF THE EDIBLE PART OF FOOD

| Food, approximate measure, and weight (in grams) | | Carbohydrate | Fat (total lipid) | Fatty Acids Saturated (total) | Unsaturated Oleic | Linoleic | Food Energy | Protein | Water |
|---|---|---|---|---|---|---|---|---|---|
| | grams | grams | grams | grams | grams | grams | calories | grams | percent |
| **Candy (cont.)** | | | | | | | | | |
| Syrup, table blends (chiefly corn, light and dark) 1 tablespoon | 20 | 15 | 0 | | | | 60 | 0 | 24 |
| **Sugars (cane or beet):** | | | | | | | | | |
| Granulated | | | | | | | | | |
|   1 cup | 200 | 199 | 0 | | | | 770 | 0 | trace |
|   1 tablespoon | 12 | 12 | 0 | | | | 45 | 0 | trace |
| Lump 1⅛ inches by ¾ inch | | | | | | | | | |
|   1 lump | 6 | 6 | 0 | | | | 25 | 0 | trace |
| Powdered, stirred before measuring | | | | | | | | | |
|   1 cup | 128 | 127 | 0 | | | | 495 | 0 | trace |
|   1 tablespoon | 8 | 8 | 0 | | | | 30 | 0 | trace |
| Brown, firm-packed | | | | | | | | | |
|   1 cup | 220 | 212 | 0 | | | | 820 | 0 | 2 |
|   1 tablespoon | 14 | 13 | 0 | | | | 50 | 0 | 2 |
| **VEGETABLES AND VEGETABLE PRODUCTS** | | | | | | | | | |
| **Asparagus:** | | | | | | | | | |
| Cooked, cut spears 1 cup | 175 | 6 | trace | | | | 35 | 4 | 94 |
| Canned spears, medium: | | | | | | | | | |
|   Green 6 spears | 96 | 3 | trace | | | | 20 | 2 | 92 |
|   Bleached 6 spears | 96 | 4 | trace | | | | 20 | 2 | 92 |
| **Beans:** | | | | | | | | | |
| Lima, immature cooked 1 cup | 160 | 32 | 1 | | | | 180 | 1 | 71 |

| Food | Measure | | | | | | | |
|---|---|---|---|---|---|---|---|---|
| **Snap green:** | | | | | | | | |
| Cooked: | | | | | | | | |
| In small amount of water, short time | 1 cup | 125 | 7 | trace | | 30 | 2 | 92 |
| In large amount of water, long time | 1 cup | 125 | 7 | trace | | 30 | 2 | 92 |
| Canned: | | | | | | | | |
| Solids and liquid | 1 cup | 239 | 10 | trace | | 45 | 2 | 94 |
| Strained or chopped (baby food) | 1 ounce | 28 | 1 | trace | | 5 | trace | 92 |
| **Bean sprouts.** SEE sprouts. | | | | | | | | |
| **Beets,** cooked, diced | 1 cup | 165 | 12 | trace | 2 | 50 | 2 | 91 |
| **Broccoli spears,** cooked | 1 cup | 150 | 7 | trace | 2 | 40 | 5 | 91 |
| **Brussels sprouts,** cooked | 1 cup | 130 | 8 | 1 | 5 | 45 | 5 | 88 |
| **Cabbage:** | | | | | | | | |
| Raw: | | | | | | | | |
| Finely shredded | 1 cup | 100 | 5 | trace | | 25 | 1 | 92 |
| Coleslaw | 1 cup | 120 | 9 | 9 | | 120 | 1 | 83 |
| Cooked: | | | | | | | | |
| In small amount of water, short time | 1 cup | 170 | 7 | trace | | 35 | 2 | 94 |
| In large amount of water, long time | 1 cup | 170 | 7 | trace | | 30 | 2 | 94 |

247

| Food, approximate measure, and weight (in grams) | | | Carbohydrate | Fat (total lipid) | Fatty Acids Saturated (total) | Unsaturated Oleic | Linoleic | Food Energy | Protein | Water |
|---|---|---|---|---|---|---|---|---|---|---|
| | | grams | grams | grams | grams | grams | grams | calories | grams | percent |
| **Cabbage (cont.)** | | | | | | | | | | |
| Cabbage, celery or Chinese: | | | | | | | | | | |
| Raw, leaves and stalk, | | | | | | | | | | |
| 1-inch pieces | 1 cup | 100 | 3 | trace | | | | 15 | 1 | 95 |
| Cabbage, spoon (or Bok Choy), cooked | 1 cup | 150 | 4 | trace | | | | 20 | 2 | 95 |
| **Carrots:** | | | | | | | | | | |
| Raw: | | | | | | | | | | |
| Whole, 5½ inches by 1 inch, (25 thin strips) | 1 carrot | 50 | 5 | trace | | | | 20 | 1 | 88 |
| Grated | 1 cup | 110 | 11 | trace | | | | 45 | 1 | 88 |
| Cooked, diced | 1 cup | 145 | 10 | trace | | | | 45 | 1 | 91 |
| Canned, strained or chopped (baby food) | 1 ounce | 28 | 2 | trace | | | | 10 | trace | 92 |
| **Cauliflower,** cooked, flowerbuds | 1 cup | 120 | 5 | trace | | | | 25 | 3 | 92 |
| **Celery:** | | | | | | | | | | |
| Stalk, larger outer, 8 inches by about 1½ inches, at root end | 1 stalk | 40 | 2 | trace | | | | 5 | trace | 94 |
| Pieces, diced | 1 cup | 100 | 4 | trace | | | | 15 | 1 | 94 |
| **Collards,** cooked | 1 cup | 190 | 9 | 1 | | | | 55 | 5 | 91 |

| Food | Measure | Weight (grams) | Water (percent) | Food energy (calories) | Protein (grams) | Fat (grams) | Carbohydrate (grams) |
|---|---|---|---|---|---|---|---|
| **Corn, sweet:** | | | | | | | |
| Cooked, ear 5 inches by 1¾ inches[6] | 1 ear | 140 | 74 | 70 | 3 | 1 | 16 |
| Canned, solids and liquid | 1 cup | 256 | 81 | 170 | 5 | 2 | 40 |
| **Cowpeas** | | | | | | | |
| cooked, immature seeds | 1 cup | 160 | 72 | 175 | 13 | 1 | 29 |
| **Cucumbers,** 10-ounce; 7½ inches by about 2 inches: | | | | | | | |
| Raw, pared | 1 cucumber | 207 | 96 | 30 | 1 | trace | 7 |
| Raw, pared, center slice ⅛-inch thick | 6 slices | 50 | 96 | 5 | trace | trace | 2 |
| **Dandelion greens** cooked | 1 cup | 180 | 90 | 60 | 4 | 1 | 12 |
| **Endive,** curly (including escarole) | 2 ounces | 57 | 93 | 10 | 1 | trace | 2 |
| **Kale,** leaves including stems, cooked | 1 cup | 110 | 91 | 30 | 4 | 1 | 4 |
| **Lettuce, raw:** | | | | | | | |
| Butterhead, as Boston types; head, 4-inch diameter | 1 head | 120 | 95 | 30 | 3 | trace | 6 |
| Crisphead, as Iceberg; head; 4¾-inch diameter | 1 head | 454 | 96 | 60 | 4 | trace | 13 |

[6] Measure and weight apply to entire vegetable including parts not usually eaten.

## NUTRITIVE VALUES OF THE EDIBLE PART OF FOOD

| Food, approximate measure, and weight (in grams) | | | Carbohydrate | Fat (total lipid) | Fatty Acids Saturated (total) | Unsaturated Oleic | Linoleic | Food Energy | Protein | Water |
|---|---|---|---|---|---|---|---|---|---|---|
| | | grams | grams | grams | grams | grams | grams | calories | grams | percent |
| Lettuce (cont.) Looseleaf, or bunching varieties, leaves | 2 large | 50 | 2 | trace | | | | 10 | 1 | 94 |
| Mushrooms, canned, solids and liquid | 1 cup | 244 | 6 | trace | | | | 40 | 5 | 93 |
| Mustard greens, cooked | 1 cup | 140 | 6 | 1 | | | | 35 | 3 | 93 |
| Okra, cooked, pod 3 inches by ⅝ inch | 8 pods | 85 | 5 | trace | | | | 25 | 2 | 91 |
| Onions: Mature: Raw, onion 2½-inch diameter | 1 onion | 110 | 10 | trace | | | | 40 | 2 | 89 |
| Cooked | 1 cup | 210 | 14 | trace | | | | 60 | 3 | 92 |
| Young green, small without tops | 6 onions | 50 | 5 | trace | | | | 20 | 1 | 88 |
| Parsley, raw, chopped | 1 tablespoon | 3.5 | trace | trace | | | | 1 | trace | 85 |
| Parsnips, cooked | 1 cup | 155 | 23 | 1 | | | | 100 | 2 | 82 |

| Food | Measure | | | | | | | |
|---|---|---|---|---|---|---|---|---|
| **Peas, green:** | | | | | | | | |
| Cooked | 1 cup | 160 | 19 | 1 | | 115 | 9 | 82 |
| Canned, solids and liquid | 1 cup | 249 | 31 | 1 | | 165 | 9 | 83 |
| Canned, strained (baby food) | 1 ounce | 28 | 3 | trace | | 15 | 1 | 86 |
| **Peppers, hot,** | | | | | | | | |
| hot, red, without seeds, dried (ground chili powder, added seasonings) | 1 tablespoon | 15 | 8 | 2 | | 50 | 2 | 8 |
| **Peppers, sweet:** | | | | | | | | |
| Raw, medium, about 6 per pound: | | | | | | | | |
| Green pod without stem and seeds | 1 pod | 62 | 3 | trace | | 15 | 1 | 93 |
| Red pod without stem and seeds | 1 pod | 60 | 4 | trace | | 20 | 1 | 91 |
| Canned, pimientos; medium | 1 pod | 38 | 2 | trace | | 10 | trace | 92 |
| **Potatoes,** medium (about 3 per pound raw): | | | | | | | | |
| Baked, peeled after baking | 1 potato | 99 | 21 | trace | | 90 | 3 | 75 |
| Boiled: | | | | | | | | |
| Peeled after boiling | 1 potato | 136 | 23 | trace | | 105 | 3 | 80 |
| Peeled before boiling | 1 potato | 122 | 18 | trace | | 80 | 2 | 83 |

NUTRITIVE VALUES OF THE EDIBLE PART OF FOOD

| Food, approximate measure, and weight (in grams) | | Water | Food Energy | Protein | Fat (total lipid) | Saturated (total) | Unsaturated Oleic | Unsaturated Linoleic | Carbohydrate |
|---|---|---|---|---|---|---|---|---|---|
| | | percent | calories | grams | grams | grams | grams | grams | grams |
| | | grams | | | | | | | |
| **Potatoes** (cont.) | | | | | | | | | |
| French-fried, piece 2 inches by ½ inch by ½ inch: | | | | | | | | | |
| Cooked in deep fat | 10 pieces | 45 | 155 | 2 | 7 | 2 | 2 | 4 | 20 |
| | 57 | | | | | | | | |
| Frozen, heated | 10 pieces | 53 | 125 | 2 | 5 | 1 | 1 | 2 | 19 |
| | 57 | | | | | | | | |
| Mashed: | | | | | | | | | |
| Milk added | 1 cup | 83 | 125 | 4 | 1 | | | | 25 |
| | 195 | | | | | | | | |
| Milk and butter added | 1 cup | 80 | 185 | 4 | 8 | 4 | 3 | trace | 24 |
| | 195 | | | | | | | | |
| Potato chips, medium, 2-inch diameter | 10 chips | 2 | 115 | 1 | 8 | 2 | 2 | 4 | 10 |
| | 20 | | | | | | | | |
| Pumpkin, canned | 1 cup | 90 | 75 | 2 | 1 | | | | 18 |
| | 228 | | | | | | | | |
| Radishes, raw, small, without tops | 4 radishes | 94 | 5 | trace | trace | | | | 1 |
| | 40 | | | | | | | | |
| Sauerkraut, canned, solids and liquid | 1 cup | 93 | 45 | 2 | trace | | | | 9 |
| | 235 | | | | | | | | |
| **Spinach:** | | | | | | | | | |
| Cooked | 1 cup | 92 | 40 | 5 | 1 | | | | 6 |
| | 180 | | | | | | | | |
| Canned, drained solids | 1 cup | | | | 1 | | | | 5 |
| | 180 | | | | | | | | |

| Food | Measure | | | | | | | |
|---|---|--:|--:|--:|--:|--:|--:|--:|
| Canned, strained or chopped (baby food) | 1 ounce | 28 | 2 | trace | | 10 | 1 | 88 |
| **Sprouts, raw:** | | | | | | | | |
| Mung bean | 1 cup | 90 | 6 | trace | | 30 | 3 | 89 |
| Soybean | 1 cup | 107 | 4 | 2 | | 40 | 6 | 89 |
| **Squash:** | | | | | | | | |
| Cooked: | | | | | | | | |
| Summer, diced | 1 cup | 210 | 7 | trace | | 30 | 2 | 96 |
| Winter, baked | 1 cup | 205 | 32 | 1 | | 130 | 4 | 81 |
| Canned, winter, strained and chopped (baby food) | 1 ounce | 28 | 2 | trace | | 10 | trace | 92 |
| **Sweet potatoes:** | | | | | | | | |
| Cooked, medium, 5 inches by 2 inches, weight raw about 6 ounces: | | | | | | | | |
| Baked, peeled after baking | 1 sweet potato | 110 | 35 | 1 | | 155 | 2 | 64 |
| Boiled, peeled after boiling | 1 sweet potato | 147 | 39 | 1 | | 170 | 2 | 71 |
| Candied, 3½ inches by 2¼ inches | 1 sweet potato | 175 | 60 | 6 | 2 3 | 295 | 2 | 60 |
| Canned, vacuum or solid pack | 1 cup | 218 | 54 | trace | 1 | 235 | 4 | 72 |
| **Tomatoes:** | | | | | | | | |
| Raw, medium, 2 inches by 2½ inches, about 3 per pound | 1 tomato | 150 | 7 | trace | | 35 | 2 | 94 |
| Canned | 1 cup | 242 | 10 | trace | | 50 | 2 | 94 |
| Tomato juice, canned | 1 cup | 242 | 10 | trace | | 45 | 2 | 94 |
| Tomato catsup | 1 tablespoon | 17 | 4 | trace | | 15 | trace | 69 |

253

# NUTRITIVE VALUES OF THE EDIBLE PART OF FOOD

| Food, approximate measure, and weight (in grams) | | | Carbohydrate | Fat (total lipid) | Fatty Acids | | | Food Energy | Protein | Water |
|---|---|---|---|---|---|---|---|---|---|---|
| | | | | | Saturated (total) | Unsaturated | | | | |
| | | | | | | Oleic | Linoleic | | | |
| | | grams | grams | grams | grams | grams | grams | calories | grams | percent |
| **Turnips,** | | | | | | | | | | |
| cooked, diced | 1 cup | 155 | 8 | trace | | | | 35 | 1 | 94 |
| **Turnip greens:** | | | | | | | | | | |
| Cooked: | | | | | | | | | | |
| In small amount of water, short time | 1 cup | 145 | 5 | trace | | | | 30 | 3 | 93 |
| In large amount of water, long time | 1 cup | 145 | 5 | trace | | | | 25 | 3 | 94 |
| Canned, solids and liquid | 1 cup | 232 | 7 | 1 | | | | 40 | 3 | 93 |
| **MISCELLANEOUS ITEMS** | | | | | | | | | | |
| **Beer** | | | | | | | | | | |
| (average 3.6% alcohol by weight) | 1 cup | 240 | 9 | 0 | | | | 100 | 1 | 92 |
| **Beverages, carbonated:** | | | | | | | | | | |
| Cola type | 1 cup | 240 | 24 | 0 | | | | 95 | 0 | 90 |
| Ginger ale | 1 cup | 230 | 18 | 0 | | | | 70 | 0 | 92 |
| **Bouillon cube,** | | | | | | | | | | |
| ⅝ inch | 1 cube | 4 | trace | trace | | | | 5 | 1 | 4 |
| **Chili powder.** | | | | | | | | | | |
| SEE Vegetables, peppers. | | | | | | | | | | |

254

| | | | | | | | | | | |
|---|---|---|---|---|---|---|---|---|---|---|
| **Chili sauce** (mainly tomatoes) | 1 tablespoon | 17 | 68 | 20 | trace | trace | | | | 4 |
| **Chocolate:** | | | | | | | | | | |
| Bitter or baking | 1 ounce | 28 | 2 | 145 | 3 | 15 | 8 | 6 | trace | 8 |
| Sweet | 1 ounce | 28 | 1 | 150 | 1 | 10 | 6 | 4 | trace | 16 |
| **Cider.** SEE Fruits, apple juice. | | | | | | | | | | |
| **Gelatin, dry:** | | | | | | | | | | |
| Plain | 1 tablespoon | 10 | 13 | 35 | 9 | trace | | | | 0 |
| Dessert powder; 3-ounce package | ½ cup | 85 | 2 | 315 | 8 | 0 | | | | 75 |
| **Gelatin dessert, ready-to-eat:** | | | | | | | | | | |
| Plain | 1 cup | 239 | 84 | 140 | 4 | 0 | | | | 34 |
| With fruit | 1 cup | 241 | 82 | 160 | 3 | trace | | | | 40 |
| **Olives, pickled:** | | | | | | | | | | |
| Green | 4 medium or 3 extra or 2 giant | 16 | 78 | 15 | trace | 2 | trace | 2 | trace | trace |
| Ripe: Mission | 3 small or 2 large | 10 | 73 | 15 | trace | 2 | trace | 2 | trace | trace |
| **Pickles, cucumber:** | | | | | | | | | | |
| Dill, large, 4 inches by 1¾ inches | 1 pickle | 135 | 93 | 15 | 1 | trace | | | | 3 |
| Sweet, 2¾ inches by ¾ inch | 1 pickle | 20 | 61 | 30 | trace | trace | | | | 7 |
| **Popcorn.** SEE Grain products. | | | | | | | | | | |

## NUTRITIVE VALUES OF THE EDIBLE PART OF FOOD

| Food, approximate measure, and weight (in grams) | | | Carbohydrate | Fat (total lipid) | Fatty Acids Saturated (total) | Unsaturated Oleic | Unsaturated Linoleic | Food Energy | Protein | Water |
|---|---|---|---|---|---|---|---|---|---|---|
| | | grams | grams | grams | grams | grams | grams | calories | grams | percent |
| **Sherbet,** | | | | | | | | | | |
| orange | 1 cup | 193 | 59 | 2 | | | | 260 | 2 | 67 |
| **Soups,** | | | | | | | | | | |
| canned; ready-to-serve (prepared with equal volume of water): | | | | | | | | | | |
| Bean with pork | 1 cup | 250 | 22 | 6 | 1 | 2 | 2 | 170 | 8 | 84 |
| Beef noodle | 1 cup | 250 | 7 | 3 | 1 | 1 | 1 | 70 | 4 | 93 |
| Beef bouillon, broth, consommé | 1 cup | 240 | 3 | 0 | 0 | 0 | 0 | 30 | 5 | 96 |
| Chicken noodle | 1 cup | 250 | 8 | 2 | trace | 1 | 1 | 65 | 4 | 93 |
| Clam chowder | 1 cup | 255 | 13 | 3 | | | | 85 | 2 | 92 |
| Cream soup (mushroom) | 1 cup | 240 | 10 | 10 | 1 | 3 | 5 | 135 | 2 | 90 |
| Minestrone | 1 cup | 245 | 14 | 3 | | 3 | | 105 | 5 | 90 |
| Pea, green | 1 cup | 245 | 23 | 2 | 1 | 1 | trace | 130 | 6 | 86 |
| Tomato | 1 cup | 245 | 16 | 2 | trace | 1 | 1 | 90 | 2 | 90 |
| Vegetable with beef broth | 1 cup | 250 | 14 | 2 | | | | 80 | 3 | 92 |
| **Starch** (cornstarch) | 1 cup | 128 | 112 | trace | | | | 465 | trace | 12 |
| | 1 tablespoon | 8 | 7 | trace | | | | 30 | trace | 12 |

Tapioca,
quick-cooking
granulated, dry, stirred
before measuring

| | | | | | | | | | |
|---|---|---|---|---|---|---|---|---|---|
| **Tapioca,** quick-cooking granulated, dry, stirred before measuring | | | | | | | | | |
| | 1 cup | 152 | 13 | 535 | 1 | trace | | | 131 |
| | 1 tablespoon | 10 | 13 | 35 | trace | trace | | | 9 |
| **Vinegar** | 1 tablespoon | 15 | | 2 | 0 | | | | 1 |
| **White sauce, medium** | 1 cup | 265 | 73 | 430 | 10 | 33 | 18 | 11 | 1 | 23 |
| **Yeast:** Baker's: | | | | | | | | | |
| Compressed | 1 ounce | 28 | 71 | 25 | 3 | trace | | | 3 |
| Dry active | 1 ounce | 28 | 5 | 80 | 10 | trace | | | 11 |
| Brewer's, dry, debittered | 1 tablespoon | 8 | 5 | 25 | 3 | trace | | | 3 |

**Yogurt.**
SEE Milk, cream, cheese:
related products.

## YIELD OF COOKED MEAT PER POUND OF RAW MEAT

| Meat as purchased | Parts weighed | Approximate weight of cooked parts per pound of raw meat purchased |
|---|---|---|
| | | Ounces |
| Chops or steaks for broiling or frying: | | |
| With bone and relatively large amount of fat, such as pork or lamb chops; beef rib, sirloin, or porterhouse steaks | Lean, bone, fat | 10-12 |
| | Lean and fat | 7-10 |
| | Lean only | 5-7 |
| Without bone and with very little fat, such as round of beef, veal steaks | Lean and fat | 12-13 |
| | Lean only | 9-12 |
| Ground meat for broiling or frying, such as hamburger, lamb, or pork patties | Patties | 9-13 |
| Roasts for oven cooking (no liquid added): | | |
| With bone and relatively large amount of fat, such as beef rib, loin, chuck; lamb shoulder, leg; pork, fresh or cured | Lean, bone, fat | 10-12 |
| | Lean and fat | 8-10 |
| | Lean only | 6-9 |
| Without bone | Lean and fat | 10-12 |
| | Lean only | 7-10 |
| Cuts for pot-roasting, simmering, braising, stewing: | | |
| With bone and relatively large amount of fat such as beef chuck, pork shoulder | Lean, bone, fat | 10-11 |
| | Lean and fat | 8-9 |
| | Lean only | 6-8 |
| Without bone and with relatively small amount of fat, such as trimmed beef, veal | Lean with adhering fat | 9-11 |

258

# INDEX

# INDEX

265

267

## ABOUT THE AUTHOR

BILLIE LITTLE, a former East Coast newspaperwoman, is now a resident of California, where she occupies herself with writing cookbooks. Her sympathy for people whose eating habits are unavoidably restricted was reflected in her previous book, *Recipes for Allergics*. That same sympathy prompted her to write this volume, assisted by Penny L. Thorup and with medical advice from Gerson A. Jacobson, M.D.

# KITCHEN POWER!

| | | | |
|---|---|---|---|
| ☐ | 23031 | **DIETER'S GOURMET COOKBOOK**<br>Francine Prince | $3.50 |
| ☐ | 23884 | **THE ARTHRITIC'S BOOKBOOK** ,<br>Dong & Bank | $3.50 |
| ☐ | 23488 | **THE FAMMIE FARMER COOKBOOK**<br>Marion Cunningham & Jeri Laber | $5.95 |
| ☐ | 22600 | **KATHY COOKS NATURALLY**   Kathy Hoshijo | $4.50 |
| ☐ | 23613 | **MOTHER WONDERFUL'S BOOK OF<br>CHEESECAKES AND OTHER GOODIES**<br>Myra Crain | $3.50 |
| ☐ | 23778 | **CROCKERY COOKERY**   Mable Hoffman | $3.50 |
| ☐ | 23418 | **COOKING WITHOUT A GRAIN OF SALT**<br>Elma Bagg | $3.95 |
| ☐ | 23344 | **THE FRENCH CHEF COOKBOOK**   Julia Child | $3.95 |
| ☐ | 13930 | **MORE WITH LESS COOKBOOK**<br>Doris Longacre | $3.95 |
| ☐ | 20656 | **BETTY CROCKER'S DINNER FOR TWO** | $2.95 |
| ☐ | 22878 | **CREPE COOKERY**   Mable Hoffman | $2.95 |

### Prices and availability subject to change without notice.

Buy them at your local bookstore or use this handy coupon for ordering:

---

Bantam Books, Inc., Dept. KP1, 414 East Golf Road, Des Plaines, Ill. 60016

Please send me the books I have checked above. I am enclosing $_____
(please add $1.25 to cover postage and handling). Send check or money order
—no cash or C.O.D.'s please.

Mr/Mrs/Miss _____

Address _____

City_____ State/Zip_____

KP1—2/84

Please allow four to six weeks for delivery. This offer expires 8/84.